A gift in appreciation of your work in
Jewish education in the Tidewater
community

Jewish Education Night

**May 10, 2010
26 Iyar 5770**

ALSO BY DR. ERICA BROWN
FROM JEWISH LIGHTS

Inspired Jewish Leadership
Practical Approaches to Building Strong Communities

the
CASE
for
JEWISH
PEOPLEHOOD

One?
Can We Be

Dr. Erica Brown and Dr. Misha Galperin
Foreword by Rabbi Joseph Telushkin

JEWISH LIGHTS Publishing
Woodstock, Vermont

The Case for Jewish Peoplehood:
Can We Be One?

2009 Hardcover, First Printing
© 2009 by Dr. Erica Brown and Dr. Misha Galperin
Foreword © 2009 by Joseph Telushkin

For information regarding permission to reprint material from this book, please write or fax your request to Jewish Lights Publishing, Permissions Department, at the address / fax number listed below, or e-mail your request to permissions@jewishlights.com.

Library of Congress Cataloging-in-Publication Data
Brown, Erica.
The case for Jewish peoplehood : can we be one? / Erica Brown and Misha Galperin ; foreword by Joseph Telushkin.
p. cm.
Includes bibliographical references.
ISBN-13: 978-1-58023-401-6 (quality pbk.)
ISBN-10: 1-58023-401-1 (quality pbk.)
1. Jews—Identity. 2. Jews—United States—Identity. 3. Jews—Social conditions—21st century. 4. Jews—United States—Social conditions—21st century. 5. Israel and the diaspora. I. Galperin, Misha. II. Title.
DS143.B8637 2009
305.892—dc22
2008033840

10 9 8 7 6 5 4 3 2 1

Manufactured in the United States of America
❀ Printed on recycled paper.
Jacket Design: Jenny Buono

Published by Jewish Lights Publishing
A Division of Longhill Partners, Inc.
Sunset Farm Offices, Route 4, P.O. Box 237
Woodstock, VT 05091
Tel: (802) 457-4000   Fax: (802) 457-4004
www.jewishlights.com

In gratitude to Ronald and Toni Paul who made this book possible
and whose friendship and support are deeply appreciated.

We dedicate this to our grandparents:
Rabbi Moshe and Rivka Rabinovich (*z"l*)
Dr. Alexander and Sophia Grinfeld (*z"l*)
Abraham (*z"l*) and Celia Raicher
who did not have to explain Jewish peoplehood because they lived it.

Contents

Peoplehood and Community

On Peoplehood and Community: Three Texts

1. Even before Ruth declared to her mother-in-law, Naomi, "Your God is my God," she first said, "Your people are my people" (Ruth 1:16). How striking that this earliest of converts to Judaism so deeply understood the significance of peoplehood in Jewish identity. We might have assumed that early converts would have simply and exclusively focused on monotheism, Judaism's singular and universal God, which indeed is what most clearly distinguished the Jews from their neighbors at the time of Ruth. But Drs. Brown and Galperin remind us that the peoplehood factor is no less distinctive in explaining Jewish continuity as well.

2. A Talmudic passage teaches: "All Jews are responsible one for another" (B. *Shevuot* 39a). The Hebrew word used for responsible, *ah-reivin*, literally means "surety"; that is one who makes himself responsible for another, perhaps as a sponsor, a godparent or, in legal terms, as guarantor of a loan. In the Torah, the model of surety is Judah. At a time of terrible famine in Canaan, when Jacob and his descendants are in desperate need of sustenance, the patriarch Jacob restrains his sons from traveling to Egypt (the one place where food is available) because they have been instructed to bring Jacob's youngest son, Benjamin, with them, and the patriarch fears that Benjamin will be harmed. As the family situation grows more desperate, Judah steps forward and says to his father, "Send the boy in my care ... I myself will be surety for him, you may hold me responsible if I do not bring him

back and set him before you; I shall stand guilty before you forever"
(Genesis 43:8–9).

A short time later, a valuable Egyptian cup is found hidden among
Benjamin's goods, and Joseph, the second-in-command in Egypt and at
that point unrecognized by his brothers, insists that he will take
Benjamin as a slave and permit the other brothers to leave. Judah steps
forward to plead with Joseph: "If I do not bring him back … I shall stand
guilty before my father forever. Therefore please let your servant remain
as a slave to my lord instead of the boy, and let the boy go back with his
brothers" (Genesis 44:32–33). Seventeen years earlier, it had been
Judah who had suggested selling Joseph as a slave into Egypt. His willingness at this point to suffer slavery himself so as to spare pain to
Benjamin and to his father is what now impels Joseph to forgive Judah
and his brothers for the terrible evil they had done him. A Midrash
teaches that as a reward for Judah's selfless behavior, the Jewish people
are subsequently named for him (the word for *Judah* in Hebrew is
Yehudah; the word for *Jews* in Hebrew is *Yehudim*).

3. One of the more unusual texts in Jewish religious literature concerns a case of an infant born with two heads. A Talmudic commentary
to *Menachot* 37a raises the question of whether such a child is entitled
to one or two shares of his father's inheritance and notes that a similar
case had been raised before Solomon (long renowned as Israel's wisest
king) who had ruled: "Let them pour boiling water on the head of one
child and see if the other one screams. If he does, then it means that the
children are not regarded as twins, but as one. However, if the second
child does not feel the suffering of the first, then they are to be regarded
as separate individuals."

One hopes that this case was hypothetical, certainly for the sake
of the child destined to have boiling water poured on its head.
Nonetheless, the late Rabbi Joseph Baer Soloveitchik, of blessed memory, argued that the implications of this case are not hypothetical at all.
In his essay *Kol Dodi Dofek* ("My Beloved's Voice Calls to Me"), he
writes: "If boiling water is poured on the head of a Moroccan Jew, the
prim and proper Jew in Paris and London must scream. And by feeling
the pain, he is loyal to the nation."

For three thousand years, peoplehood has meant that the Jewish people recognize that the God of other Jews is our God as well, that the community of other Jews is our community. Recognition of this fact means that we cry and cry out for each other when necessary (as was the case with the Soviet Jewry movement and is the case with support for Israel), and that the bravest and most devoted of us see Judah's selflessness as models for ourselves. Drs. Brown and Galperin, themselves two exemplary models of communal leadership, have presented in *The Case for Jewish Peoplehood* an important statement of peoplehood, one that can guide and inspire Jews in the twenty-first century as this idea has guided and inspired Jews over the past thirty centuries.

—RABBI JOSEPH TELUSHKIN

Acknowledgments

We would like to acknowledge Alan Hoffmann, Dyonna Ginsburg, Eric Levine, Meredith Woocher, Jonathan Woocher, and Sheryl Friedlander for reading this book in its entirety and for helping us think through the many and complex issues of Jewish peoplehood. We are grateful for their insights.

Erica Brown: I want to acknowledge my students, friends, and fellow Jewish communal professionals for showing me the importance of creating invisible bridges. I particularly want to single out my colleagues at the Jewish Federation and the Partnership for Jewish Life and Learning. Across the life span and across the denominational and geographic divide, you have demonstrated what it means to sustain a collective sense of *kehilla*, a community of meaning. I thank the Jewish institutions that educated me and gave me a wonderful appreciation of Jewish literacy, the bedrock of peoplehood. Every day I count my blessings—I thank God for giving me energy and a sense of purpose. I thank my parents and in-laws and am eternally grateful for the support of my loving husband, Jeremy, and my children: Talia, Gavriel, Yishai, and Ayelet, who teach me every day about the relationship between family and community.

Misha Galperin: I would like to thank my wife, Alisa Guyer Galperin, and my mother, Irina Galperin, for reading this manuscript carefully and for sharing their thoughts. I forever thank my late father for having made the decision that our family leave the Soviet Union and reconnect to the Jewish people. He transmitted the fragile yet powerful memory of my family's Jewish history. Just as I thank my father for giving me a past, I thank my children for showing me the future: Anna, David, Ezra, and Sofia. Bob Kogod, I thank you for being a devoted friend and mentor, and I am grateful to John Ruskay for stimulating conversations and joint work and for establishing the topic of peoplehood as a worthwhile and urgent endeavor for Jewish communal service and the federation movement, in particular. I would also like to acknowledge the lay leadership and staff of the Jewish Federation of Greater Washington for providing daily inspiration.

We both want to thank Stuart M. Matlins, publisher of Jewish Lights, for believing in this project; and Emily Wichland, vice president of Editorial and Production, Michaela Powell, assistant editor, and the staff at Jewish Lights who worked miracles to get this book to press.

INTRODUCTION

Jews in the 'Hood

Peoplehood seems to be the word of the hour in the Jewish community. Everyone is talking about it. But we are not convinced that we are all working with the same definition or meaning. To date, there has been no single full-scale treatment of Jewish peoplehood. A Jewish journal recently devoted an entire issue to peoplehood and asked some probing questions:

> [W]hat exactly is "Peoplehood"? Is it just another empty phrase carted out by Jewish communal professionals determined to keep Jews procreating with other Jews? Or does it have intrinsic meaning beyond catch-phrase pabulum? Where does Peoplehood end and tribalism begin? Is it possible to articulate Peoplehood in a manner that is inspiring yet not exclusionary?[1]

The questions are familiar. The answers seem amorphous or out of mental reach. This book was written in the throes of an immense debate taking place in the halls of Jewish institutions, at universities, and among Jewish thinkers and writers of note about what being Jewish means today in a collective sense. We are writing this to bring together aspects of this discussion and expose it broadly so that we can *all* be part of a conversation we have been delaying for too long.

Why is this conversation important? Why does it merit your attention? If you care about Jewish identity and community, then you know that we have no trouble identifying the problems that fragmentize us as

1

a people but have far less success identifying that which unites us. Without a unifying, collective notion of Jewish identity that is meaningful and robust, it is virtually impossible to make a strong case for Jewish continuity.

By Jews in the 'hood, we don't mean neighborhood; we mean peoplehood. The 'hood is not only a geographic reference; it is a shared identity that may be characterized by joint assumptions, body language, certain expressions, and a host of familial-like behaviors that unite an otherwise disparate group of people. But how do we get a Jewish community splintered by factionalism and ideological divides to feel collectively attached to each other as part of a global family? Like the 'hood, how do we create a quiet sense of acknowledgment, care, understanding, and special language and behaviors to exist among a people with profoundly different orientations and interests? *And*, how do we do this without sacrificing the universal concerns that extend far beyond communal boundaries?

For many, the answer is peoplehood. We need to intensify a sense of family, belonging, connection, and caring that can seem almost tribal in appearance and behavior. For many, this ethnic identity is too weak to be taken seriously. Some argue that peoplehood is a lowest-common-denominator term when we dilute everything else that being Jewish has ever meant. In other words, it comes down to this: we are united by Jewish*ness* in some hard-to-articulate way rather than by *being Jewish* in an active way through portals such as religion, language, and culture. For peoplehood to be a meaningful term that is truly engaging, peoplehood must demand a greater threshold of intensity than other sentiments that vie for our attention.[2] The success of Jewish experiences today—from Birthright to Jewish camping—has less to do with content and behaviors and more to do with the intensity of the way that Jewish content and behaviors are experienced. Generally, few experiences and expressions of modern Jewish life are intense at all. Mostly, they feel tepid, passionless, stale, or conventional. For peoplehood to be central to Jewish identity building, Judaism must be experienced as authentic, immersive, creative, meaningful, and deeply resonant.

This last sentence reminds us that peoplehood is still a concept of importance even among those who are Jewishly literate and engaged daily in an array of Jewish behaviors. We all know that personal Jewish choices do not always extend to ethnic connectedness for those outside immediate social or religious circles. Among those who lead unquestionably rich Jewish lives—those who enjoy high levels of Jewish education and who will marry Jewish, live in a Jewish neighborhood, and join and support Jewish institutions—peoplehood still matters. Peoplehood extends the boundaries of personal Jewish life so that everyone matters. We all know people who are religious or traditional yet unconcerned about the Jewish community at large. Their lack of involvement in the peoplehood part of Judaism is a cause for grave concern. They do not suffer any sense of lack or loss at being unengaged with those who express their Jewish commitment differently—through charity, culture, or institutional service. In fact, they may feel that involvement with the broader Jewish community may diminish themselves religiously and, therefore, actively disassociate themselves from peoplehood concerns.

We would hardly call such individuals unaffiliated, but in many ways that is exactly what they are from a peoplehood perspective. In other words, peoplehood is not merely a means to engage those who are unaffiliated or create a very loose umbrella of Judaism that "covers" everyone. Peoplehood is not a means but an end that brings together a concern and connection for Jews from all walks of life, affiliations, and points of commitment.[3]

As the expression *Jewish peoplehood* makes its way into institutional jargon, it is regarded as an overarching loose membership in a tribe, a faith, and an ethnicity that shares a common history, religion, and set of basic values. We would like to suggest an alternative meaning that incorporates these characteristics but engenders greater consilience and intensity. Peoplehood means sharing a mission or a purpose with an extended family with whom we have a collective history and a shared language of faith, ritual, and culture. If peoplehood were merely about shared history, it would always be retrospective. I am who I am in the future because of who I was in the past. This is rarely true in the creation of collective identity. A definition of collective identity must also be futuristic in orientation, and it must be meaningful. A professor we know who studies, among other things, the success of mega-churches asked why people attend such institutions in such great numbers. It is not predominantly because of passionate leadership, inspiring services, or great programming, although these are all component parts of their success. People come in droves because of a shared sense of mission and belief. Above all, it is a shared purpose that colors and animates participation.

This book is an attempt to come to some consensus of meaning that will allow us to think carefully about the purpose, possibilities, and limitations of peoplehood as a unifying concept of community for a people struggling profoundly with Jewish identity. It will also suggest ways to strengthen the feelings engendered by peoplehood through a host of experiences and community-wide conversations. We accept the fact that, statistically, notions of Jewish peoplehood may not be as unifying as they once were, but we are not resigned to the fact that there is nothing to be done about it. We believe powerfully in the collective—in *klal Yisrael*—as a concept that needs strengthening and that *can* be strengthened. Failure to strengthen peoplehood will be a failure of the imagination and a relinquishment of the essential Jewish "glue" that has held the Jewish people together for thousands of years. We are not prepared to let go of that legacy.

In these pages, you will find chapters defining what peoplehood is and is not. To further that discussion, we will take a step back and explore both collective and personal Jewish identity and the nature of identity construction. From that point forward, we need to establish some of the obstacles that challenge a shared notion of peoplehood: the plethora of personal choices, the construct of membership and boundaries, the growth of Jewish illiteracy, the identity fragmentation between Israeli and Diaspora Jewry, and the generational divide affecting traditionalists, baby boomers, and generations X and Y. We conclude with a vision forward and desired outcomes that should emerge from a community-wide conversation on peoplehood because, without practical guidance and recommendations, our conversations on peoplehood would remain just that: talk. We need more than talk today. We have also included vignettes at the beginning of each chapter and throughout to illustrate in a narrative way the ideas we are framing. In addition, we have added questions at the end of each chapter to illustrate the challenges and also to stimulate much-needed communal discussion.

We decided to write this together because we both have a profound commitment to Jewish peoplehood even though our backgrounds are quite different. If together we could sustain a fascinating conversation that stretched beyond our professional responsibilities to our own personal Jewish identities, then it was conceivable that we could also bring others into a meaningful conversation about Jewish identity and the ties that bind.

We feel that it is time to bring this conversation to more people in more ways. The discussion of a collective purpose and meaning for modern Jewish living cannot remain in the purview of Jewish academics and professionals alone; we are all stakeholders in this enterprise called Jewish life. And, in several decades of being participant observers of Jewish communal life, working predominantly for organizations that serve large Jewish communities with complex infrastructures, we have both come to the same conclusion: for too many people, being Jewish no longer means having a joint language of shared commitment at all. For some Jews, humanitarian activism creates their Jewish connection. For others, it is Jewish legal and ritual observance. Some define their Jewish commitment through a Zionist lens, while others regard Judaism as a rubric for caring and nurturing those who are most vulnerable. We may agree to disagree on the nature of Jewish life today, but one thing is clear: the lack of a shared language of Jewish commitment has led to splintering and conflict, a plethora of Jewish institutions often at odds with each other for limited resources—both human and financial—and tensions that have resulted in crisis, division, and mutual recriminations.

We want to share our backgrounds to give you a sense of where our conversation begins and how you can join it.

My Background: Misha Galperin

I am a former Soviet Jew, born of the deep secularism attendant with Russian communism. I had virtually no Jewish education before coming to the United States more than thirty years ago, but—like many other Soviet Jews—I benefited from feeling part of an extended family, nurtured by Jews far away who were strangers to me. My grandfather was a rabbi before the communist era, but my father had no Jewish education. My grandfather, a victim of the Holocaust, was killed when my father was only six years old. My father watched his father get shot as he crouched in a mulberry tree. It is a haunting image that I carry with me about the high price we have paid to be Jewish.

My father had a PhD in engineering, but when he brought us to America he told our social worker that he wanted to be a rabbi. He wanted to carry on the professional inheritance of his father that skipped a generation because of communism. No one took him very seriously. He was already forty years old. He was offered a job in a textile factory that paid $2.35 an hour and was supposed to study Judaism early in the morning and late at night; this was the only way he could make good on his dream. It did not take him long to realize that his meager salary was not going to feed us. So he passed his dream on to me and sent me to Yeshiva University in New York. I made my way through the American college and graduate system to find a career of meaning in clinical psychology (sort of like a rabbi but without the sermons!) and later in Jewish communal service.

My work is largely informed by the commandment of *pidyon shvu'yim* (redeeming captives). It is not that this particular commandment drives my professional commitments; it was the realization I had when I first learned the term. For centuries, we as a people have been drawn together under a rubric of shared ethics. Someone in the Talmudic period who was captured by a Roman may have been ransomed, and the Jewish community would have come instantly to his defense. That would also have been true for an Ashkenazi Jew at the time of the Crusades. It was true for me as a former Soviet Jew. It will be true for all of us who pray and work for the freedom of Israeli soldiers currently held captive. It was the sense that I am personally linked to a chain of tradition and responsibility that changed my life and that has changed the lives of others and will continue to do so in the future.

I have never been willing to let go of the importance of Jewish texts and Jewish values, even though I am not a religiously observant person. After all, it is these very values that inform our commitment to each other and the world at large. Without Jewish values, there can be no real *tikkun olam* (repair of the world). My understanding of *pidyon shvu'yim* has given added meaning and impetus to give back to my community. It has helped me understand that personal spirituality is never enough. Being Jewish is also a statement of responsibility to others.

My Background: Erica Brown

Like Misha, the Holocaust played an important role in my formative Jewish identity. I am the daughter of a Holocaust child survivor and two grandparents who survived Auschwitz. They all separated after leaving their village and miraculously found each other and reunited after the war. I have never regarded this miracle of survival and reunification as a coincidence. Because I exist as a result of this miracle, I and the rest of my family will have to make our own miracles for the Jewish community. My grandparents were Gerer Hasidim before the war, like many Polish Jews. When they came to America, my grandparents and mother experienced much of the same assimilation patterns that we know about from history books. They began to work on Shabbat to rebuild a life out of poverty. They had a chicken farm in Jackson, New Jersey, and my mother collected eggs before she went to school. Then they opened a dry-cleaning business. They always worked hard. It was the key to an American future. My grandparents cared passionately about a college education for their daughters so that the next generation could live successfully in America. They helped build a synagogue, but their affiliation was more about nostalgia and friends than religion. Belief mostly died in the ashes.

My mother had a poor Jewish education, which she has worked to repair as an adult. My father is an American for many generations. I was raised with the unengaging Hebrew school education shared by so many in this country. My house reflected few spiritual Jewish behaviors. I turned to religion through a synagogue youth group and made my way to religious observance in my first years of high school. I fought to go to Jewish day school. I began to observe holidays. I became a vegetarian because my home was not kosher. I learned through a tortuously long process how to pray and speak Hebrew and learn Talmud. I found myself and my faith in these ancient pages and rituals. I wanted to be Jewishly literate so that I could belong to something larger than myself, to reclaim something that my family had lost.

Eventually, my family was also drawn back to this tradition; we found something that our family once died for, and we started living for it. My grandfather, of blessed memory, began to put on *tefillin* (phylacteries) once again when he was seventy-five. My mother and siblings became religiously observant and now live in Israel. My life has also included two major stints in Israel and Israeli citizenship for me, my husband, and our four children. Our lives are informed by religious Zionism even though we do not currently live in Israel.

My work as a teacher of Jewish texts and as a Jewish community professional reflects a strong drive to give others a chance to consider a spiritual journey that changed my life. Jewish study has an enormously transformative capability once we get beyond the diffidence or the negative associations and have personal encounters with a tradition of ritual and study. I believe strongly in the power of community, spirituality, and religious observance. At the same time, like Misha, I know that the personal is not enough to sustain a religion and a culture. I feel frustrated that many of my Orthodox coreligionists do not seem to care enough about the Jewish community at large. Jewish preschools, senior facilities, and group homes for the developmentally disabled are usually important to them only if they are conducted through an Orthodox lens. Caring about the demographics of Jewish life today seems to be somebody else's job. At the same time, I wonder at so many of my Jewish colleagues who downplay the importance of religion, spirituality, and literacy, placing their Judaism solely on the altar of Jewish communal service. If we cannot find a why for our work, then the hows will matter less. The office is not the synagogue. There has to be more. Together, we are all investors and owners in Judaism, and we have a responsibility to ensure that it passes safely from one generation to the next. Judaism does not have to look the same in each generation, but it does have to be meaningful and substantial in each generation.

Our Shared Vision

Together, we are compelled by a definition of Jewishness that is more expansive than our respective histories, faith commitments, or educations reveal. Conversation after conversation with each other revealed a similarity in our attitudes about Jewish identity that required greater articulation. As Jewish communal professionals, we both pursued similar career paths but from very different starting points. And yet, we are and remain joined by an energetic, enduring, and emotional connection to the Jewish people that has gone far beyond our personal Jewish narratives. Our shared Holocaust connections propelled us into a strong commitment to the Jewish future and peoplehood. Yet we realize that with the death of survivors, the Holocaust identity card is losing the hold it once had on American Jewry. And we independently struggled with articulating what peoplehood and Jewish identity means succinctly and uniformly. That conundrum forced us to spend more time examining these concepts and coming up with a language that *does* capture the dilemmas of Jewish identity today and *does* define what peoplehood is and is not. The language of this dialogue appears on the pages ahead.

These conversations of ours were mirrors of discussions that we have had with Jewish leaders, students, and communal professionals in classrooms and conferences. We find that there is a deep need to talk about what being Jewish means, and there is not one exclusive meaning. The ambiguities are driving the conversation. In our respective personal backgrounds, the deprivation of religion in both our cases created a deep yearning. When you can't have something, you begin to want it desperately. You have a hunger for it. This longing for religion has changed over time and now includes a strong desire to understand what it means to have a collective Jewish identity when the boundaries of ritual observance, faith, and shared culture can no longer be assumed.

We are not writing this book as sociologists or as Jewish academics, although we both share an academic background and value research. We try to keep up with the latest writings and trends in demography and sociology and, between us, have many close friends and colleagues who are engaged in the everyday academic practice of studying the Jewish community. We deeply value the contributions they have made to contemporary Jewish life. We are neither qualified nor wish to replicate their work. At the same time, we have arrived at a sad conclusion. Many Jewish lay leaders and Jewish communal professionals do not read extensively in sociology, nor are they acquainted with the work of Jewish demographers. There is an increasing distance between practitioners and academics that has made Jewish institutional life intellectually impoverished and allowed academic conversations to become highly specialized and less relevant than they should be to the practice and study of Jewish life.

We have also written this book to share academic literature more broadly with our coworkers and lay partners and to request greater involvement on the part of Jewish sociologists, demographers, and historians with today's Jewish communal institutions. We have brought together a lot of recent important studies in a compact way to expose our readers to the wealth and breadth of research today and, at the same time, to point out gaps where there is still more work to be done. The work ahead is not necessarily in producing more research but in finding more collaborative and creative ways to *integrate* the research into the sacred work that we do, both as professionals and as committed volunteers. We recognize the urgent need for greater innovation, vision, and expansive thinking as we try to understand the Jewish present and plan for the future. And, perhaps most importantly, we have kept this to a trim volume in the hopes that it will get read.

In addition, we both struggle with the fact that institutional Judaism seems to be constantly on the defensive, trying to prove its worth at every turn. In a recent forum on reimagining the federation, it was notable that the article questioning and criticizing federations appeared before all the others, setting up every other article in a defensive posture. The federation system, and its network of agencies, has long been criticized for doing business in an outmoded way, an old boys' network of connections, a leadership scheme built on money, not ideas, with an outdated emphasis on Jewish continuity and community, at a time of profound individualism. We are moved by calls to change and recognize the intense alterations that institutional Judaism has already made and is continuing to make to accommodate changes in philanthropy and technology.

At the same time, we refuse to be defensive about our concern for a collective voice of Judaism built on a web of communal connections. Rather than defend communal institutions, we choose to strengthen them to a point where they need no defense. The word *federation* is from the Latin for *covenant*. The notion that we are part of something larger than the individual infuses our belief in communal institutions. We wrote this to provide a positive and proactive platform for reinvigorating notions of the collective without a posture of defensiveness. We need to define, affirm, and assert a positive approach to peoplehood that captures the sense of mission and struggle that has always characterized Jewish history and global Jewish accomplishments. We make no apologies for our deep sense of Jewish pride.

Having said that, we recognize that civic Judaism, described so eloquently by Jonathan Woocher, chief ideas officer of the Jewish Education Service of North America, as "a way of being Jewish and program of Jewish activity within which the role of the synagogue and the rabbinate—the life of study, prayer and ritual observance—is no longer primary." [4] Membership on a board is not an ideology or a meaningful alternative to a Judaism of faith, spirit, and social activism. Those whose Jewish lives were encapsulated by affiliations with Jewish institutions alone have found that they have not provided the substantial heft of meaning that Judaism and the collective voice of the Jewish people once had. Peoplehood cannot be divorced from religion. It is an outgrowth or offshoot of religion. In the words of a contemporary Jewish thinker:

> "Spirituality" has come to complement "ethnicity" as a portal to
> Jews who cannot think of themselves as religious because they

think of "religion" as overly formalistic and restrictive. To be sure, Judaism is a social affirmation and an inheritance, but it is more: a mode of understanding human life that, moving through time, has encountered great systems of thought that have spurred its own unfolding. Judaism is one of history's paradigmatic attempts to comprehend the human in the context of the whole.[5]

Whatever definition of peoplehood we offer cannot have an appeal limited to those who are religiously observant, those who are cultural and culinary Jews, those who are Zionists, or those who serve Jewish institutions as the sole expression of their Jewish commitment. It has to be more, and it can be more.

Our hope is that the feelings and experiences that have shaped our friendship and our joint notions of belonging to an extended Jewish family will include many readers of this work anxious to arrive at a notion of Jewish peoplehood that can be understood and shared. We need to find the net, the web, the meaningful, unifying, and overarching reason for involvement with a Jewish legacy, tradition, and people that can hold us all, no matter where we come from. We need to find the joint anchor that stabilizes us and the collective compass that will determine our direction for the future.

1

DEFINING PEOPLEHOOD

I have been in this country for more than thirty years. I wanted so much to be an American when I first came here, just like many other immigrants. And I also wanted to be Jewish, really Jewish, not the Soviet Jewish of having your religion stamped in your passport by someone else but to be Jewish through knowledge and personal commitment. I wanted to own my Judaism. When my daughter—who was born in this country—applied to college, she wrote her essay on her own struggle with Russian-American-Jewish identity and the search for self. When I read it, I realized that I had inadvertently passed down my own hyphenated identity and that it was a rich, hyphenated identity, a complex identity and one that filled me with pride.

—MISHA GALPERIN

How long does it take for a good game of Jewish geography to get started? You visit someplace new. Someone asks you for your family name or where you live. Instantly, this person begins reciting the names of others with the same last name or the same zip code. Are these relatives of yours? Do you know any of them? Where is your family from, really from? Could it be Eastern Europe, some generations ago? Maybe together you will find some connection in the distant past. By chance,

13

do you know so-and-so from your neighborhood? He used to live there, went to graduate school there, has a first cousin there. Sometimes you disappoint. Much as you would like to, you simply cannot connect with any names or geographic locations. More often than not, you both try until you stumble upon some connection, however remote. The six degrees of separation in another culture is only one or two in yours. With a "discovered" connection, there is a small and inconsequential sense of relief. As a Jew, I am not alone in the universe. I am part of a remarkable network where the possibilities of belonging are only a few questions and answers away. I am situated among my people.

The game of Jewish geography—superficial as it often feels—is played to reinforce peoplehood, the feeling that Jews the world over are part of an extended family: that a Star of David necklace on one links to the concentration camp numbers tattooed on the arm of another to the Jewish-sounding last name of yet another to the Israeli-born aunt of someone else.

The unusual strength of the peoplehood bond is so intense that it is hard to believe we lack a clear definition for the word. Until very recently, the word *peoplehood* did not appear in the dictionary. It first appeared in the *Supplement to the Oxford English Dictionary*, volume III, only in 1982.[1] It is usually regarded as a nonexistent word in a computer spell-check. That does not negate the idea of peoplehood. It merely implies that it is a term begging for definition and better articulation before it can expect greater usage and familiarity.

From a Jewish perspective, the term *peoplehood* is often credited to the founder of Reconstructionist Judaism, Mordechai Kaplan, specifically in his use of the term in a 1942 issue of *The Reconstructionist*, a publication of the Reconstructionist movement. Kaplan was seeking a word that would capture a sense of communal identity beyond nationalism:

> Kaplan's immediate hope was that a strong sense of communal identity would strengthen Jews' connection to Jewish life and to each other—something he felt was in danger of being weakened by the restrictive visions of the Orthodox and Reform movements. But his ultimate goal was nothing less than universal sal-

vation, a healing of the world brought about by people's commitment to one another.[2]

Kalpan began a conversation without obvious conclusions. The conversation about peoplehood continued through the conclusion of World
War II, the founding of the State of Israel, and the development of
Jewish organizational life in North America. It continues today. It has
been called by different names or spurred by different concerns: continuity, identity, renaissance, solidarity, unity. In Hebrew, peoplehood is
amimiyut, from the root word *am*, or nation. These words are inevitably
part of this conversation but do not explain it in full. Peoplehood is
about all of these terms but goes well beyond it.

Kaplan may have used the word *peoplehood* in a specific way, but
his terminology should not be understood in isolation from the language
of Jewish texts and history, as if the idea were original to him. Just as
other cultures have multiple words to refer to something inherent or
important to that culture, the Bible and subsequent historical and rabbinic texts have many Hebrew words to describe the notion of a people:
am, chavurah, edah, kehilla, minyan, kevutzah.

In this book, *peoplehood* is roughly defined as the collective aspects
of Jewish identity and community that create connections among individuals, even strangers. It is the mutual voice of Jewish responsibility
that most closely resembles being members of an extended family with
all of the joys, anxieties, frustrations, idiosyncrasies, and responsibilities
that membership in a family brings.

Jewish peoplehood signifies kinship based on a common history,
culture, values, and future. Peoplehood involves an attempt to unify a
group that is diverse and identify those inside and outside often imaginary boundaries: the collective self and the other. It is this, but it is also
so much more than this. In its strongest Jewish definition, it also means
a global community joined by covenant—a definite sense of purpose.
This covenant was originally established in the Hebrew Bible between
Israel and God and has extended to include each other. A covenant is a
special partnership that implies joint and conditional responsibility,
love, and respect. We care, inspire, look after, and connect with each

other across the horizontal boundaries of geography and the vertical boundaries of time. We are connected to rabbinic scholars in fourth-century Babylonia just as we care about the Beta Israel Jews of Ethiopia in the twenty-first century. We not only *exist* together, but by virtue of this invisible yet powerful covenant, we also *act* together to improve ourselves and the world. Our sense of global membership and mission transcends time and place.

In an interview between Susan Berrin, editor of the journal *Sh'ma*, and Alan Hoffmann, director of education for the Jewish Agency of Israel, we are offered an explanation of peoplehood that also goes beyond literal boundaries:

> The unique character of Judaism, the combination of religion and ethnicity, was shaped by the formative experience of living in Diaspora unconnected to soil and boundaries, so typical of most other nations. We are therefore a spiritual community, a sociological entity, a series of ethnic islands—a conglomerate that is difficult to pry apart.
>
> The notion of a Jewish "people" in relationship—something larger than individual existence—gives many Jews a sense of connectedness to a bigger something, which is especially important as collective bonds weaken in the general society and also amongst Jews. But a danger lurks if this becomes a diluted lowest-common-denominator concept, not nearly as powerful or robust as Jewish religious identity or national identity.[3]

Hoffmann warns us against the danger of a definition of peoplehood so all-inclusive that it lacks substance and heft. It cannot be a fund-raising slogan or a way to diminish or minimize responsibility. He asks, "What are the minimal conditions of being an active member of this people? What contents, acts, or behaviors create the commonalities that give Jewish peoplehood an active rather than passive meaning?"[4] His questions are critical if peoplehood is to be more than a clever label that reinforces Jewish charity while "permitting" ignorance of Jewish history, Hebrew, texts, rituals, and responsibilities. Hoffmann poses the question in yet another way that is equally difficult: "What kind of threshold of intensity is necessary to preserve a Jewish people no longer anchored at its traditional moorings?"[5]

Hoffmann's question unnerves us because it reveals a conundrum. To be Jewish is a matter of birth or choice. The former requires no threshold of intensity; it requires nothing more than one's birth, a simple fact of existence. But the issue of peoplehood today is not so much about *accidental* membership—you belong simply by virtue of birth—but about *intentional* membership, about generating meaning and purpose around your Judaism. Being Jewish makes a visible, notable difference in your life.

Jonathan Ariel, executive director of Makom, offers an exploration of peoplehood that is worth mentioning here because, like the one just offered, the term cannot be reduced to a simple catchphrase or glib sentence. It manages to discuss personal choices within a communal framework. Ariel offers a parallel to family relatives:

> Jewish Peoplehood is a shifting, evolving, dynamic sense that the sum total of the different parts is greater than its aggregate components. It sees a family resemblance between certain siblings, or cousins, even distant ones, rather than looking all of the time for identical twins. It posits that you can make a claim on each other at a time of need, and that you have the potential for a different kind of conversation with each other than you do with non-Jews: one that is at turns warmer, livelier, more heated, more aggressive, and more intimate about Jews, and the meaning of life.[6]

Ariel offers less of a definition than a description of what peoplehood behaviors and interactions may resemble. The family dynamic he describes allows for more intimacy in both the positive and the negative ways in which those behaviors may be manifest. In many ways, Ariel describes peoplehood as psychic closeness because it can ostensibly be felt toward strangers. We may make all kinds of assumptions involving cultural stereotypes that attract or alienate us by virtue of knowing that someone in our ambit is Jewish. The fact that we know someone is Jewish or are unexpectedly told that a celebrity or an office coworker is Jewish gives rise to other kinds of family interest and invasiveness. The expression "Funny, you don't look Jewish" is open to all kinds of interpretations and suggests a family resemblance that is assumed to be shared and causes alarm or raises curiosity when it is not.

Both Hoffmann and Ariel imply levels of commitment that assume transmission. We care deeply about familial connections and understand that being part of a family means a connection to those who came before us *and* those who will come after us. But one of today's great challenges is the passing down of peoplehood; the unarticulated commitment to an ethnic identity must be stated today precisely because continuity is coming under question, some would even call it siege. The "traditional moorings" Hoffmann mentions are also not guarantees that one generation can—through ritual, text, or any other mechanism—transmit its value to the next.

> *In one of our basic Jewish literacy courses, I ask participants to think of an object that tells the story of their Jewish commitment. Very often—in virtually every class—at least one adult learner will mention a set of Shabbat candlesticks or a menorah that was passed down from a grandparent or parent. Sometimes it is a necklace with a Jewish star or a mezuzah. Often they will mention that this object has no aesthetic or material worth but comes packed with memories of a different time or place in their lives, and that this object connects them powerfully to people whom they associate with love and a nostalgia for things Jewish. Just at the point of "Jewish rhapsody," I remind them that they are not only descendants but also ancestors. I ask them to reflect on the responsibility of being an ancestor and to wonder which Jewish object or memory a family member three or four generations hence would associate with them. This question is usually followed by deep silence, the kind of silence that suggests challenge. I allow that silence to penetrate. Silence is a remarkable teacher.*
>
> *After one such class, a couple shared with me their observation of this exercise: "My husband and I were talking over the break and*

realized that we have never bought a Jewish ritual object that we would consider an heirloom, something we'd really like to pass down to our children. And yet we both feel attached to memories and things given to us by others. Maybe it's time to create those memories and attachments now for our children."

—Erica Brown

Passing Down Peoplehood

In his momentous book, *Kaddish*, Leon Wieseltier analyzes a Talmudic quotation that questions the very nature of what collective language means across generations. In the Talmud, Rabbi Yose says, "Ready yourself for the study of Torah, because it is not your inheritance." Is the Torah not our inheritance? How can it not be? It is not a natural inheritance. It is an inheritance that must be taught, and even then it may not make it. In the act of transition from the ownership of one generation to the next, it may get lost, dropped, misplaced.

> Rabbi Yose is a realist about continuity. He cautions that in the transmission of tradition there is a moment between the giving and the receiving, a moment when it is no longer the possession of the father and not yet the possession of the son, a moment of jeopardy, like the pause in a beating heart, a moment of discontinuity, a beat skipped, when what has stopped has still to start, and what has been transmitted can slip away or run out. This is the moment for which you must "ready yourself."[7]

To borrow Wieseltier's expression, we are living in the generation between the heartbeat, when whatever has held our interest in Judaism and brought us to a place of care and responsibility cannot be assumed or easily passed down to the next generation. A recent study by preeminent sociologist Steven Cohen affirms this by concluding that the commitment to Jewish peoplehood is in decline.[8] Cohen amasses statistics to show that American Jews are less committed to a common destiny with Jews around the world than they have perhaps ever been in Jewish history. They also feel less compelled to rescue or have responsibility toward Jews more than others in a humanitarian circle. And yet, despite this fact, "Being Jewish is not only about God, faith, rituals, worship and spirituality. It is also about friends, neighborhoods, community, Israel, and peoplehood. In fact, 'people,' 'nation,' and other variants of the Jewish collective appear repeatedly in the Bible; religion does not."[9]

We might challenge Cohen's assessment of religion in the Bible, but we cannot argue with the fact that the social and emotional ties that were once so critical to Jewish life are on the wane. The assumption that these Jewish ties are eternal is being profoundly questioned today. We have not readied ourselves for this enormous task of transmission. And we no longer have a shared language of peoplehood with which to transmit this integrated sense of Jewish culture, responsibility, ritual, text, and history. Defining peoplehood is only the beginning. We must also manage the discrete moment of transition when continuity, if not handled with love and care, may turn into a time of discontinuity.

Although we may need to strengthen a shared language of continuity, we are more accepting today of the fact that the expression of peoplehood can take various forms. A chosen method is only emblematic of the commitment to membership and is not the exclusive way to express it. We define peoplehood as being part of an extended family with a mission, a people connected by a purpose. Within that extended family, individuals can express their commitments differently, just as they do in a nuclear family. Peoplehood presents the collective aspects of Jewish identity—as opposed to our individual choices—and our relationship to those outside Judaism. For these emotional bonds to be significant, peoplehood should ultimately be a conscious choice rather than an accident of birth. Rabbi David Gedzelman, executive director for the Steinhardt Foundation for Jewish Life, writes

> That being Jewish is both of birth and of choice, of belonging
> to an extended family and subscribing to a wisdom and spiri-
> tual tradition, makes the definition of Jewish Peoplehood

complex and essentially of a dialectical nature. The idea of the Jewish People cannot be neatly fit into either/or categories of nation, religion, biology or culture. Because the Covenantal Family of the Jewish People combines birth and choice, its very existence teaches the values of both openness and belonging as well as the value that affirms both the particular and universal at once.[10]

In the universe of philosophy, there are aspects of virtually anything that are accidental and those that are essential. The essential quality of a chair is that it provides seating. An accidental property may be that a chair is blue or green, wooden or plastic. Our chair can be configured in many different ways, and as long as it does not lose its essence—its ability to provide seating—then it is still a chair. If we were to use a similar construction—albeit an oversimplified one—Jewish peoplehood is about both an ethnic and a spiritual identity that is created through shared language and shared concern. The notion of community is an essential characteristic of Jewish commitment. Being hip, being funny, having good marketing, or providing interesting programming is an "accidental" property of "doing Jewish," even though all of these features may be very intentional and well thought through. Community, on the other hand, has always been an essential property of Jewish initiatives.

Being Jewish has never been understood as a solitary spiritual or cultural identity that favors isolation or can exist in the absence of a group. Steven Cohen, who authored the above study, also coauthored a well-known essay in the magazine *Commentary* on this very aspect of Jewish existence:

> Embedded in notions of Jewish peoplehood are strong familial or "tribal" associations. But the openness of the Jewish people to converts makes plain that the familial bind is itself a function not solely of biology but of a shared history, closely similar religious customs and practices. Through centuries of life as a minority group, Jews could thus function as something of a global

polity. Leaders of far-flung local communities, both lay and rabbinic, maintained contact with each other, coordinated action, and, insofar as possible, strove to provide mutual assistance.[11]

Many new Jewish or spiritual initiatives have at their heart an exploration of personal identity with a Jewish twist. They are not aimed at bringing people to something larger than self as much as they are concerned with the development of the self within some Jewish context. It's all about the journey and not about the destination. The Jewish piece is voluntary and may be just a stimulus; rather than the beginning of a journey to Judaism, such initiatives have yet to demonstrate that they are more than a means to personal discovery and that they manage to communicate and even advance commitment to this sense of a global polity.

Peoplehood and Familism

Definitions of peoplehood keep returning to the theme of familism, the feeling of being part of an extended family, with all of its benefits and disadvantages: the caring and overcaring, the presumed knowledge of each other or the kindness to the stranger, the compassion and ironic complacency, guilt, triangulation, the heightened interest and pride, the heaping of responsibility and the denial of responsibility in the quest for comfort. All of these conflicting notions exist within families, so they should also exist within extended families to varying degrees. The Yiddish word for *family* is *mishpoche*, from the Hebrew word *mishpacha*. In the *Joys of Yiddish*, Leo Rosten defines this word and illustrates its meaning as follows:

1. Family, including relatives far, near, remote and numerous.
2. Ancestors, lineage.
   The closest thing in English to *mishpoche* is "clan."
   Parents, grandparents, siblings, uncles, aunts, cousins (first, second, once removed) all form part of the extended family Jews call *mishpoche*.

Nothing is more flattering than to say someone comes from a fine or distinguished *mishpoche*.

"All Jews are *mishpoche*" means that all Israel is one family. This intense feeling of a common heritage, common obligations, common values, has led the State of Israel to accept, without exception, Jewish immigrants of the widest, sharpest cultural differences.

The Chase Manhattan Bank's memorable advertising campaign is built around the slogan "You have a friend at Chase Manhattan." 'Tis said that a sign in the window of the Bank of Israel reads, "But here you have *Mishpoche!*"[12]

We may laugh at this joke, and that laughter would signify that we understand Rosten's meaning. Or we may not find it funny but understand it anyway. What if we were to pick apart the term *mishpoche* to determine its exact meaning, not only in a dictionary but to us as a people?

How can we transition from *mishpoche* to peoplehood without losing some warmth in the translation? Perhaps we cannot. Yiddish is the funny, sad, expressive language it is precisely because it joined people in communication who felt a shared sense of fate and destiny. It was also a unique language to the Jewish people, like Hebrew or Ladino. Idiosyncratic quirks in a language "owned" by one people reveal just how much a language expresses values particular to that people, like a signature or an odd way of dressing. In fact, Michael Wex, in his wonderful discussion of Yiddish, *Born to Kvetch*, concludes that Yiddish is a language with expressions and nuances designed to separate Jews from non-Jews: "Yiddish arose, at least in part, to give voice to a system of opposition and exclusion."[14] All families and peoples use language as a means of creating intimacy, privacy, and insider/outsider status. Relating *mishpoche* to peoplehood and its transition and translation to English—a language shared by millions across racial, religious, and national lines—seems crazy but is worth an attempt.

To be in a family means to be joined by some common ancestral ties that create a natural bond, even if this bond is not meaningful in any practical terms. A second cousin once removed is still related, whether or not we know much about each other or ever get together outside family celebrations. There is nothing that we can do to remove his status as cousin, even if we do not like each other. His "cousin-hood" is a *fact*. This fact often generates warmth and sometimes generates disappointment precisely because people within families often do not take the time to make natural bonds meaningful; it is as if they do not need to ask questions or strengthen a relationship as they would with a friend simply because they are in a family unit. There is presumed knowledge. You may hear an adult sibling complaining that her brothers and sisters know little about her and seem uninterested in the details of her life, who she is and why, when they may just assume that this information is, to some degree, unnecessary to the relationship. After all, they are siblings regardless of intimate knowledge.

Intimate knowledge *is* important because it extends worth. I am related to someone, *and* I have taken the time to know that someone because that is what makes my family genuinely meaningful in my life. This also explains why in our definition of peoplehood the notion of an extended family is not enough; familism must be accompanied by purpose, because the existence of a family is not enough of a reason to take pride in a family.

This tie by birth and mutual family has one component that is rarely discussed but, in its absence, can generate great tensions within families: responsibility. Being in the same family signifies a shared fate as a group, but it should also imply a collective sense of responsibility toward each other. Neglecting responsibilities within a family setting can lead to profound emotional and physical dysfunction and the breakdown of relationships. In order for the collective bonds of family to have meaning, they must be characterized by two qualities: comfort and obligation. Families where people only take comfort from each other but share no tasks or offer no assistance will break down because no one is accountable. Such weak ties feed into personal narcissism or self-indulgence. Tragedy can disrupt such groupings when no one picks up the pieces. To illustrate, imagine a family table where one person invites the guests, cooks, cleans, and takes care of all chores while the other family members look on with bored detachment. Resentment builds in the host, the one family member who looks at his lazy blood relatives and decries the situation, swearing never to host his family for a dinner party again.

The responsibilities within families can range from just showing up at family gatherings to taking an active role in the preservation of family history and/or sustaining and caring about the health and welfare of those in the clan. In purely biological terms, it is this enduring concern created by the bonds of birth and ancestry that helps ensure survival. The moment a baby is born, he or she has a group of diverse individuals who immediately care about his or her existence and will often go to extreme measures to make sure that that child is able to live and thrive in conditions, pleasant or adverse.

But there is another side to family health and vibrancy: comfort. If individuals were connected merely by collective responsibility without getting any pleasure or personal growth from these bonds, these ties would soon cease to be meaningful and would weaken over time. People take pleasure and comfort from families that demonstrate concern and pride in the achievements of individual members. They take comfort from having a web of emotional connections to people who care about their mental, spiritual, physical, and fiscal health. Individuals who have friends at work and in their neighborhood and on the golf course understand that their friends are often limited by contexts. A sports partner may see only a piece of the total life of his friend; his colleague at work will see another. One of the benefits of family is that there is, or should be, a holistic concern for each of its members. Whereas friends often come with "contexts," family members rarely do. They are related to you in every setting in which you can imagine. Again, the existence of this bond of *mishpoche* is a fact, whether we like it or not and whether we like our family members or not.

> *Several years ago, I was invited to address a small group of young Jewish social activists on Jewish responses to poverty, issues about which I care passionately. I spoke from a point of commitment about three types of poverty affecting different Jewish populations. I*

began with what I thought was a cogent explanation of tikkun olam (repairing the world), and I traveled with these college graduates across the Jewish globe to give them examples of different types of poverty and how the Jewish community responds to each tragic situation. A young woman raised her hand and said something that I'll never forget. "Is this what the federation spends its money on? I don't want to spend money on people somewhere else. I want to spend it on people in the inner city." Fair enough, I thought. I applauded her ideological commitment; people like her make an enormous difference in the world. We help all in need, not just the Jewish community. It was the dialogue that followed that hurt me most. I responded to her question with an unapologetic "yes." Supporting efforts to alleviate Jewish poverty worldwide is a major pillar of the work that the federation does. But I also told her why, in my mind, this kind of support is critical. "This is our family," I said. Yet she quickly retorted, "These people are not my family."

—MISHA GALPERIN

If we mark personal identity through relationships, it is natural to believe that certain relationships will matter more than others. We naturally expect parents to find their own children cuter than the children who live down the road. We do not judge parents for being too biased and not subjective enough. Being a parent not only entitles you to subjective treatment of those you love, but it also positively demands it. If you did not find your children cuter, smarter, better behaved, and more lovable than your friend's children, you may not parent them with the degree of love, affection, and responsibility that are integral to parenthood. And if a parent did not offer preferential treatment to his own children, we would question whether something was amiss.

But what if definitions of family are extended beyond those in our gene pool to those in our "tribal constellation"? Would the same feelings apply? Or, asked differently, can we extend the definition of family to connections beyond our direct gene pool? Specifically, the same people who feel that it is okay to love family more than friends or strangers may not feel that being a member of the Jewish people should allow for any kind of preferential treatment at all. In fact, such individuals may say that giving your own people preferential treatment is racist, biased, and not acceptable in a pluralistic and diverse society.

Some people regard being Jewish as being a member of a large interconnected web of people who treat each other with special regard. This feeling manifests itself as a fierce loyalty to individual Jewish people, to the State of Israel, and to Jewish values. It may mean feeling a peculiar kinship with someone standing in an airport simply because she is wearing a T-shirt with a Jewish symbol, or it may mean opening up the newspaper and first scanning it for articles about Israel. Beyond surface attachment, it may mean that my ethnic affiliations come first in terms of volunteer time, charitable giving, or my choice of life partner or neighborhood. Is it justifiable for someone who lives in a multicultural environment that espouses tolerance to offer this treatment to others just because they are Jewish or to make life choices that prefer ethnic affiliation?

Philosophers have long discussed whether we can show loyalty to one particular group over another, particularly in cases of lifeboat ethics or triage, where selection of one individual out of a group may have life or death consequences. Can we save someone who is in our own family, for example, over a complete stranger, simply because we have blood ties to that individual? If we believe in the famous Talmudic teaching that no one's blood is redder than anyone else's, then it would seem that we are not allowed to show preferential treatment to anyone. Showing preferential treatment would liken us to a divine being, possessed of ultimate judgment, who could measure the worth of one life over another. How do we know that when we save an uncle from a building on fire before rescuing anyone else that he will find the cure for cancer or love more people during his lifetime or do something that changes humanity as we know it? Perhaps we should save someone younger, smarter, richer, or more compassionate than this uncle, whom we are merely saving because he is our mother's brother and has joined our family for Passover Seders from time immemorial? The factors mentioned for such an evaluation seem almost absurd the moment they hit the paper.

The answer is that we do not know how to measure the worth of a life except in very limited ways. Membership in a family is simply one of those ways. Kenneth Feinberg, the grand master of the 9/11 compensation fund, was given the task of assessing the worth of life in distributing compensatory funding after the bombing of the Twin Towers in 2001. He discusses the impossibility of this task in his book, *What Is Life Worth?*[13] Reading it, one can instantly see that the complexity of the task is not answering *why* but *how*. How do we go about analyzing the factors that contribute to grief once we have already measured and compensated for financial loss? It's a wonder that the work of helping the victims ever came to an end. And yet, despite the difficulty, Feinberg met with every family who was willing to share their family story. What is revealed in story after story is just how much personal identity is contingent on personal connections in ways beyond measure. Philosophers *do* entertain and justify the selection of a family member first in making a difficult choice because the fiber of family connections is one of the most important ways that we relate to others and build lives in society.

Within every family, there are takers and givers. Within this constellation, there are also sustainers and joiners. Virtually every family has individuals who take the family more seriously than others. They are the members who organize the cousins' club, the annual family barbeque, the fiftieth wedding anniversary parties. There are also family recorders who care about the family history and carry within them a lot of "institutional" memory. They may be the ones to write down several volumes of family genealogy or never forget a card on a birthday. These figures—the family organizers—are the cement of a family. They consciously create events, communicate regularly, or record family memories so that the family has a sense of belonging to something larger than self in a real and possibly meaningful way.

Along with this type—who are more rare—are those who are happy to be on the receiving end of such deliberative crafting of family and show up at family events and celebrations and show others the impressive family history drawn up by some great uncle. They are actively proud of their family but do not see themselves as actively sustaining these ties in the extended sense. Their foremost commitment is to their immediate family. Any additional layers are a value add-on but not something they seek out. These are the joiners.

The sustainers and the joiners are not alone in the extended family model. There are also those who do not want to join and are certainly not going to create conscious family ties or sustain them. They are simply members, those who take a more aggressive stance in questioning their place in the family unit and become kvetchers (complainers). Complainers are simply genealogical facts. They are born into families and regard this birth as purely accidental and not meaningful in any particular way. They do not seek to strengthen ties, quite the opposite. They are only or mainly interested in a universe of their own construction and not the inherited world of family. If they are particularly unlucky and inherit a place in a family riddled by dysfunction, they become complainers. They try to escape the predestined universe of family because they regard it as destructive.

If peoplehood is integrally connected to familism, then we have to ask ourselves how we can best deal with members and kvetchers, sustainers and joiners. There are approaches that suggest that we concentrate on strengthening interested parties and ignore the accidental members, while marginalizing the kvetchers for fear of their potentially destructive impact on the unit. Enhanced focus on the sustainers and joiners will stabilize the central magnet of the community to bring in more members. Some fraction of these new members, over time and with increased participation, may go on to become sustainers. Thus, the core will keep growing and will be self-sustaining. Investing in the margins may or may not yield results.

Others argue that there should be no core or margin; identity is not a bull's-eye with the most committed arrows landing in the center ring. Community affiliation is a series of interlocking and overlapping networks into which individuals move in and out. How, then, would it be possible to work on the center? Instead, if we engage those least affiliated, they will bring along others. We are not here to take sides in this well-contested debate, as much as to show that without any feeling of family or connectivity, there is virtually no possibility of outreach.

Not My Family

What about individuals who don't share the feeling of family at all, as represented by the comments of the young activist in an earlier vignette who did not regard Jews as family? Or, let's take a look at this observation from www.jewcy.com's webmaster Joey Kurtzman:

> I don't regard the Jewish people as my family. I feel a great affection for Jewish culture. I value Jewish tradition, and I feel a connection to other Jews. But there's no point in pretending that this is at all comparable to what I feel for my family. A Jewish life ought to be one in which the wisdom and insights of Jewish scripture and Jewish history help us more effectively engage with, and navigate in the world in which we actually live. It shouldn't serve as an alternative to that world, a sort of soft Amish-ism by which we retreat to the narrow particularistic concerns of one traditional community.[15]

Kurtzman raises an important issue. Does being Jewish have to mean a familylike feeling toward fellow Jews, or is this too particularistic? Surely, we can have affection and appreciation without believing that we are somehow related?

The familism of which we are speaking is not a replacement or even similar in degree to the feelings we have for our own blood relatives, nor should it be. But it should consist of a sense that being Jewish is a statement of uniqueness; uniqueness is not the same as being particularistic. Uniqueness is the recognition that there is something different about you that joins you to a group that is happy to have you as a member, that takes pride in a collective sense of identity in which you are included.

What these competing or complementary definitions of peoplehood do is force us to narrow the language and create the holding ground for a concept. And this concept of peoplehood needs to be both about feeling *and* about doing. If we merely have feelings about belonging that are not backed by actions that show membership, we will soon find that the feelings pale into insignificance.

If peoplehood is best expressed through common sentiment, then we need to generate experiences as a community that will enhance and expand that feeling so that it will touch more individuals and deepen from a superficial sweep of nostalgia to a demanding and lasting commitment. Again, Ariel offers a challenge to notions of peoplehood: "[F]or a vital sense of Peoplehood to hold sway, the Jewish people as a people have to stand for something, and be working on a shared project, even if they are doing so in a multitude of ways."[16] We know that shared Jewish experiences are the most powerful identity markers of Judaism today, be it a Jewish camping experience, a group trip to Israel, or joint projects in social activism. These are immersion experiences that soak up all of our thoughts and senses for a time and help deepen our level of engagement with Judaism so that a small emotional tug grows into something greater and more profound. A community-wide discussion of how to create such initiatives and engender such feelings should become, if it has not already, an important part of the communal agenda.

What Peoplehood Is Not

In a recent essay that questions whether peoplehood is really a meaningful and useful term, one writer concluded emphatically that peoplehood can only be understood by what it is not rather than by what it is.

> I think peoplehood is better understood negatively, i.e., by that which it is not: not a religion, nor a nationality, nor an ethnicity, nor a culture. Peoplehood is none of these things because many Jews don't identify with them, and peoplehood is meant to be universal. Really, peoplehood might be best understood as devoid of any meaning. It says: we don't know what this Jewish thing is, but we're here and we're in it together. In this negative sense, there is something appealing about peoplehood. It adds no normative content, and thus excludes no one. Each of us can fill it with our own meaning, and color it with whatever

emotional connection we happen to have.... Peoplehood
embraces it all and by saying nothing, includes everything.[17]

Can a word mean something if it can mean everything? Can a concept
that is stretched to hold so much, hold anything at all? The author is
being cynical in his plea for peoplehood to signify something universal
in nature that is nonexclusionary. Without any limits, peoplehood
lacks inherent meaning and, therefore, any substance. There have
been other outcries against the use of peoplehood as a term with little
substance. This criticism must be confronted honestly. Neil Gillman,
professor of Jewish studies at The Jewish Theological Seminary of
America, calls peoplehood an agenda whose time has passed: "It no
longer will work to inspire people to be serious, committed Jews."[18]

For the record, peoplehood is not a discussion of nationality as it
might be if we were all citizens of Israel and a dimension of our
Jewishness included being legal participants in the national affairs of
the state. This definition would limit peoplehood to those living in
Israel (to be discussed later). Peoplehood is also not an antireligious or
a nonreligious definition of Jewish life, as it is often accused of being. It
is not a way to dilute and strip a religion/culture of its rituals and beliefs
in order to find some common composition that Jews share regardless
of religious behaviors. Judaism cannot be fully meaningful without the
faith, the history of belief, and the rituals that have connected Jews for
centuries. Peoplehood is not merely a leveraging tool or hook into support for charities and Jewish institutions. Peoplehood is also not solely
about an ethnicity that reduces Judaism to certain cultural or culinary
activities, as important as these activities may be. Such a definition of
peoplehood may be pleasurable, but it is not demanding, nor is it deep.
To demonstrate why ethnicity is a poor substitute for peoplehood, one
need look no further than a popular Israeli ad for Jewish study that, in
striking white lettering on a black background, asks the question: "Has
Judaism Come Down to This?," and beneath the block letters sits a
solitary bagel. Judaism must be more and is more. If it is not, then we
have failed our historic tradition and reduced it to simple shared food
associations.

There were challenges that once offered charge and purpose for the Jewish community—endangered Jewish populations around the globe, the building and support of Israel (especially in wartime), and combating anti-Semitism. In the absence of these urgent needs and causes, the Jewish community has found itself in the "pareve" neutral ground of a passionless Jewish existence. Urgency and crisis must be replaced by strategic thinking about a Jewish future that is complicated and subtle and not only crisis driven. If we want to attract people to this extended family, we must also and predominantly show off our successes.

Creating a House

Our chapter presented definitions of peoplehood and a discussion of the relationship between peoplehood and membership in a family. To define our terms with greater clarity, we also discussed what peoplehood is not. Research shows us that peoplehood is on the emotional decline as a shared notion of collective identity. Some may regard this news as no news at all or not very noteworthy. And yet, a commitment to peoplehood has, among other dimensions, practical implications for research, funding, and communal priority setting. There are Jewish leaders today who believe that those who do not share a sense of Jewish peoplehood—either through apathy, intermarriage, or the cultivation of other interests—are not worth investing in as a Jewish community. Once such people have chosen to move out in some fashion, our responsibility is first and foremost to strengthen the core—those with strong levels of commitment. There are other Jewish leaders who see the enormous shift in American Jewish identity and have a more inclusive inclination that has policy implications: create an open tent and make room for everyone in it because, sadly, there *is* plenty of room. Often, this position is without any boundaries. Anyone can enter the tent and benefit from belonging.

In between these extremes is a position more nuanced than either of these strident voices of debate. A shared notion of peoplehood can unite and unify, but not without borders and boundaries. Instead of a tent, we like the metaphor of a house, a *bayit*, a space that houses a family and has more solid walls than a tent but has plenty of open windows and doors. Without a shared commitment to peoplehood, it is hard to achieve *shalom bayit*, a bit of peace within our divided house. Without a collective commitment to peoplehood, it is difficult to ensure that the commandment of *hakhnasat orkhim*, inviting and welcoming guests, is a *mitzvah*—a sacred commandment—that takes place within this large Jewish house. More people will join our extended family, come into this *bayit*, if there is energy, warmth, and creativity within, if they feel welcome as family.

Sir Jonathan Sacks, chief Orthodox rabbi of the United Congregations of the British Commonwealth, also used the metaphor of home in his book *The Home We Build Together*. In contrast to the country home to which one may be invited as a guest or a hotel which one has temporary ownership of space but no responsibility, Sacks argues that to create a genuinely diverse society with common values, we need to use the metaphor of home. "'Home' means that we care about belonging ... 'build' means that we focus on responsibilities, not just rights; contributions, not claims ... 'together' means integration, not segregation."[19] Working together to build a structure we can all live in requires unity amidst diversity.

Within each house is a table, and seated around our community table are those who may not normally eat or socialize together. Our respective roles in the Jewish communal world have enabled us to create many such tables of unlikely company, and we recognize that there are fewer and fewer Jewish institutions today that are capable of creating community tables. The conversation and debate at these tables does not have to and should not reflect agreement. The conversations should continue the tradition of debate that began with the Talmud and has characterized Jewish life ever since. Our tradition remains alive when it remains a serious object of conversation among Jews who are not like one another. The message is twofold. Create a house of warmth and inclusivity. Place a table in that house where Judaism is taken seriously. Build a better house.

QUESTIONS FOR CONVERSATION

1. Do you see yourself as part of an extended family? Explain your answer.
2. Do you feel that associations with family are generally positive or negative?
3. Some regard the notion of familism as racist or too particularistic. Where do you stand on this?
4. Describe an incident that provoked your own feeling of alienation from the Jewish community.
5. Now describe an incident that encouraged strong feelings of belonging within the Jewish community. What can you do to create those feelings for others?

2

COLLECTIVE JEWISH IDENTITY

I am with a group of students teaching about Jewish identity for college credit. Our syllabus is extensive and ranges from textual-ity to gender, persecution to redemption, Diaspora to homeland, and the impact each of these factors has on collective Jewish iden-tity. Some students have taken an active role in their campus Jewish lives. Others are far removed from it. One young man shakes his head when we talk about the impact of denomination-alism on Judaism. "While everyone is fighting about what it means to be a Jew and who is a Jew, I just figured I would do something else. These kinds of arguments are just a turnoff, really."

—Erica Brown

A young professional recently quipped, "If I want to find out if some-one is Jewish, I ask them if they are an M-O-T (member of the tribe). If they have no idea what I'm talking about, then I know they're not one of us." But what is the "us" to which she is referring? The "us" may be defined in very specific ways. "It encompasses Jews joining together to form organizations, charities, industries, and political move-ments. It may represent an attachment to Jewish friends, to American Jews, to Israel, and ultimately, to the Jewish people."[1] In other ways, the "us" is not about formal or institutional affiliations at all. It is a simple, often inexplicable web of attachments to a people that often expresses itself most strongly as an emotional claim. To unlock and develop a shared language of peoplehood, we have to take a step back and formulate a way to understand the creation of both collective and personal identity.

Being Jewish today may be more complex than at any other time in Jewish history. In his novel *Operation Shylock*, Philip Roth conducts a fascinating literary exploration of Jewish peoplehood today that places us at the center of an identity storm:

> Why couldn't the Jews be one people? Why must Jews be in conflict with one another? Why must they be in conflict with themselves? Because the divisiveness is not just between Jew and Jew—it is within the individual Jew. Is there a more manifold personality in all the world? I don't say divided. Divided is nothing.... But inside every Jew there is a *mob* of Jews. The good Jew, the bad Jew. The new Jew, the old Jew. The lover of Jews, the hater of Jews. The friend of the goy, the enemy of the goy. The arrogant Jew, the wounded Jew. The pious Jew, the rascal Jew. The coarse Jew, the gentle Jew. The defiant Jew, the appeasing Jew. The Jewish Jew, the de-Jewed Jew. Shall I go on? Do I have to expound upon the Jew as a three-thousand-year amassment of mirrored fragments?... Is it any wonder that a Jew is always disputing? He *is* a dispute, incarnate.[2]

Roth's mirrored fragments force us straight into the complicated, uncomfortable, but somehow familiar arguments of what it means to be Jewish. This time, the debate is taking place internally within each person. And the dispute is taking place within each Jew who ponders the curious inheritance of multiple layers of identity. From persecution to prosperity, the Jewish people have wrestled with their destiny and their identity. We give ourselves names and are given names by others. As a result, being Jewish today also seems more confusing than ever.

Isaac Bashevis Singer communicated this multiplicity of selves in an anecdote he liked to share with audiences when questioned about Jewish fragmentation:

> A man has returned from Warsaw and he is telling his friend, "I saw a Jew who vas poring over the Talmud day and night. I saw a Jew who vas vaving the red flag of communism. I saw a Jew who vas passing out leaflets to come see his new play on Spinoza."
>
> "So? Vhat's so unusual about that?" his friend answers. "There are a lot of Jews in Varsaw."
>
> "But don't you understand, my friend?" the man yelled. "It vas all the same Jew!"[3]

Singer's joke is just as true today as it was when it was originally told. The many portals into Jewish life today—from ethnic hip-hop to high-brow literature, spiritual searching to Jewish board involvement—have made Judaism richer and more expansive in some ways, but have also created great ambivalence about Jewish identity generally. Tiffany Schlain, in her short film history of the Jewish people called *The Tribe* offers us a written discussion guide to her film, stating:

> Who's perplexed? We are. And so is everyone we know. What does it mean to be a Jew today? Going to synagogue? Supporting Israel? Eating bagels and lox? Knowing what *chutzpah* means? All of the above? Or something completely different? ... It's very Jewish to be perplexed.[4]

Collective identity is more than language, food, musical preferences, or social networking. Identity formation must also involve an active engagement, a wrestling with the self and the collective conscience. One "option" Schlain does not entertain is apathy. Instead of the "all of the above" choice she presents in this passage, what happens when Jewish identity is "none of the above"—namely, it is not even a consideration? The wrestling or struggle is nonexistent, although struggle has been an inherent part of our collective Jewish identity for millennia. To return to this sense of struggle we must turn back to the very beginning of Jewish identity and advance forward through history.

What's in a Name?

We meet the first Jew, Abraham, at the end of Genesis 11. He is from a small family who wanders in search of a better life and settles in an ancient city until Abraham hears a resounding call from God to leave his homeland and travel to Canaan. There, he will become the father of a nation in its own homeland. There is a great sense of promise and possibility in this nascent journey. We do not know why Abraham was chosen for this mission. We know simply that he answered the call and, in so doing, began a fledgling tribe that, over time, became the Israelites. If you asked whether someone was a member of the tribe in Abraham's day, the question would have been quite literal.

And yet, the Jewish people as a collective entity are surprisingly not named after the first Jew. The Jewish people acquired the name Israel from one intriguing biblical verse found in Genesis. Our patriarch Jacob was traveling with his large family and crossed them over the Jabbok River. Returning on his own, he had an encounter that changed him and eventually transformed the Jewish people from a small family to a people of faith, influence, and achievement: "Jacob was left alone. And a man wrestled with him until the break of dawn."[5] When they parted, this "man" asked Jacob for his name, and Jacob complied. At that point, the man, a divine messenger whose own identity was concealed, said: "Your name shall no longer be Jacob, but Israel, for you have striven with beings divine and human and have prevailed."[6] Jacob faced many obstacles in his path that shaped his personal identity, but one identity prevailed—that of the wrestler.

Our people call themselves "Israel" because Jacob wrestled with God and humans and prevailed. We are also called Hebrews from the term ivri'im, which means "those who crossed over." The word Jew comes from the Hebrew yehudi, which originally referred to the descendants of

Jacob's son Judah and the name for a geographic area in the Land of Israel. All these names signify a faith, a nation, and a tribe while also suggesting particular characteristics of this membership: tenacity, difficulty, alienation, otherness, connection to a land, and remarkable perseverance.

To contemporize the biblical conversation, professor Michael Walzer contends that collective Jewish identity today is anomalous. We do not know who we are, not because Jewish identity is so limiting but, conversely, because it is so expansive:

> [T]he Jews are a people, a nation, for a long time a stateless nation, but nonetheless a collective of a familiar kind. There are many nations, and we are one among them. And, at the same time, the Jews are a religious community, a community of faith, as we say in the United States—which is another collective of a familiar kind. There are many religions, and ours is one among them. The anomaly is that these two collectives are not of the same kind, and they don't ordinarily or, better, they don't, except in the Jewish case, coincide.[7]

Walzer argues that Jewish identity is confusing precisely because we have more than one collective identity, and each identity is in itself a way that people create familiar and lasting connections. Yet these two identities together—nation and faith—have difficulty overlapping or assume characteristics that actively work against each other. Other scholars have tried to find and define the areas of overlap.

Leading political scientist Daniel Elazar described the Jewish community as a "unique blend of kinship and consent." Kinship and consent assume a level of conscious choice. No longer do Jews share the common language of ritual practice and Jewish law, nor are they joined by the shared insecurity of oppression and persecution. In the absence of these historical markers of cohesion, the Jewish community of the twenty-first century is struggling for a shared language of anything. Some have argued that the very term *Jewish community* is a misnomer, giving the impression of group loyalty and ethnic affiliation where none really exists. Elazar's description of kinship and consent is problematic because the boundaries of kinship have been stretched beyond recognizable borders. The word *consent* implies a decision to belong. But we know that many unaffiliated Jews are not involved or engaged simply as a result of ignorance or apathy.

Some would argue that being Jewish in this day and age is different than at any other point in Jewish history because the level of affluence and security that Jews enjoy today has reached a previously unimaginable zenith, particularly in America. Without the fear for survival, Jews in North America have been able to blend into American society and accept American norms as self-defining. Two prominent sociologists, Roberta Rosenberg Farber and Chaim Waxman, have concluded that for Jews without Jewish education or little Jewish background, "being American was the more prominent and the more important identity."

> Tolerance and diversity are American values and as such have largely been accepted by the American Jewish population. America's greatness has always been in the multiplicity of religious, ethnic and racial groups that claim adherence to the same national identity. The price of this pluralistic diversity, combined with a lack of persecution, is a fluidity of personal commitment and a subsequent weakened and/or symbolic sense of minority group identity.[8]

The competitive advantage that being American has over being Jewish for Jews of the twenty-first century in North America has, until recently, not presented significant challenges for community building. A commitment to equality and diversity is regarded as a Jewish value by many Jews. National, religious, and cultural identity was and still is regarded by many Jews as a condition of confluence, not conflict. But this union of multiple identities is increasingly raising questions that bring the issue of Jewish identity into the foreground:

- What happens when these identities *do* find themselves in conflict?
- When Jewish identity is deeply entangled with American identity, how do American Jews relate to and unite with Jews from other parts of the world?
- Specifically, what happens to Jewish identity when it confronts Israeli nationalism in politics, policy, and cultural norms that do not conform to American values? Where is Jewish loyalty stronger?
- Jews have always "enjoyed" an insider/outsider status in most geographic locations, particularly before Jews were granted citizenship in their host countries. This status has been both harmful and helpful. It often gave Jews a countercultural edge in both adapting to surrounding norms and questioning them. What happens to Jewish creativity, innovation, and achievement when Jews lose this outsider status?

These are only a sampling of questions that have to be asked in considering Jewish identity. Before any of these questions are examined atomistically, it is critical to develop some notion of identity construction generally.

Jews believed that their identity was, at one point and for many centuries, determined by revelation tinged with struggle. God determined our identity through a revealed text that offered us a covenant of laws and a master story—the narrative of Jewish peoplehood in the Bible—that stretched across time and experience. The story begins with the patriarch Abraham, who was given a charge through an act of revelation to travel to Canaan, leave his past behind, and build a nation in a homeland. Abraham, through an act of covenant, set about his task of acquiring land through alliances, conquest, purchase, and the hard manual labor of digging wells and building altars. And yet, although the homeland piece of his calling was demanding, it was still possible. The struggle for Abraham came in the charge to father a nation because his wife was barren. Chapter after chapter of Genesis takes us through the trials of Abraham to have a child so he can begin the task of nation building. The mission and the struggle. These two facets facing the founder of Judaism were to face every subsequent generation of Jews. Driven by a promise and an enduring sense of purpose, Jews struggled with external and internal obstacles that stood in the way but did not deter them.

Our next significant chapter in Jewish biblical history is slavery in Egypt and the redemption that comes with a host of responsibilities formed in the face of oppression. We cannot persecute strangers because we ourselves were strangers. Each layer of experience adds a layer of responsibility, shaping Jewish identity through immersion in a culture antithetical to our own. The wilderness years that followed were filled with leadership crises. They also represent the transition from slavery to freedom with the giving of law at Sinai and the building of a *Mishkan*, a Tabernacle, to house the divine presence. The *Mishkan* was built with private donations and represented the building of the people; unlike the half-shekel commitment that everyone was obliged to give later, the *Mishkan* was built through individual contributions of money, building materials, and labor. Remarkably, Moses had to turn away these voluntary contributions because the communal pot was overflowing. The initial sense of ownership was very powerful and palpable.

Later, when the Jews arrived in the Promised Land, the commandments they received through revelation were coupled with the new commandments related to a homeland of their own. The possession of land and the move from slave to traveler to homeowner brought about significant identity changes that are reflected in the Bible's prophetic texts. Anxieties about the harvest replaced the fears and complaints of wilderness living. Jews outside a homeland had a different identity than Jews within a homeland. Jews in their own homeland enjoyed greater autonomy and self-reliance, but this often came at the price of belief and dependence on God, as the prophets were quick to remind the people.

In the later prophets, we read of the Temple's construction and a new phase of Jewish identity—a mediated relationship with God through the agency of the priest. Jerusalem became the spiritual center of the Jewish universe. People came to Jerusalem three times a year for pilgrimages and sought expiation for their sins by bringing sacrifices.

When the first and second Temples were destroyed, both biblical and rabbinic literature reflect the profound anguish of a people who had lost their spiritual center. So much of Jewish identity was, at that point, tied into Temple worship that rabbinic debates ensued about how to best worship God without a communal altar. There were those who gave up meat and wine because these were sacrificed at the altar. One rabbinic sage went so far as to say that Jews without a Temple could experience no happiness in this world. That emotional change represented a very significant change of identity.

The next stage of Jewish identity was wrapped in study. The study hall became the new Temple, due, in large part, to the visionary thinking of a few scholars who radicalized Jewish identity. They claimed that in the absence of Temple worship, the study of Jewish texts was the new path to God. In this new identity of scholarship in place of worship, the texts of divine revelation were still the same, but the relationship to the text for the majority of Jews changed. Jews were expected to be the owners and interpreters of these texts. Imagine, if you will, a textual identity that mirrors the look of the Talmudic page or a page of a Bible embellished by commentary. The text lies in the center, and all around the text is a conversation spanning time and place. A sixth-century Babylonian scholar is arguing with a fourteenth-century French Talmudist. These scholars come from particular places and centuries, but they all viewed the texts in front of them as part of the masterworks that determine Jewish life.

Over the next centuries—from roughly the sixth century BCE to the middle of the eighteenth century CE—Jewish identity largely consisted of an ongoing relationship to Jewish texts mediated through rabbis and scholars and the personal observance of commandments. The Jewish Diaspora changed radically after the Spanish Inquisition and the expulsion of Jews from the Iberian Peninsula. The spread and prominence of the Diaspora added a new layer to Jewish identity; the insecurity and instability of living outside a homeland was coupled with relatively constant threats of anti-Semitism depending on the host country. Christian and Muslim anti-Semitism created an extreme picture of Jewish subordination and even physical deformation that was bound to make an impression on the Jewish soul. From small identity markers such as anti-Semitic woodcuts to pogroms and blood libels, anti-Semitism became yet another layer in Jewish self-identity.

The "last chapter" that is still evolving in Jewish identity is the post-Enlightenment modern identity of the Jew. No longer constrained by ghetto walls or the denial of citizenship, many Jews broke the traditional mold of observance and study through assimilation and intermarriage, the forming of new religious denominations, and their increasing presence still further out in the Diaspora, from Europe to the United States. In 1806, Napoleon convened a Jewish court, the *Sanhedrin*, to force the French Jewish community to face its own new identity and probe the question of multiple allegiances. Who are you? French or Jewish? This externally coerced questioning would come to represent and signify the deeper inner questioning taking place for Jews confronting modernity all over Europe.

Modern Jewish identity is deeply nuanced and complex. As Jews learned most painfully, modernity did not prevent anti-Semitism. Giving up on core aspects of revelation and tradition did not mean easy acceptance into the mainstream culture. This pattern was to repeat itself in the two most identity-shaping events of modern Judaism: the Holocaust and the creation of the State of Israel. Although both anti-Semitism and Zionism were building a following throughout Eastern and Western Europe, it was not until both movements reached their apex that their respective impact on Jewish identity was fully felt. The impact of both is still being felt.

Before the Enlightenment, traditional Judaism was the only Judaism. This did not mean that everyone was observant of biblical commandments and a believer in divine revelation. It simply meant that this was the only "version" of Judaism that people defined themselves through or against. Today, we have both a vibrant Israel and a full and active Diaspora Jewish community. Our core identity no longer comes from the study of Jewish texts. This once constant or persistent sense of identity cannot work today because Jewish texts are not central enough to the construction of a Jewish self. Many people can no longer read these texts in their original language or are uninterested in them even in translation. But if we were to break down the challenges of translation and study, a fundamental problem remains. Most Jews do not care about their intellectual heritage. If the text at the center of the page is not at the center of their lives, then it cannot possibly serve as the beginning of a collective language of fate and destiny for a people at large. Text is not at the center, nor is commandment. We have not found a comprehensive replacement. Responsibility for other Jews is waning as multiculturalism is on the rise. Anti-Semitism is still sadly alive and well, but—blessedly—is not used as an externally driven push to stronger Jewish affiliation. Nor is a sense of homeland shared by all Jews today. In addition, for the past several decades, Israel has struggled not only with being oppressed but with being in power, a status for which we prayed but for which we had little historical practice. Jewish political autonomy is still relatively new to us. Our challenge today is to form a meaningful Judaism in the absence of the old challenges and assumptions that once took us by storm.

Sir Jonathan Sacks observes that the real test Judaism faces today is affluence. Putting this within its historical context, he argues that most nations and empires fell not as a result of military weakness or debt but through the decay of purpose or morality.

> When times are hard, people grow. They come together. They bury their differences. There is a sense of community and solidarity.... The real test of a nation is not can it survive a crisis, but can it survive the *lack* of crisis? Can it stay strong during times of ease and plenty, power and prestige? That is the challenge that has defeated every civilization known to history.[9]

This, Sacks argues, is the challenge that Judaism faces today. In the absence of obvious crisis and in the face of affluence and influence, can we sustain a sense of purpose and unity?

In Steven Cohen and Gabriel Horenczyk's book, *National Variations in Jewish Identity*, the authors question what happens to identity when it is not as all-enveloping as it once was, as our sweep of Jewish history affirms. "Once Jewish identity had become less than total, it seemed the more imperative to argue for the significance of what remained. Paradoxically, sometimes the grandeur of the claims made for it increased proportionally as its scope declined."[10] We may be grasping for straws to define ourselves now that the totality of Jewishness no longer embraces us.

At every turn in this survey of Jewish history, there was reaction and preservation; those who craved innovation and change and those who desired stability and continuity. There was always a group that held fast to the old ways and those who searched vigorously for a way to a different future. The desire to preserve, conserve, and sustain fights powerfully against the impetus to innovate and change. And then there are the means of change that actually help sustain Judaism. Jonathan Sarna concludes his *American Judaism* with the thesis that historic revolts that challenged assumptions about Judaism, such as feminism and individualism, have ended up enriching Judaism in immeasurable ways. It is, in his words, the power of discontinuities that inform Jewish continuity. Reflecting on three hundred and fifty years of Jews in America, Sarna asks some of the critical identity questions every communal leader today juggles:

> Jews feel bewildered and uncertain. Should they focus on qual-
> ity to enhance Judaism or focus on quantity to increase the
> number of Jews? Embrace intermarriage as an opportunity for
> outreach or condemn it as a disaster for offspring? Build religious
> bridges or fortify religious boundaries? Strengthen religious
> authority or promote religious autonomy? Harmonize Judaism
> with contemporary culture or uphold Jewish tradition against
> contemporary culture? Compromise for the sake of Jewish unity
> or stand firm for cherished principles?[11]

And yet, through all these changes and despite the kind of questions that can easily cause paralysis, the presence of a collective Jewish identity remains. Throughout all these earlier phases, some sense of joint mission and purpose persists and endures. And, over time, Jewish group identity reflects all of these fragments—chosenness and oppression, textuality and assimilation, insider and outsider status, exile and statehood, anti-Semitism and citizenship, social activism and apathy.

All of these disparate pieces together, over time, created a modern Jewish identity filled with dialectic forces and contradictions: Philip Roth's perplexed Jew who argues within his inner self. These component parts combined to create a unique collective identity, as Leon Wieseltier observed in a discussion of his own Jewish identity.

> I think to be a Jew is not to be an American or a Westerner or a New Yorker. To be a Jew is to be a Jew. It is its own thing. Its own category, its own autonomous way of moving through the world. It's ancient and thick and vast and it's one specific thing that is not like anything else. And though it converges with other identities and other traditions and other ways of going through the world, it's not them.[12]

There is something different about Jewish identity from other identities, and perhaps there is a relief in allowing it to be different.

Ironically, one of the most astute observers of Jewish "difference" was the biblical Haman from the book of Esther, regarded as an arch-enemy of the Jews. In a Persian empire of 127 provinces, he singled out the Jews because he noticed that they did not act like other peoples over whom King Ahasuerus ruled. "There is a certain people, scattered and dispersed among the other peoples in all provinces of your realm, whose laws are different from those of any other people." Haman makes an observation that uncovers Jewish distinctiveness. Jews are a nation yet live among nations, scattered and dispersed yet ideologically aligned. This was an anomaly, and Haman observed it. Sadly, Haman was the first in a long line of irrational anti-Semites because of the conclusions he drew from this observation. The verse continues "… they who do not obey the king's laws and it is not in your Majesty's interest to tolerate them."[13] Haman's conclusion exemplifies *intolerance* of difference rather than the *observation* of difference. Jews, in his scheme, must pay a high price for their differences rather than be seen as contributing to an environment of diversity. Mordechai and Esther's gift to the Jewish people was in promoting the differences that Haman noted into a positive force for influence in ancient Persia.

The Challenge of Language

Defining the terms of peoplehood implies a concern for the impact of language on identity. What are the terms, expressions, and even body language that we associate with being Jewish?

Why, if it is so hard to come up with a lexicon of meaning, is it important to find unifying language at all? Language is a container, a holder of cultural ideas, principles of faith, and mechanisms of cohesion within groups. That language is the bedrock of Judaism is evident from the very first chapter of Genesis, where God speaks the word and only then creates the fish and the birds, the sun and land masses. Words of the Bible created more words, generating centuries of commentary. Talmudic pages are filled with debates about the meanings of words. In a fascinating letter sent to Maimonides by the famous convert Obadiah, the convert asks the renowned scholar whether he can recite "the God of my fathers" in his prayers because he was not born Jewish. The answer Maimonides offers is that conversion is also retroactive. Once someone converts, he takes on a new ideological lineage. His very genealogy changes, and that is reflected in the language he uses.

> I have just conducted a class in western Massachusetts and am kindly given a ride to the airport by two women who have been active in the federation world for decades. They are proud of being Jewish; they are passionate about their commitments. They would also like to see more young people stepping up so that, as volunteers, they can "retire" soon. I am both participating and eavesdropping on the conversation they are having. Always attuned to language, I hear them complain that things have fallen apart since the federation stopped using the motto "We Are One." It is dark in the car; this enables me to hear the words with greater clarity because the visual images are blurred. "Maybe no one thinks that we are one anymore, but I do. We are one. I still feel it, and it's the reason that I do everything I do. It was always the single most important expression that inspired me, and now we've let it go. Why did we let it go?"
>
> —ERICA BROWN

A famous feminist, in her review of the impact of feminism on society, concluded that in her twenty years of activism, she is still unsure how much male/female norms and behaviors have changed. She did conclude, however, that the use of language had changed, and that no revolution can take place without a linguistic revolution. Language both holds ideas and creates them, in as much as language gives people the tools to articulate feelings and observations that are elusive, ambiguous, confusing, or obtuse. Jewish institutional life has not done much to offer a lexicon for contemporary Jewish life. For a while, the fad words of Jewish purpose were "Jewish continuity." People struggled with their meaning in an age steeped in Jewish assimilation and intermarriage. What the term did not denote was a *reason* for being Jewish other than to keep a dwindling flame alight, or continue something that perhaps lacked any inherent personal meaning or attachment. The term communicated responsibility to a past and a future without a sense of presentism. Words such as *renaissance* and *Jewish future* suffered the same fates. One looked too much like a revival of the past to offer current meaning. The other seemed to emphasize a day too far off in the future to hold much current attention.

Large Jewish institutions are indeed struggling to come up with a language of meaning and inspiration to overcome seemingly insurmountable challenges. Organizations once started to represent Jewish needs and strategic thinking have lost a sense of collective visioning, often for the more banal role of communal fund-raising. Even on a fundraising level, the landscape has changed radically and dramatically. Institutional life is not keeping up, and we have to be bold and honest enough to say the truth.

> After the mid-80s ... the federation movement began to lose power and authority. A combination of trends ranging from the growth of privatism in American life, which led people away from organization activity and commitments, to the greater desire for hands-on giving, where the donors could choose the objects of their support directly and follow them personally ...

and new divisions in the Jewish community with regard to Israel and religious matters. All combined to weaken the ability of the federations to draw in their share of the voluntary funds raised in the community and, to a lesser extent, to exercise the power that flowed from those funds.[14]

As Judaism has gradually moved from communal religious ties to communal organizational ties, we are finding a pushback. Our organizational affiliations are not always as meaningful as they need to be. Board meetings and leadership roles are not a replacement for spiritual connections and the *hesed* (acts of loving-kindness) to be found in strong communal settings and informal networks. Today, many Jewish organizations are wringing their hands trying to understand why membership and funding are down:

> Institutional vitality is a burning issue in contemporary American-Jewish life. Numerous organizations are engaged in self-evaluation and re-definition, as they attempt to meet new challenges, such as attracting and retaining members, volunteers and philanthropists in order to maintain established infrastructures and programs. In addition to internal institutional anxiety, Jewish organizational participation is currently a crucial concern not only for the institutions involved but for the entire Jewish community.[15]

Organizations provide structures; they do not provide language, other than the often insider language and abbreviations that characterize so much of American Jewish life today. We have made institutional Judaism an end in and of itself and are now trying hard, too hard, to backpedal and figure out where we went wrong. We have not gone wrong in creating strong institutional scaffolding to support a dynamic and complex community. It is one of our great communal strengths. It is not, however, a replacement for the person-to-person language of caring that constitutes peoplehood. Daniel Elazar, cited earlier, gives us the language to understand this conundrum:

The American Jewish community is built on an associational base to a far greater extent than that of any other in Jewish history; that is to say, not only is there no inescapable compulsion, external or internal, to affiliate with organized Jewry, but there is no automatic way to become a member of the Jewish community. Nor is there a clear way to affiliate with the community as a whole. All connections with organized Jewish life in America are based on voluntary associations with some particular organization or institution.[16]

The nature of these voluntary associations is that they cannot be forced. In terms of meaningful communal life, Elazar recommends "persuasion rather than compulsion, influence rather than power." These, he says, "are the only tools available for making and executing policies."[17]

A Case Study in Confusion

Because policy making is a matter of persuasion and not compulsion, we find that the personalization of Judaism has brought some thorny problems to the community table. We will use an example to illustrate. In an exercise given out in one of our leadership development programs, board representatives are given a case study to analyze and asked to make recommendations to resolve a sticky issue. The problem: a board member of a Jewish organization whose mission is to fight anti-Semitism and any form of racial discrimination is outraged that the annual dinner is turning kosher to welcome all members of the community and make every attending individual feel comfortable. He expresses his own discomfort at the fact that the group's reason for existence is to promote tolerance and openness but that this new "religious" policy is working counter to the organization's express purpose. For him, being Jewish means being a social activist who fights against discrimination of any form directed at anyone. He is an outspoken person who has done a great deal of good; consequently, the board is very torn about how to approach the issue.

This case almost always generates strong feelings about the nature of Judaism and Jewish organizations. There are those who come to the board member's defense, who feel uncomfortable with Jewish organizations that are "too Jewish." Others are annoyed that one person's discomfort with religion would prevent everyone from eating comfortably at a dinner. Some say that the dinner is just emblematic of an increasing stranglehold of the religious right and question where it will stop. What if everyone in attendance were asked to observe the Sabbath or dress in a particular way? Some believe that being part of a democracy means protecting those who are in the minority, and they look at this principle relative to the dinner. Others suggest that even if no one were to keep kosher at the event, it should still be kosher, not to accommodate any one person, but to be a visible and distinctive sign that the event is under Jewish auspices, much like wearing a yarmulke (skullcap) in a synagogue even though one may not engage in that ritual regularly.

The responses to the case study are interesting and varied, but more interesting is the meta-conversation that it raises every time it is presented. People claim that they know exactly the case and when it happened. Although it is a composite case, they are almost certain that they know the institution in question. There is something familiar about the problem and something hauntingly troubling about it. On every level, it brings up issues of what being Jewish means, especially for individuals within Jewish institutional settings.

Dennis Prager, radio talk show host, author, and ethicist, writes in an article that the "greatest problem confronting the Jewish people is the lack of a rational and persuasive response to the question: 'Why should I be a Jew?'" He offers ten answers, including that living a meaningful life requires a manual and that Judaism can provide that manual. Judaism is a religion of moderation that places a prime value on human life and outlines values of good and evil unequivocally. Judaism provides immense joy through holiday and ritual observance. It also provides community at a time when human beings are acutely aware of their aloneness. Judaism is a religion that emphasizes accomplishment in this world, rather than the afterlife, and Judaism allows and encourages individuals to argue with God. Prager mentions that Jews have distorted Judaism into various other "isms," including Marxism, socialism, feminism, and environmentalism, but these are only a slice of what Judaism is or what some Jews believe.

One could argue that Prager's view may prove compelling for many who suffer alienation. Because Judaism is an act of birth (or conversion), and not belief, being Jewish has an array of meanings that include attachments to culture, history, language, Israel, social activism, and community in addition to its religious appeal. When struggling with the case study above, adult learners often question what the "J" in the organization's title means or try to understand the mission of the organization with a view, again, as to why the organization calls itself Jewish at all if there is nothing distinctly Jewish about it.

A case like this is further proof that a definition of peoplehood that is substantive and comprehensive is necessary. We must deal with the challenge that striving for a shared language is not an attempt to create artificial, overly nostalgic, or backward-looking scaffolding for the Jewish present. In his book, *Studying the Jewish Future*, Calvin Goldscheider says:

> [T]he diversity of paths taken by Jewish communities should be encouraged, not lamented or neutralized through attempts to culturally construct one worldwide Jewish community or nation.[18]

We encourage the diversity of portals into Jewish life and the rich and creative layers this diversity has contributed to meaningful and vibrant Jewish living. At the same time, we do worry that these diverse approaches can create schisms in understanding and cooperation between generations and across geographic boundaries. Consequently, Michael Walzer, the Jewish thinker who began the conversation in this chapter, asks us to be more patient and accepting of the contradictory forces that shape Jewish identity today:

> In a world where there are many ways of being different, an extraordinary diversity of customs and beliefs, what justice requires is respect for difference—and our own differences are among those that demand respect. To make that demand effective, we must respect ourselves, and that means, right now, embracing the anomalies.... We are what we are, and we need

to make a secure place for ourselves in the world—a place for ourselves *as we are*. If we do that, one or another kind of normalcy might follow in time.[19]

Walzer asks us to embrace our contradictions and contends that only if we are able to live with an identity that goes against "normal" definitions of identity will we be able to find security and normalcy.

There is an unhealthy, constant questioning that we as a Jewish community engage in that prevents us from embracing multiple collective identities. The search for boundaries, the attempt to secure membership, and the need to pin down what it means to be Jewish and who can be Jewish has engaged us in a battle of insecurities that has prevented us from progressing and advancing our successes. Imagine that a couple kept asking themselves whether they were really a couple, whether they really loved each other, whether they were really right for each other. These questions, when asked continually, would prevent the couple from really loving each other, from really being together securely and advancing their relationship. Progress can be stultified by asking and reasking who we are.

There is an uncomfortable paradox here of probing and rethinking but not questioning to the point of instability. This paradox is signified by the wrestling image we cited earlier. Our patriarch Jacob fought for his name but, at the same time, all of his wrestling and struggling was also accompanied by an act of blessing. He deceived his brother to receive a blessing. He fought with an angel, and then, surprisingly, received a blessing. Later, upon arriving in Egypt to see his son Joseph and escape from famine, Jacob was escorted to Pharaoh's palace and, although he complained at the time about the impoverishment of his life, he began and ended the dialogue with an act of blessing Pharaoh. Wrestling is an act of challenge and insecurity. Blessing is an act of stability and dignity. Jacob was a wrestler armed with blessing. He was also a dreamer. These complex and perhaps contradictory identities live in tension within one person, the very person who created the twelve tribes and whose name was transferred to a nation.

Establishing a language of peoplehood is *not* asking who we are or who we might become. It is also not an artificial umbrella that squeezes everyone together to avoid the rainy day of a history of persecution or an overarching concept so wide that everyone can fit in. It is a powerful statement of connection and association that pairs comfort and support with responsibility across time and denominational and geographic boundaries. Establishing a shared notion of peoplehood is not about the kind of arguing that leads to fragmentation that has characterized so much of Judaism in America in the twenty-first century. It is not an argument for the sake of argument, but an argument for the sake of heaven, to establish a concept that is accessible, enduring, and universal in its particulars.

In thinking about the strengthening of a shared past through the lens of history, education, and experience to form the bonds of responsibility for the present and future, we would like to share a story told to us by a friend of our federation, Maury Atkin. He told us that on February 23, 1967, David Ben-Gurion, with a Bible in his hand, took him outside his house in Sde Boker in the Negev, Israel's southern region. He pointed to the hills and said, "Our Bible tells us of the riches in those hills. Our past will guide our future." He then went on to share some of his vision for what would come out of the Negev. In this encounter the present, past, and future came together beautifully and harmoniously. When people feel a powerful, meaningful connection to a joint past, they feel inspired to realize a communal future.

QUESTIONS FOR CONVERSATION

1. What historical events have most shaped your own view of Jewish identity?
2. What contemporary trends in Jewish living today do you feel will endure the test of time?
3. How is Jewish identity for you essentially different than other personal identity markers? How is it the same?
4. How has the influence of anti-Semitism impacted your identity, if it indeed has?
5. What factors do you believe will most change or influence Jewish identity for the positive?

3

CONSTRUCTING A PERSONAL JEWISH IDENTITY

As a clinical psychologist, I am well aware of the ways that people construct identity and also run away from identity. One Yom Kippur several years ago, I was asked to speak at a large Washington congregation and tried to find something appropriate that would combine some of my thoughts about the seriousness of the day and the need to strengthen Jewish identity in our community. I came upon the book of Jonah and discussed the escape from responsibility that many of us feel. Jonah runs away from the tasks that he was assigned, imperiling his life and others in the process. But he is confronted by his destiny and eventually embraces it. He leaves us with this very personal message about identity. We cannot escape fate; we have to make peace with it. Constructing identity is complicated. Sometimes it's about running toward. Sometimes it's running away. Sometimes it's about standing still.

—MISHA GALPERIN

Any conversation about peoplehood has to include some basic parameters about personal identity building. How is our individual sense of self constructed? There are many different understandings of identity brought to us from the worlds of psychology, philosophy, theology, and neuroscience. In writing this, we were also conscious of the fact that we chose particular ways to describe identity construction out of many other possibilities with the understanding that the very expression *Jewish identity* is not uniformly or universally understood. "In most uses of the phrase 'Jewish identity,' the word 'Jewish' does not refer to any agreed-upon or universal set of Jewish beliefs or behaviors, and the phrase does not imply what Jewishness itself means."[1] We have chosen to highlight some theories that are particularly relevant to the topic even with these limitations.

We know that identity is a fluid characteristic of self-definition and group cohesion. We may view our sense of self as stable and consistent, but when we consider the changes that affect our personal notions of self, we find that we are not really on solid ground. At different stages in our lives, we may have been more athletic, compassionate, ideological, spiritual, or academic. Increased or decreased responsibilities change the way we think about ourselves. Illness can radically change personal notions of self, both bodily and mentally. Changes in career or a move to another state or country create yet other layers of self-definition. At some points in life, our identities are powerfully shaped by particular relationships—that with parents, partners, and children—and at other times, these relationships place fewer demands on us or are less pressing in the ways in which we construct notions of the self.

Accepting that identity changes over time and is influenced by both external and internal factors is critical to understanding how group identity mirrors personal identity constructs. In *Sources of the Self: The Making of the Modern Identity*, philosopher Charles Taylor presents the complex nature of modern identity constructs influenced by our relationship to nature, morality, and the need for inner expressiveness.[2] As we wade through the murky waters of modern identity, we find a two-tiered notion of self emerging: thick identities and thin identities. Thick identities reflect core aspects of a person's sense of self that remain somewhat timeless and relatively unaffected by change. Others—thin identities—are malleable, less significant, and often bounded by place and time. Personal identity is constructed through a complex process of individuation that begins with the way a person begins to think of him- or herself in unique terms. How am I different than my siblings? Friends? Parents? Teachers? How am I aligned to the major institutions that have shaped me? How am I different?

As part of this process, the individual begins to distinguish him- or herself not only through life choices but also through the "persistence" of identity—the noticeable patterns of behavior and reactions that repeat themselves over time and through life changes. With the enormous amount of change that modernity has presented us, these constants of character and behavior help create and anchor identity so that the push and pull of identity variables can be experimented upon within a relatively stable environment. Some measures of identity are relative; they depend on time, place, and the social constellations that surround us. Others are less open to manipulation. If everything were experimental in identity formation, the chaos alone might prevent personal, spiritual, and professional growth. Determining a Jewish thick identity is critical in forming a personal notion of Jewish peoplehood that will be meaningful across space, will not be as fluid over the vagaries of time, and will join with a larger, collective identity.

From a psychological—rather than a philosophical or sociological—perspective, identity is composed of three component parts: the cognitive, which represents the way we think; the behavioral, which reflects what we do; and the emotional, which signifies what we feel. In Jewish terms, we might break this down loosely into our relationship with texts or the cerebral parts of our tradition (the cognitive), the rituals we observe or do not observe (the behavioral), and our sense of belonging or alienation (the emotional). For Jewish identity to be a force within our lives, these three parts must be well nurtured independently and brought together in some organic fashion.

Jewish communal organizations generally structure their appeals to the cognitive and behavioral aspects of the Jewish self. Formal educational institutions try to strengthen Jewish identity through study. Books and journals on Jewish history, sociology, and communal life also attempt to reach us through an appeal to the mind. Yet, Freud let us know that humans are less rational beings than rationalizing beings. Rituals and emotions, contradictions and confusion, usually play a much larger role in the formation of identity than we would like to believe. The feelings that overlay cognition are often much more influential in forming our opinions and connections to Jewish peoplehood.

To illustrate, in one of our courses on Jewish literacy, we ask participants to mention an object of Jewish significance that tells a piece of their Jewish story. One woman in a course offered in Arlington, Virginia, unapologetically let us know that her object was brisket. The other adult learners laughed and then nodded with the body language of recognition. Slowly, student after student piped up with a Jewish food that was significant for him or her. Bagels and *matza brei*. A corned beef sandwich from a local deli. Their grandmother's chicken soup. At once the room brimmed with both hunger and positive feeling. The energy in the room was more than it had been when discussing rituals from passages in the Talmud. The foods came with all kinds of associations of people and places, smells and tastes that transported our participants out of the room and to all different stages of their lives. Traditions of the stomach are not to be scoffed at because, in so many ways, they outlive the traditions of the mind. Food associations are deeper than food preferences, which do not in and of themselves reflect a deep Jewish identity.

One of the greatest advances in psychotherapeutic treatments of the twentieth century was systematic desensitization, based on the work of the South African psychologist Joseph Wolpe. Wolpe identified the fact that mammals cannot remain in an anxious or fearful state while eating or digesting because the sympathetic and parasympathetic nervous systems cannot be engaged simultaneously. One system controls food intake and the other anxiety. The treatment Wolpe developed essentially taught people to remain in a relaxed state while imagining or placing themselves in a fear-provoking situation. He recognized that people who are relaxed cannot also be anxious. Intake of food is an antidote to anxiety. The link between eating and comfort may explain the existence of comfort foods and also the existence of certain eating disorders. This may also explain physiologically why culinary associations with Judaism are so emotionally important and powerful.

In Aaron Lansky's astonishing *Outwitting History*, a book about saving one million Yiddish books, he cites a conversation between Golda and Tevye, the main characters in Sholem Aleichem's *Tevye the Dairyman*, the basis for *Fiddler on the Roof*. Tevye is arguing with his daughter Chava about her relationship with a non-Jewish villager. The conversation moves into universalism versus particularism. Golda interrupts the heated debate: "My *milkhiger* (dairy) borscht," says Golda, "may be just as important as all those important matters of yours." Lansky observes, "When the rational, scholarly, masculine, Hebrew side of Jewish tradition fails, the *hefmish* (warm), workaday, down-to-earth, feminine, Yiddish side prevails." In the end, Golda suggests it is borscht more than Hebrew quotations that will hold the Jewish people together.[3]

> *Although my father was the son of generations of rabbis, as I mentioned in the introduction, my mother was the daughter of German Jews who were completely assimilated. She was a third-generation Russian whose family had been transferred from Germany in a political move to bring well-educated specialists, such as engineers and doctors, to Russia. My great-grandfather was one such engineer; he built the first power station in Odessa. He did not speak Yiddish or practice Judaism in any meaningful way. My grandmother inherited few Jewish practices, and yet she made a legendary gefilte fish, and this was passed down as a sign of being Jewish. My father was drawn to a Judaism of the mind. My mother was given a Judaism of the stomach. The stomach is actually closer to the heart. And that is what they both passed on to me. I cannot judge which is more important, only that both exist within me.*
>
> —MISHA GALPERIN

Mordechai Kaplan, the father of the Reconstructionist movement, understood that before there is believing there is belonging. People need to feel welcome and a sense of the familiar before they begin to construct a cognitive approach to their Judaism. Day school and Hebrew school education places greater emphasis on cognition than on the experiential side of identity formation, preferring instead to shape ideas. But we know that the believing side of ourselves often emerges out of a powerful sense of Jewish emotion. First we feel, and then we want to know. We know that experiences such as Jewish camping, travel, missions, and Taglit-Birthright Israel—targeted immersion experiences for particular age groups—are helping Jewish communal institutions understand the need to help form positive emotional connections to Jewish peoplehood in ways that other approaches cannot. We also know that much of Hebrew and day school education focuses on the teaching of religion and not on other experiences and disciplines, such as group singing, cooking, or the teaching of history, Zionism, and Yiddish literature, which each provide alternate portals into Jewish life. We need to generate exponentially more positive associations with Judaism to fill out the three legs of Jewish identity that we identified: what we think, what we do, and how we feel. More will be said about the importance of behavioral and emotional experiences in the last chapter. For now, suffice it to say that a Judaism that is meaningful is multidimensional and also mimetic—it comes with a feeling of home, of welcome, of doing, and not only of thinking.[4] It is consciously but also unconsciously compelling.

Horizontal and Vertical Identities

Another important layer in understanding identity is how we prioritize aspects of the self, that is, what is most important in our placement of values and use of time. To gain insight into how this process works, we will use a simple framework of horizontal and vertical identity constructs. In vertical identities, we list—in rank order of priority—the characteristics and qualities that are most important to us in our own definitions of self. An example of such self-definition might look like this:

- Jewish
- Father
- Husband
- Graphic Artist
- Vegetarian
- Chess Player

Usually, the first few self-defining characteristics tell an important story of personal identity because these selected top qualities usually manifest themselves in many different settings and in varying ways. So, for example, defining yourself as a vegetarian may not appear at the top of the list because it is generally a chosen behavior at mealtimes and not at all times, unless you were, let's say, an animal rights activist, in which case, your eating habits may have a lot to do with more profound life decisions. A characteristic such as being Jewish may influence much of your being across a spectrum of time, decisions, and relationships, or it may be taken out and dusted off occasionally.

In addition, in vertical identity constructs, people often define themselves in relation to others, and these relationships are usually very significant in the way that a person sees him- or herself. An individual who places his marital or familial status as first or second in self-classification is stating loudly, "Being a husband is a key characteristic in the way that I see myself" or "I am a parent above all else." The test of whether or not this is true is to explore how well an individual prioritizes his or her relationship to others in the hierarchy of life concerns and tasks. This may manifest itself in what he or she does, says, or believes. Harry S. Sullivan, an American psychiatrist, posited in his theory of personality that an individual personality can only be defined in relationship to others.

In horizontal identity constructs, the same qualities may be listed as part of self-definition but will not necessarily be persistently regarded as priorities. Rather than being connected to the past and future, such identity constructs are very much subject to presentism, whoever we are at any particular moment. These self-selecting qualities may shift in placement and be added or dropped over time. To illustrate, the same qualities used above would, instead, appear like this:

Jewish • Father • Husband • Graphic Artist
• Vegetarian • Chess Player

At another stage in life, this construct might look like this:

College Student • Vegetarian • Chess Player
• Fraternity Member • Son • Jewish

And at another, the construct may look like this:

Golfer • Father • Jewish • Vegetarian • Single
• Gourmet Cook

The first set of identity markers clearly appears at midlife. The second comes during late adolescence; the last, at retirement after the loss of a spouse. The fluid part of identity here is the way that we spend our time and our lifelong habits, behaviors, and hobbies. Changes in relationships also add a fluid rather than stable aspect to identity across a lifetime, although these relationships give off the impression of permanence at any particular life stage because they may be so important to self-definition.

Often, our identities are really the nexus of vertical and horizontal constructs, where the order of importance of parts of ourselves over time meet the present, again and again. The nexus of these identities is mediated by the enduring characteristics of our personality, lifelong habits, patterns of coping and cognitive styles, and the way we intellectually respond to the world. For example, you may choose to become a supporter of Planned Parenthood—a cognitive choice—and be passionate in this advocacy, which would be an expression of your temperament. Your behavior reflects your horizontal and vertical identities as well as your enduring personality traits.

Note: Horizontal and vertical identities are not defined by emotions such as happiness, fear, or excitement, because these qualities are subjective and generally contextual. Certain circumstances may bring out these emotional responses more or less dramatically. Our construction is more a matter of the defining characteristics that may influence decisions, life choices, and the formation of critical relationships. Particular characteristics keep showing up in the way that we see ourselves despite the fluidity of circumstances.

Some commitments may shift in relative importance through the developmental stages in life, but may be persistent throughout. In identity constructs, we search for persistent behaviors and characteristics. Relationships may seem persistent and may, over a lifetime, prove to be that. Relationships, however, can skew identity constructs because they *do* change, although they may form the most passionate or committed sense of who we are. We view being Jewish not only as a statement of history, birth, or activity but also as an aspect of relationship.

Blended together, collective and personal Jewish identity, conscious and unconscious approaches to Judaism, can form a powerful connection to Jewish peoplehood. Throughout Jewish history, there have been competing collective voices that have added to a rich, mosaic-like approach to Jewish identity. Within a single self, competing voices of cognition and emotion fight and unite over identity.

Identity as Fact

In his slim but potent book *Against Identity*, Leon Wieseltier understands that identity cannot be only a matter of vision; it also has to be a matter of facts.[5] It is a fact that you are born of certain parents, in a certain place, at a certain date, and of a certain faith or ethnicity. You may want to change aspects of yourself, but there are some aspects of existence that simply cannot be avoided. The fact of our existence is one of them. Being Jewish, if you are indeed Jewish, is another. You may try to deny it, but you cannot escape it. Weiseltier plays with identity, understanding that at times we want to be one thing, and at other times, something else entirely:

> We have a craving for specificity, but we love also to slip away from specificity. We want to be one thing, but not any longer this thing or that one thing. We have a fear of being nothing and a fantasy of being everything, but we do not see that everything is a busy version of nothing. So one cheer for identity: it imposes discipline.[6]

Conversations on identity have so often lacked the discipline that Wieseltier commends. We cannot be everything. Once we are everything, we become nothing, and nothing is not an acceptable conclusion for an almost four-thousand-year history. When we turn back the hands of time, we find that Abraham, the first Jew, was given an unambiguous purpose that has stood the test of time: "[T]hat he may instruct his children and the generations that follow to keep the way of the Lord by doing what is just and right."[7]

On the heels of this famous biblical expression, Sid Schwarz, in his book *Judaism and Justice* (Jewish Lights), has argued that being Jewish today must bring both our particularistic and our universalistic impulses together, and that the question of purpose is not one that can go unanswered. "Why be Jewish?—because it is a heritage that extends the boundaries of righteousness and justice in the world and invests our world with holiness."[8] Here we hear all of the echoes of Abraham's mission ringing loudly in our ears. Why can we not hear this mission that so many of us identify with naturally? Because for centuries, our need to equate Jewish values with American values has weakened and flattened our particularism, which has also had an impact on our universalism. Schwarz goes on to say:

> Increasingly, it is obvious that secular American culture is not the neutral setting it was thought to be a century ago, a setting that would allow for a multiplicity of faiths and ethnic groups to co-exist, leading to a rich cultural mosaic in a tolerant and pluralistic America. This country's affluence and its love affair with consumerism has created a culture that is at odds with Judaism's emphasis on justice and holiness.[9]

Some American values meld easily with Jewish values. Others find themselves in uneasy tension and conflict. That is why, more than anything else on our institutional agenda, we need to have conversations on Jewish identity and sort the meaningful from the meaningless, the kitsch from the mission. How are we different or similar to those who came before us and those who will come after us? How are we different or similar to Jews who live in other countries or live in the Jewish homeland? When are those differences insurmountable and when are they simply superficial? Most importantly, why do these differences separate us instead of making us comfortably aware of diversity? "In the modern world, the cruelest thing you can do to people is to make them ashamed of their complexity," Wieseltier notes.[10] We are many things, not one thing. We can hold many conflicting notions of self and identity at the same time and be richer and stronger as a result.

But, ultimately, we can only have a richer notion of self as Jews if that self is also part of a larger, developed notion of peoplehood that is not fractious but universally accepted. We have offered a simple but potent definition. Peoplehood is a sense of belonging to an extended family with a mission, a people with a purpose. The image in our last chapter of Philip Roth's divided Jewish self is the microcosm for a Judaism that this divided self has generated personally and collectively. Many of the problems of fragmentation that we began with need to find resolution in something that unites. Aimee Landman, a university student, puts it succinctly when she writes, "A solution, while idealistic, needs to be creating a stronger collective identity. It is not about what different groups of Jews are doing, it is about what the community as a whole represents; if it manifests weakness and fragmentation, so will its followers."[11]

We have searched for a way to bring a sense of unity to the conversation, a gratifying approach to connection, a way to find a thread—not a braid or a rope or a net—to different ways of looking at identity while still cultivating a feeling of belonging. Without any unifying element, the Jewish people will lose their wholeness. They will lose a sense of collective purpose and their mission. We cannot afford that loss, not because we are at a time of potential extinction or assimilation but precisely because we are more influential than we have ever been. We cannot be afraid of our own excellence, and at this time of strength, it is incumbent upon us to create a collective understanding of peoplehood that will connect and deepen the cognitive, emotional, and behavioral aspects of Judaism.

QUESTIONS FOR CONVERSATION

1. We've discussed many different ways to construct identity. Which most resonates with you?
2. Can you name a single event or moment that was transformational in your Jewish identity?
3. Describe an aspect of a "thick Jewish personal identity" that you believe will remain in place in the future.
4. What are the constituent parts of your collective Jewish identity? Is there anything about them that is fluid?
5. How can the organized Jewish community strengthen certain aspects of identity so that they will become core components in collective Jewish identity formation?

4

PRO-CHOICE JUDAISM: ARE THERE TOO MANY IDENTITY OPTIONS?

I remember my first trip to a supermarket in the United States. We were taken by a couple who volunteered to escort my family through the ins and outs of American consumer life. At first, I could not believe how much food there was, how spacious the aisles were, how small the lines were. It seemed that everything was the exact opposite of the Soviet Union I left behind. Here was choice at every turn. It was incredible, until ... until I got to the coffee aisle and had to actually buy something. How do you know what to buy when there is so much of everything? I turned to our new friends and asked them to pick something out for me. I was paralyzed by too much choice. Little did I know then that this was a problem that went far beyond the coffee aisle.

—MISHA GALPERIN

Jewish choices in our tolerant, multicultural society have yielded an ability to shape Judaism with an astonishing degree of personalization that has led to puzzlement. One can say in jest that Jews are pro-choice; they believe in a self-definition of Judaism that is based on layers of personal choice. But this very boon to the individual has the potential to be calamitous for the Jewish community at large. And, within the framework of possible choices, there remains the choice of apathy, a conscious decision that Judaism will not touch one's life in any considerable way. This chapter and the chapters that follow present obstructions and obstacles to a shared notion of peoplehood. Today's level of choice and personalization is the first obstacle we will explore on the path to peoplehood.

Alan Greenspan, the former chairman of the American Federal Reserve, once characterized ours as an age of "irrational exuberance." There was a time not long ago when people invested, not out of rational decision making but because they were caught in powerfully good feelings about their ability to create wealth and move ahead. Exuberance in this expression is a joyful willingness to ignore reality, preferring instead an irrational attitude or feeling of entitlement. We suspend reason, spend money, make certain choices, and engage in certain behaviors because we *can*, not necessarily because we *should*.

This irrational exuberance has an impact on identity that has been only marginally explored for its effect on faith and ethnicity. Sir Jonathan Sacks addressed the World Economic Forum on this very issue and concluded, "Reverence, restraint, humility, a sense of limits, the ability to listen and respond to human distress—these are not virtues produced by the market, yet the attributes we will need if our global civilization is to survive, and they are an essential part of the religious imagination."[1] In other words, the forces of the market, as pervasive as they are, are also misleading in terms of the human spirit. He continued:

> Never before have we been faced with more choices, but never before have the great society-shaping institutions offered less guidance on why we should choose this way rather than that. The great metaphors of our time—the supermarket, cable and satellite television and the Internet—put before us a seemingly endless range of options, each offering the great deal, the best buy, the highest specification, the lowest price. But consumption is a poor candidate for salvation. The very happiness we were promised by buying these designer jeans, that watch or this car, is what the next product assures us we do not yet have until we have bought something else. A consumer society is kept going by an endless process of stimulating, satisfying, and

re-stimulating desire. It is more like an addiction than a quest for fulfillment.[2]

Our consumer culture has indeed enhanced the number of choices we have and the degree of customization we can have, from large purchases to relatively insignificant ones. From toothpaste to computers, we can have our conveniences any way we like them. The marketing line "Have it your way" represented a change in the way Americans purchased food and signaled an era of customization that few realized would have such significant consequences for faith communities.

Barry Schwartz, in his book *The Paradox of Choice*, says that a world without choices seems bleak and constraining, but too much choice, especially regarding relatively insignificant issues, can also tyrannize. We spend so much time trying to decide matters of little consequence that our minds are too cluttered to consider some of the larger issues. We have a harder time committing to something because something new and improved awaits us around the corner.

> The United States was founded on a commitment to individual freedom and autonomy, with freedom of choice as a core value. And yet it is my contention that we do ourselves no favor when we equate liberty too directly with choice, as if we necessarily increase freedom by increasing the number of options available. Instead, I believe we make the most of our freedoms by learning to make good choices about the things that matter, while at the same time unburdening ourselves from too much concern about the things that don't.[3]

From a Jewish perspective, the freedom of choice that is so culturally rich in the United States has not found easy integration within the framework of ethnicity and faith. Ethnicity is a fact rather than a choice. Many concepts that are core to virtually all major faiths, such as belief, sacrifice, submission, authority, and community are not regarded as matters of choice but as component parts that lead to deep religious feeling and behavior. Personal choice can eat away at these spiritual values and reduce or dilute them to a meaningless veneer. Spiritual guide and leader Rabbi Yitz Greenberg contemplates the pros and cons of choice:

> I, too, believe that choice should play a greater role in our religion, but having thought about it for ten years, I think the movement toward pure choice is excessive. Life is more subtle than that.[4]

We would be naive if we believed that everything in our lives is a result of personal choice and not also and often predominantly fact, election, selection, luck, hard work, intention, or connections.

Putting Choice Onstage

Tyranny of choice is the unstated theme of a play, *Immigranti*, that presents in a fictional fantasy the immigrants' dilemma. The play begins with a spotlight on two writers, communicating a sense that each is similar to the other and each character could have the fate and destiny of the other. A young Russian Jew takes up a pen-pal relationship with a Jewish boy from Brooklyn. Over time, the young Russian is given the opportunity to come to the United States and finally meet the friend he knows only through correspondence. Judaism in Russia is very limited in its possibilities, but not in the United States. His American teenage friends take this immigrant to a supermarket, but instead of purchasing food, this is a supermarket of Jewish identity. He watches an array of Jews around him—the ultra-Orthodox Jew in his black gabardine suit and the Reform Jew who is virtually indistinguishable from his American neighbor—before having to shop for his own Jewish identity.

The play is intriguing if not difficult to digest. We may think that we do not shop for identity, but, in fact, consumer norms have affected us in formerly unimaginable ways. The play is subtle in its judgment. The lack of choice in the former Soviet Union is regarded as a deficiency and weakness but also as a boon and a reality. And the fact that one boy comes from one part of the world that has certain cultural norms and the other from a wholly different society is interspersed with the feeling that their lives could easily have been swapped. When it comes to consumer spending and wealth, we often divide ourselves into the haves and the have-nots. *Immigranti* opens its viewers to the possibility that the geographic and material circumstances we have are fleeting and insecure.

Parenthetically, this reasoning champions why collective philanthropic giving must still be a norm at a time of growth for family foundations and individual givers. Such individuals may have fortunes and lose them. They may care passionately about certain issues, and then change their minds or redirect their giving. Communal giving has to be the bread-and-butter care of central institutions that value and support the everyday concerns that do not go away because we suddenly care about them less. We must be stewards and custodians of this collective, because financial fates may change but community needs are constant and growing. At no time have we realized this more than in the most recent collapse of the financial market, personal fortunes, and philanthropic family foundations. And yet, through all of the market's erratic behaviors, one thing remains constant: charitable needs. The homeless, the elderly, the uneducated, the disabled become only more vulnerable without a strong, communal safety net.

As a young man, my grandfather considered coming to America. He and a rabbi from the next town, Rabbi Byk, had synagogues waiting for them on the Lower East Side of Manhattan. In the end, my grandfather, Rabbi Rabinowitz, decided to stay in the former Soviet Union. His friend decided to go to America and start a new life. Years later, my grandfather reconsidered his decision and wanted to go to America, but by the time he chose to go in the 1920s, America's doors of immigration had already closed.

Generations later, when I was working in the Lower East Side, I arranged to meet the local Jewish community leader. We got to talking, and he asked me about my family and my own background. I shared with him the fact that my grandfather almost came to his part of the world to be a pulpit rabbi decades earlier. He asked for my grandfather's name, and then picked up the phone. He spoke quickly in Yiddish to someone on the other end of the line. That person was Rabbi Byk's grandson, currently a rabbi in Borough Park. I sat back in my chair, astonished. That rabbi could have been me. Here we were, two grandchildren working for the Jewish community with grandfathers who were friends, yet each made a different decision that shaped his own life and the lives of those who came after him. At one point in time, our fates were linked. Generations later, they became linked again.

—MISHA GALPERIN

Back to our conversation on choices. We have all heard the expression "shul shopping," where individuals and couples visit multiple synagogues before investing membership dues in any particular one. We all know that tuition in Hebrew and day schools is on the rise and has turned many parents into consumers rather than partners and supporters. We may not want to believe that we shop for faith, but it is hard to escape the pervasive assumptions that choice and consumerism have made on Jewish identity at large.

Pro-choice Judaism has had both a positive and a negative influence on Jewish identity. Its positive contribution lies in the competition to make Jewish institutions excellent. People will not simply join or fund institutions for being there, on the basis of their existence. There was a time when people moved into a neighborhood and joined synagogues and JCCs and gave money to federations because that was the way to establish yourself in a new community. It was a way to meet friends and to continue patterns of affiliation that may have been learned from parents and grandparents. Today, institutions have to prove their worth; they have to compete. They have to appeal, or they will lose their membership base or their financial support. But on the flip side, personal choice and consumerism have made us almost too savvy as buyers. We do not see ourselves as stakeholders and owners with the "corporation" being the Jewish community. Instead, we are purchasers who can buy and exchange, complain and walk away, give and take back. Our commitments are less permanent. Our loyalties are more easily compromised. The emphasis on personal choice is potentially grave for institutions that need regular members, dues, and a core committed group of adherents and supporters to continue to provide service.

A recent *New York Times* article captured the dilemma among young Jews experimenting with synagogue services. Traditional services are not appealing for many in the younger generation. Young Jewish individuals are not looking for their parents' synagogue services. The photo accompanying the article shows a Torah scroll spread out on a table for many feet long, surrounded by young adults on either side of the table looking at its columns. One founder of just such an alternative *min-yan* says that the congregants are looking for "redemptive, transformative experiences that give rhythm to their days and weeks and give meaning to their lives."[5] Few could argue with a noble cause like personal meaning. And yet, this trend has consequences. In the words of one leader in synagogue research, "Established synagogues are worrying about how to attract and engage younger people, and younger people are looking for a sense of sacred community, and they are going elsewhere."[6] The competition is potentially wonderful, since synagogues must do more thinking about recruiting younger members and serving their needs. But the crowd in such services can shift and may be transient. There may not be a sense of loyalty to a place or an institution over time to grow institutions through a core membership. The trend also raises other questions:

- Who pays dues and funds these *minyanim* without buildings?
- How do they stay in business when there is no membership or "brand loyalty"?
- What happens to such prayer circles when their members age and go on to different life stages where their own needs change?
- What happens to the originality and innovation of such services over time, when repetition and established patterns fall into place? Will the idea still feel new and fresh?
- Who leads such communities over time?

- What is lost when communities are composed of members who are very similar in age, socioeconomic bracket, and interests? Can communities educate us about living diversely when they are composed so homogeneously? In ultra-Orthodox communities, there is no claim made about valuing diversity. Quite the opposite: homogeneity is valued. Open societies say that they value tolerance but rarely create the kind of diverse communities that express it.

These are just a few of the many questions and observations that excessive choices about Jewish living raise. Without choice, Judaism can feel constrained, monochromatic, and uninteresting. With too many personal choices, we relinquish the effort to build bridges of understanding to people and customs unlike our own that take us out of the shell of ourselves. We can imagine that taken to the extreme, too many choices creates Jewish narcissism. The individual orientation that characterizes our example has been studied extensively in the annals of contemporary Jewish sociology and is worth a brief review.

The Sovereign Jewish Self

In the now well-known data of *The Jew Within*, coauthors Steven Cohen and Arnold Eisen presented characteristics of the "sovereign Jewish self," a term that emerged from their extensive qualitative interviews. Surveys were distributed to more than 1,400 American Jews. The authors arrived at a list of basic qualities and mindsets that characterize the Jew of the twenty-first century:

- A sense of inalienability (I'm Jewish regardless of what I do or do not do)
- An orientation toward volunteerism
- A supposition of personal autonomy
- A highly developed sense of personalism
- An aversion to judgmentalism
- A sense of journey without commitment to a particular stance or belief[7]

These characteristics revolve around a highly personal commitment to Judaism, disconnected from an involvement with communities and not bounded by rules and regulations. One respondent named Sheila was asked what kind of religion she believed in, since it was largely of her own making. "Sheila-ism," she replied.[8] Her answer was honest, but taken to the extreme, such an orientation makes the creation of a collective voice of Judaism near impossible.

In analyzing the impact of individualism on the sovereign Jewish self, contemporary Jewish thinker Jonathan Woocher has posited that the challenge to peoplehood and community comes in two related directions:

> On the one hand, we see an accentuation of individualism, personalism, and choice as dominant features in our society and culture. This thrust ... undermines all a priori loyalties, and especially loyalty to collectives that are perceived as seeking to impose limits on personal freedom or as setting standards of behavior that contravene the ultimate decision-making power of the individual. On the other had, we also witness today, especially among young people, a heightened commitment to globalism, multiculturalism, and universalism. This commitment renders what might be seen as particularistic loyalties—e.g., loyalty to a specific ethnic group or nation—as morally problematic. Why should we single out members of one people for special concern when so many need so much?[9]

Woocher argues the case for enhanced experimentation in confronting this double-edged sword of personal autonomy and recommends an expansion of Robert Putnam's notion of social capital from his highly popular and influential book *Bowling Alone*. To build a stronger sense of peoplehood, we have to strengthen the individual connections and relationships that undergird Jewish institutions rather than strengthening the institutions alone. It is only through relationships that we are able to build trust and concern for each other in a noncoercive way that highlights community without compromising the value of personal autonomy that is so highly prized. This would mean, for Woocher, creating more Jewish experiences of meaning that build Jewish social capital and generate interactions that do not involve Jewish institutions that once were our standard spaces for community building. We have to expand our platform and swap inward, parochial initiatives for more humanitarian, global projects that are less limiting for Jewish identity.

Woocher's analysis and recommendations are an important way to engage individuals who fit the description of the sovereign Jewish self. His paper raises two critical questions. First, why should we try to bring people who have a less developed Jewish impulse to the table by possibly diluting an intense commitment to Jewish life to suit their needs? After all, there are still so many Jews committed to active Jewish life who may be feeling that all of the attention we are giving to outreach has minimized attention to those with a core commitment. Second, given the assumption that trends are not permanent orientations, at what point do we begin to question cultural norms in an attempt to move the pendulum back? When does an overemphasis on self become truly deleterious to Jewish life? Rather than cater to it, when do we begin to act counterculturally?

A commitment to a journey with no destination and an aversion to judgment sounds too wishy-washy and undetermined for institutions. This research has spurned a host of conflicting responses from a "we'll show them" attitude for countercultural education to financial support of initiatives that feed into the mentality that Cohen and Eisen described—a sort of "if you can't beat them, join them" resignation.

Philosopher Charles Taylor has argued that the self-orientation of current society does not have to be regarded as such a negative and pervasive threat. He contends this on the grounds that the placement of the self in the faith/tribe equation has created a greater level of personal investment, or what he calls "authenticity." Taylor considers some of the existential worries that have accompanied modernity. In his words,

> The first source of worry is individualism. Of course, individualism also names what many people consider the finest achievement of modern civilization. We live in a world where people have a right to choose for themselves their own pattern of

life, to decide in conscience what convictions to espouse, to determine the shape of their lives in a whole host of ways that their ancestors couldn't control.... In principle, people are no longer sacrificed to the demands of supposedly sacred orders that transcend them. Very few people want to go back on this achievement.[10]

Taylor has identified two worries: the concern that individualism has generated selfishness and self-absorption along with the conflicting concern that the price to be paid to relinquish personal freedoms is one that few would willingly make. He develops these fears to an even greater extent later in his writing:

Once society no longer has a sacred structure, once social arrangements and modes of action are no longer grounded in the order of things or the will of God, they are in a sense up for grabs. They can be redesigned with their consequences for the happiness and well-being of individuals as our goal. The yard-stick that henceforth applies is instrumental reason.[11]

Society needs structures. Once the old orders that used to guide us are relinquished and outdated, it seems that anything can determine behavior, modes of existence, and attitudes. There is a black hole that faith or religion once filled. To avoid the vacuum, reason and rationality create structure. Unfortunately, many of the structures that reason creates have to do with cost-benefit analysis and efficiency. These measures are important in and of themselves but are not a holistic way to measure a life.

As ritual and religion become less significant markers of identity, religion becomes more privatized in America and the world over. In public religion, rituals, texts, and symbols form a language of identity shared by many. In privatized religion, this language, too, becomes private. It is spoken in smaller groups. Its customs and symbols may be quieter forms of expression shared among fewer individuals. This privatization of a once public language has its own impact, as the late sociologist Charles Liebman observed:

> Ethnic Judaism ... has given way to a form of privatized religion.
> This religion speaks in softer terms of individual meaning,
> journeys of discovery, spirituality, and the search for fulfill-
> ment. Its emphases are interpersonal rather than collective. It
> values authenticity and sincerity over achievement or efficiency.
> Typically it is non-judgmental, consoling, intuitive and non-
> obligating. There are distinct signs that privatized Jewishness is
> having a substantial impact, especially on younger Jews....
> Organizational work, once a common Jewish avocation, is now
> seen by many as excessively impersonal, power-centered and
> perfunctory.[12]

The appeal in private religion is not what is good for the many or the
sacrifice or subordination of personal desires for the good of the whole.
Jewish identity becomes a personal affair. When it is personal, it is about
choices and decisions rather than an education in shared norms, values,
and behaviors.

There is inherent value in reaching out to those marginally affiliated
because their distance or criticism about the mainstream, when taken
seriously, can generate more innovation and creativity at the core.
Nurturing those who feel disenfranchised can create greater responsive-
ness and sensitivity for those who stand at a community's center. This
kind of push-pull can force communal leaders to confront problematic
norms and behaviors at the center that have gone unquestioned. If you
like, enriching and expanding the core is a metaphoric way of increasing
the gene pool of ideas within any community. And it is critical to increase
that idea pool for the ultimate survival and substance of any community.

In terms of countercultural education, we have to challenge current notions of the sovereign Jewish self and ask whether this is the
legacy that we are prepared to leave the next generation of Jews. We
can change the trend through deepening our community's sense of
history and memory—our shared past—which can pave the way for
responsibility to a shared future. We also need to create more meaningful experiences for individuals to build peoplehood capital. According
to Einat Wilf, an Israeli writer and activist, we should identify the

"*mitzvot* of peoplehood."[13] Although she does not offer solutions, she offers a powerful question: "What should we all do as Jews, no matter where we live and how religiously observant we are?"[14] We need to create experiences and determine *mitzvot* that reach out and touch the cognitive, behavioral, and emotional aspects of identity above and beyond an investment and expression of social capital. One such direction is a countercultural education in consequences; personal choices may be an expression of personal freedoms, but they come with costs. And, for every choice we make, we reduce the pool of possible choices in any one area. Choice has a price. Choice limits other choices.

The Case for Consequences

One of the unpleasant but realistic corollaries of choice is consequences. We are all entitled to make choices about our lives in general and our Jewish lives in particular, but we have to understand that choices have consequences. With every choice, we have to educate ourselves about the price and contemplate the consequences. These consequences do not only affect us; choices in the aggregate impact community building. To avoid Jewish narcissism, we have to consider both the long-term and the collective impact of our personal choices. That we have largely divorced choice from consequences has been a failure of the personalist orientation that Cohen and Eisen presented.

The message of Jewish consequences and accountability is as old as the first chapters of Genesis. Adam was shown a magnificent tree in an orchard of trees designed to sustain him and Eve. He was told not to eat from only one tree; he was told that disobedience would have consequences. Adam chose not to pay attention. The consequences for Adam were not insignificant. He would have to work for his food; his wife was to have pain during childbirth. The couple was banished from the Garden of Eden. Adam and Eve were given free will, but free will is not free. The story continues in the next generation with more serious consequences. Cain and Abel are the first brothers of Genesis. They also take part in the first murder. Cain, out of anger that God rejected him and his sacrifice, took his rage out on Abel. Right before he does, God offers Cain a discourse on free will. "Sin crouches at the door, but you can control it." The message is visually graphic. Sin sounds like an animate being, poised and ready to pounce at any moment. But despite its strong and forceful presence, every human being can overpower it. The message seems too abstract for poor Cain, who goes out into the field, engages his brother in conversation, and then, unprovoked, takes his brother's life. God challenges Cain and wonders where Abel is. Cain retorts, "Am I my brother's keeper?" (Genesis 4:9). Do I have any responsibility to this person? God makes the question simpler: "What did you do to your brother?" (4:10). After God explains that Abel's blood is crying out from the ground, Cain finally has a moment of recognition: "My sin is greater than I can bear" (4:13). Cain now understands that a moment of uncontrolled rage took his brother's life permanently and that he, Cain, is unable to carry the weight of his own guilt.

The Genesis lessons in free will and consequences have found modern-day relevance during a time when choice is rampant but consequences may appear less clear or less instructive for the individual. Choices have costs that are both obvious and hidden. Understanding that our choices have consequences and that private choices about religion and ethnicity still have public consequences may offer us pause in the Jewish identity equation. We may act alone at times, but that does not mean that our acts in isolation do not have a ripple effect on Judaism. After all, Sheila thought her Sheila-ism was okay for her. Imagine that every American Jew had his or her own version of Sheila-ism. Would it not impact the majority? Would it not create stumbling blocks in conversation and communication about Jewish issues that need collaborative and collective thinking? Would it not minimize the responsibility that we have to each other?

The federation system is a good case in point. For many decades, the federation of each local community stressed an expansion of membership. Like the giving that built the ancient *Mishkan*, or portable desert sanctuary, the idea of charitable giving was to create a notion of communal responsibility and ownership. Everybody gives. Over time, federations gradually shifted their orientation. They began to see financial goals as more important than collective membership. Federation lay leaders and executives began to woo the top local philanthropists and spent their energies investing time and resources in a small percentage at the very top of the giving pyramid. Today, we are living with the consequences of this decision. We sacrificed community-wide giving for individual giving, ultimately shrinking our donor pool and the number of participants in active Jewish life. Now, with many family foundations challenged, we are once again turning to our community donors for help. But they are no longer looking back at us. We lost them. Here in the Greater Washington, D.C., area, we are trying to buck the trend by concentrating on new donors, not only on new gifts, and have made some small but significant gains in reversing the trend. Nationally, most federations in the country are raising much more money from far fewer people. People have begun to question the value of communal giving altogether since the end goal has become the dollar amount and not community-wide generosity.[15] Choices have consequences.

Choices can tyrannize, and they can embolden. We cannot turn back the hands of time and limit the ways that people express their Judaism, nor should we want to. We are living in an age of Jewish creativity and innovation that has created multiple portals into participation. Why would we want to limit such possibility at a time when we are trying to reach out to more disengaged, unaffiliated Jews? Instead, our task is to expand the field of choice to include an enhanced commitment to Jewish responsibility. As Jonathan Woocher emphasizes, our goal is not to minimize the psychological approach of choosing freely among options but rather to beef up the collective *along with* the tendency to individualism.

> We have to be prepared to discuss how Judaism can answer the questions of the psychological Jew. That language is not evil, it is not inherently selfish. Judaism is a pathway to self-fulfillment, and it urges us to choose affirmatively. But we should also note that in today's spiritual climate what needs to be defended is not freedom of choice or self-realization; it is precisely the claims of community, memory, and responsibility.[16]

Memory can be personal and individual, or it can be communal. Within Jewish tradition, we are called upon to share memories that we have not personally experienced. At the Passover Seder, we are all to see ourselves as having left Egypt, although none of us has taken that journey ourselves. When it comes to memory, we can obligate individuals to share in the collective. When it comes to responsibility, there is no such thing as personal responsibility that does not have an orientation to the other. The nature of responsibility is that one person must go outside the self to answer to the other. Choices must have that degree of otherness to them if we are to create an overarching Jewish identity. We begin with the self, but we do not end with the self, to paraphrase the great Jewish thinker Abraham Joshua Heschel on prayer. Our identities include our relationships to others, even those we do not see or hear. Speak to anyone who has stood at dawn on Masada or said *kaddish* on the train tracks to Auschwitz and you realize that sometimes this psychic connection to those who are invisible can carry more weight and mission than the existence of people in our actual everyday lives.

QUESTIONS FOR CONVERSATION

1. Would you say that decision making—especially regarding significant issues—comes easily to you? Please explain.
2. What do you think about the impact of choice on Judaism today?
3. In your own Jewish life, what kinds of choices would have led to different consequences or outcomes?
4. How has the privatization of Judaism contributed to collective identity changes within the Jewish community?
5. How do you think consumerism has and will affect Jewish life?

5

MEMBERSHIP AND BOUNDARIES

We are sitting, about twenty of us, in a class on basic Jewish liter-
acy in the nation's capital. I am convening a session on personal and
national journeys. Few people in the room know each other. They
represent a range of ages and have different levels of Jewish literacy.
They are happy that we give out books and a good dinner. The con-
versation is initially slow-paced until there is more trust in the room.
A young woman introduces herself and her Jewish journey: "I am a
convert, but you have to understand something. This is going to
sound strange, but I know that I was always really Jewish. I was
always drawn to Jewish people and Jewish ideas. Converting was
the most natural thing in the world. I wanted to be part of this
people. I knew my soul was always Jewish. But now that I am
Jewish, I don't know how to get other Jews to realize that."

—ERICA BROWN

If we follow our definition of peoplehood as membership in an
extended family with a mission or a people with a purpose, then we
run up against the age-old problem of exclusion. Not everyone is a
member of the same family. In a political age where we are more inclu-
sionary than ever in our use of language, our attempts to strengthen
minority voices and our sensitivity to universalism make the idea of

peoplehood seem almost quaint or outdated. Others may judge it more harshly; perhaps peoplehood is countercultural, offensive, or even racist.

One of the risks of strengthening a sense of belonging is the heightened sensitivity of those on the outside. If you have no chance of belonging to a club, then you may not be offended by the fact that you cannot join. If you are not a graduate of a particular college, you cannot be miffed when you fail to receive alumni updates. If you do not have the money to join a local country club, you cannot possibly get angry when you do not get invited to their annual dinner. The problem with feeling kinship or membership is that this feeling can backfire into anger when it is not translated into any meaningful outreach. We will offer a telling example. Working in a federation means sitting in a community seat that is often assumed to be all and know all about the Jewish community. Our receptionist often fields calls on a wide range of Jewish issues that may have little to do with our core business. Here are some samples of real issues we may hear about:

- "I am a Muslim writing a term paper on Judaism. Can someone explain an idea from the Old Testament?"
- "I am angry because no rabbi showed up for my father's funeral!"
- "Where do I buy gluten-free matzo for Passover?"
- "How come my daughter moved to the area three years ago and no one from the federation has the decency to call her? I thought you were a Jewish organization!"

Hidden in each of these questions/statements is an assumption that there is an entity called the Jewish community that should be all-knowing. If a person moves into our area but does not let us know she is Jewish through membership at any Jewish organization, how would we know she lives among us so that we can offer her a proper welcome? We would not have any way of knowing. But if we were truly a large, extended family, then we should know where our members are, even those on the margins, through a network of informal connections. An aunt told a second cousin once removed, and then the news made its way to the family barbeque. In reality, we do try our best to get information and make connections so that in each case, the person in question gets answers or explanations. The point is not the answer but the assumptions hidden in the questions about the way extended families work.

Families also embrace multiple members because anyone born with a particular genetic makeup by virtue of that birth is a member. The individual may engage in behaviors that marginalize him- or herself, but—as we said earlier—birth is a fact that cannot be taken away or changed. In extended family constructs, the same assumptions may or may not hold true. We tolerate a range of membership through an emphasis on pluralism, but these words are not the same. Although we use the words *pluralism* and *tolerance* as synonyms, this blurring of distinctions has not helped us understand what can and cannot be imagined in an identity that embraces more than one collective notion of peoplehood. Rabbi Donniel Hartman, author of *The Boundaries of Judaism*, offers a helpful formulation:

> Pluralism is that category which assigns equal value to certain differing positions. At the foundation of pluralism lies, as Isaiah Berlin states, the recognition that "human goals are many, not all of them commensurable, and in perpetual rivalry with each other." Those in a pluralist community are cognizant of the differences among members but are able to perceive equal value in a multiplicity of positions. While pluralism does not necessitate the acceptance of all positions, and is not equated with relativism, it does recognize the possibility of equally valuable though differing goals and values which "cannot be graded on a scale so that it is a matter of inspection to determine the highest."[1]

When we tolerate a position we do not share, we are offering it a limited form of acceptance that is not essentially positive. Tolerance is not open-armed acceptance; it is almost a teeth-grinding patience that is forced upon us. Pluralism is the acceptance of multiple paths, characteristics, and orientations as sharing equal value and equal entitlement to significance. Tolerance is not.

Returning to our example of family, we tolerate family members who are not like us or are annoying or different in some significant way, and we understand that families are constructed of many different types of individuals who live together in some form of acceptance. This concept is essential to an understanding of peoplehood. Some would argue that multiple Judaisms are emerging precisely because we are not really pluralistic; in point of fact, we are barely tolerant of difference.

Imagined Communities

To explore the impact of intolerance on peoplehood, we need to turn our attention to membership and boundaries. In Benedict Anderson's influential book, *Imagined Communities*, the author argues that national identities are formed through three basic mechanisms: census, map, and museum. These symbolize the number and type of individuals counted in a particular community; an agreed-upon understanding of the physical borders and boundaries of a place; and a sense of common or collective past that shapes an understanding of history, values, and the future. In the creation of statehood, Anderson writes that these three institutions "profoundly shaped the way in which the colonial state imagined its dominion—the nature of the human beings it ruled, the geography of its domain, and the legitimacy of its ancestry."[2]

Using Anderson's framework, it is not hard to understand the current Jewish confusion about identity. In terms of a census, we have a hard time knowing who to count and why given the differing opinions about who is Jewish, what is an acceptable conversion and by whose standards, and whether or not to count patrilineal or matrilineal descent. Outside of these obvious identity markers, there are those who want to be counted because they feel profoundly Jewish, live in a household with other Jews, or live in partnership with Jews. Many of the recent demographic studies of Jewish communities around the country counted Jews only through affiliation records of institutional membership of schools, social agencies, and synagogues. But we know today that many people "do Jewish" outside institutional walls. Are they not counted?

When we turn to physical borders—Anderson's map—we encounter similar difficulties. On purely physical terms, Israel's borders are still not stable and determined because land that was annexed in previous wars is still not counted as an official part of the state. This may seem minor to some, but Israel's map is certainly not minor to most. It is not minor to those who live on either side of these amorphous borders, places that have become moving targets of violence, protest, ambiguity, and instability. In many cases, it is these very imaginary lines that are the cause of untold anguish and insecurity.

Moving beyond maps to museums, we find the importance of sharing a joint past as a marker of national identity. A museum is not only a national repository of history, and history is not only the recording of dispassionate facts told objectively. It is also a place that provides the heritage stance of national pride, and the shaping of facts to present particular values. Within Jewish tradition, it is memory that forms one of the most substantial ancient mandates and one of the most oft-used contemporary Jewish expressions: never forget. Always remember. We use history and memory as a way to form and inform Jewish values, as the contemporary writer Peter Novick observes:

> The most significant collective memories—memories that suffuse group consciousness—derive their power from their claim to express some permanent, enduring truth. Such memories are as much about the present as about the past, and are believed to tell us (and others) something fundamental about *who we are now*.... For a memory to take hold in this way, it has to resonate with how we understand ourselves: how we see our present circumstance, how we think about our future.... We embrace a memory because it speaks to our condition; to the extent that we embrace it, we establish a framework for interpreting that condition.[3]

Thus, memory is a mechanism to recall the past because it tells us something about our current and future identities. In support of shared history as a marker of Jewish identity, we turn to a staggering law recorded in a sixteenth-century code of Jewish law regarding conversion. A potential convert to Judaism is only taught about Judaism in broad strokes. The question that is posed to the convert is this: do you know that Jews have been persecuted throughout history, and are you willing to become Jewish despite this? In other words, we place more stock on peoplehood as an initial determinant of future Jewish life than we do on observance of the commandments. A meaningful Jewish life is not hard to construct; a willingness to accept Jewish destiny is a much harder commitment.

Although we may have questions about census, map, and museum and their applicability to the current Jewish condition, Jewish history has been relatively stable as an identity marker. Our catalog of persecutions punctuated by high points and humble victories is something that should be, out of Anderson's three symbols, the easiest one to help us form some loose boundaries around collective identity. It should be, that is, until we come to terms with the fact that different Jewish groups manipulate history for different political or spiritual ends. It should be, until we come to terms with the fact that memory is often unreliable. Yosef Yerushalmi, in his book *Zakhor*, opens with the remarkable number of times that the word *memory* appears in the Hebrew Bible: 169. He also reminds us that memory is remarkably subjective: "Memory is always problematic, usually deceptive, sometimes treacherous.... We ourselves are periodically aware that memory is among the most fragile and capricious of our faculties."[4] Do we look back at Jewish history positively or negatively? Do we look at Jewish tragedy and say "never forget," or always forget, because the painful memories give us a sense of Jewish isolation, dispersion, and oppression? History should be a loose marker of collective identity until we realize that so few members of the Jewish people today know Jewish history. Between active manipulation, human capriciousness, and an almost willful ignorance, we find that history, too, is problematic in creating collective identity.

In trying to figure out who is in and who is out, Anderson's scheme is helpful but limiting. It also shows us why the issue of basic unification to counter all the differences that pull us apart is still elusive. It is not, however, as problematic as being defined by others. We know that if we do not define peoplehood, someone else will step in the breach and do it for us—usually to our detriment.

Self-Determined Boundaries

In 1844, Karl Marx—a Jew by birth—took on the same question that has occupied these pages. What does it mean to be Jewish? His book, *On the Jewish Question*, helps us understand what happens when this question is asked for reasons other than to secure an objective answer based on research or observation. Marx equated the Jews with the worst kind of middle-class capitalism. They became, in his eyes, the epitome of a people endangered by their own greed. Ironically, Marx ignored the Jewish support of communism that would eventually metamorphose into the very vision that David Ben-Gurion had for an Israel that was "a socialist Jewish State." But outcomes are beside the point. Marx defined Jewish identity in a pernicious and harmful way. Yet, in the absence of a clear, unified picture of Jewish identity, it was relatively easy for an outsider to create labels and descriptions that we might find problematic. Marx reminds us of the importance of Jewish self-determinism. If we cannot identify ourselves, we leave ourselves open for others to identify us.

One of the most difficult and vexing issues affecting peoplehood is defining who is in and who is out of the entity called the Jewish people. And yet, as we see from the Marx example, we would rather define identity than have it defined for us. And while it would feel good and politically correct to be as inclusive as possible, no structure can be boundless and still exist as a defined entity.

Many Jewish leaders today, in particular Rabbi Kerry M. Olitzky, executive director of the Jewish Outreach Institute, prefer the expression "an open tent" to describe the Jewish community. The tent signifies something ancient and biblical; the open tent takes us back to rabbinic images of our patriarch Abraham, welcoming and embracing strangers in a tent reputed to be open on all sides. But something as porous as open membership taken to the extreme does not result in expansion. It can result in the collapse of the tent altogether. Donniel Hartman reminds us of the importance and inevitability of boundaries:

> There is no viability for social life without some notion of boundaries and limits on the difference which it can accommodate. Without these boundaries it becomes impossible to locate that common core by virtue of which fellow members affiliate with one another and form a social entity.[5]

The problem is that too many people want to determine who is in and who is out of any community. There are those who say that anyone who wants to be in is in, and those who argue that very few can make their way in. Our unwillingness to make any uniform demarcations has created a Judaism that is anything that anyone wants it to be, as well as narrow and unchanging. Translated into terms of meaning, this weak, stretched definition has allowed for fluid membership and flagging interest because the collective core lacks sufficient substance, form, and meaning.

> Contemporary Jewish life seems to be left in the predicament of having to choose between a policy that undermines the possibility of a coherent collective Jewish life by rejecting boundary policies altogether, and one that achieves the same end by advocating socially destructive boundaries.[6]

Who chooses such policies that may end in socially destructive boundaries? Individuals living within families make decisions about Judaism as either an inclusive or an exclusive entity that informs their choices as a unit. More significantly for collective Jewish identity, any number of Jewish institutions make boundary decisions. Synagogues decide who can join and who can and cannot be called up to the Torah. Jewish day schools decide which children to accept based on loose or firm Jewish identity markers or birth facts. Jewish social service agencies regularly make decisions about whom to serve and why. On some level, there is logic in allowing boundary decisions to be made locally rather than globally, but the unwillingness to discuss an overarching framework of membership has hurt our notion of peoplehood as an extended family with a mission because we are not sure who is in our family.

One of the problems in handling this tension is the poor judgment that institutions and individuals so often use, making boundary decisions alienating and a source of friction. Too often, institutions make rash decisions about who can be in or out without really exploring the possibility of a relationship that may become transformative. What do we mean? Institutions and individuals are each making decisions about membership. Generally, institutions make decisions about membership first. They determine the criteria for admission and participation. Individuals can suffer the consequences of these decisions and experience profound rejection as a result. But, just as Jewish study is predicated on the belief that knowledge is part of acceptance, knowledge should also be part of rejection. Who are we turning away?

Many people who are rejected from Jewish institutions turn around and then reject Judaism wholesale. Logically, we all know that institutions do not represent an entire belief system, but emotionally, we can't help ourselves. The repercussions of these decisions can be devastating. Sometimes the stories of pain that Jewish institutions have caused through rejection have not been sufficiently told or heard. We have heard countless such stories and have even experienced this rejection ourselves.

I was sixteen years old and had made the most momentous decision of my young life. Growing up in a nonobservant Jewish home, I decided to become observant myself in early adolescence. As a result of taking off many days during High Holy Days season, I forfeited my merit scholarship at a local prep school that did not allow students to take off for religious reasons. I begged my parents to send me to Jewish day school, but there were no local high schools; the decision meant living away from home. I went to visit various schools, nervous and excited about the adventure ahead. One morning, I went to visit a school far from home by myself. I walked through the doors and the principal started shouting at me that I was late for school. I said, "But I am not a student here. I am here to take an entrance exam." This did not generate any smile or welcome. I proceeded to the front office. They gave me an exam in Hebrew and one in English and directed me to an empty room to take the tests. When I said that I did not know enough Hebrew to take the test, the secretary just barked that I needed to take it anyway. I sat for forty-five humiliating minutes, with a preschool scribble of my Hebrew name in the right-hand corner of a totally blank page. A black cloud spread over my head. What was I doing? Why would I give up a perfectly excellent education for this? I had journeyed so far and felt that I had run into a wall of friendliness. Fortunately, I went to a wonderful, warm Jewish day school that really helped me grow as a person.

P.S. I never got accepted to the school. But then again, after my visit, I didn't want to go there anyway.

—ERICA BROWN

Imagine a different scenario. Imagine that our initial response is always to embrace people and open up possibilities for them. We don't make a conscious decision to be friendly, as if we could turn on warmth at will. We are friendly and open regardless of where it will go, simply because all people are created in God's image and deserve respect and kindness. Then we give people the language of belonging—enough explanation and information to decide for themselves whether they want to join before an institution makes its boundary decisions.

At the same time or in parallel stance, individuals are also exploring their own personal boundaries and thinking about joining and rejecting. They also make boundary decisions. In other words, an individual decides whether he or she is in or out, and then an institution decides to accept or deny membership. This does not mean that an institution needs to lower its entry standard, although low-barrier, high-content programs and events tend to help Jewish outreach the most. Simply put, it means that people are given the opportunity to think about who they are, their needs, and their narrative in relation to an institution in a dignified, thoughtful, and respectful way as the institution explains its boundary policies to potential joiners. An attitude to peoplehood that says, "We are all in this together. This may not be the right place for you. But we will help you find the right place" is a recruitment policy that goes beyond walls and opens doors.

Questions for Conversation

1. Do you think the organized Jewish community needs to answer the question "Who is a Jew?"
2. If so, who should answer that question?
3. How do issues of boundaries and membership affect your Jewish life today?
4. Describe how such issues are avoidable or unavoidable.
5. What would happen to Judaism in the absence of boundaries?

6

PEOPLEHOOD AND INTERMARRIAGE

A woman in her thirties with young children shared with me her thoughts on her marriage to someone outside the faith. "I am committed to raising my children Jewish but am doing that alone. Listen, Joe is a lapsed Catholic but incredibly supportive. He let go of his religion in college, so he was fine to go with mine. In a way, we bring the best of both worlds in helping the kids grow up with values." When I asked her about potential challenges, she confessed that it was not all smooth sailing. "The holidays are always a challenge. Every interfaith couple says that. My parents never cared that much about Judaism, and they really love Joe. The days of sitting 'shiva' for a kid who intermarries are over. But I do struggle as my oldest asks me questions about Judaism. He can be confused about the differences between Judaism and Christianity. To tell you the truth, I don't know enough to educate him, and I'm starting to realize that it's fine to raise your kids with two faiths if you know what you're talking about. But for me it feels like a game that I don't know all the rules to. There are some real differences between Judaism and Christianity. It's as if we smooth it all down, pick a few rituals, and give the kids double the presents. That's not really raising your kids with faith, is it?"

—ERICA BROWN

It is tempting to think about intermarriage in purely numerical terms.

- How many Jews are intermarried?
- What percentage of the Jewish population chooses intermarriage?
- How many raise their children Jewish?
- How many significant Jewish donors are intermarried or have intermarried children, and how does this influence their thinking about giving?
- How many dollars go into outreach to the intermarried in contrast to the in-reach of those struggling with high Jewish day school tuition or Jewish institutional memberships?
- Why do we use the scare tactics of statistics about intermarriage to advance in-marriage?

All of the hows in these questions mask the importance of the whys of intermarriage. In terms of the peoplehood equation, the whys matter much more than the hows.

Unquestionably, one of the great challenges of boundary setting for Judaism and peoplehood generally is the issue of intermarriage. Today, we find ourselves in an unusual paradox. Research demonstrates that individuals who intermarry are not necessarily making a decision to leave Judaism but making an affirmative statement about today's multiculturalism when it comes to choosing a life partner. They are not saying good-bye to Judaism as a life option by choosing a non-Jewish spouse, as might have been true in the past. Historically speaking, intermarriage today is not about achieving social status or opening the doors to social or professional success, as it was once regarded. On the other hand, contemporary academic debates indicate that intermarriage is not necessarily succeeding in enhancing the commitment to Judaism of individuals in this relationship either. In other words, there is no animus against Judaism, but neither is there a move toward it.

In such a portrait of faith-based stasis, notions of peoplehood suffer. Peoplehood, unlike Jewish rituals or even beliefs, is much more difficult to simulate in a household committed to two faiths. It is much easier to light Hanukkah candles, sit at a Passover Seder, or even pray in a shared language than it is to share the mysteries of Jewish identification: the jokes, the food predilections, the body language, the modes of expression. Ironically, it is often these unspoken behaviors that cause the most distance in an interfaith marriage. They create the insider/outsider tensions that many non-Jews feel in an intermarriage; they bolster the claims that Jews are exclusive, biased, or noninclusionary. Some partners do not even realize that they engage in these peoplehood behaviors and that these are alienating for their non-Jewish spouses. Such relationships can experience marital strife that is never consciously attributed to deep ethnic differences but regarded instead as a matter of personal idiosyncrasies.

Paul and Rachel Cowan, intermarried before Rachel converted, wrote a book called *Mixed Blessings* that shares vignettes of group work they have done with interfaith couples that reveal the extent to which peoplehood issues become divisive in interfaith families. They use techniques in ethnotherapy to surface some of the deep-seated differences that many couples fail to realize are there. In these workshops they have discovered undercurrents of conflict that were not previously acknowledged, much less managed:

> We have heard honest disclosures of the ways Jews and Christians see themselves and each other inside the privacy of their homes. In these relationships, pressures mount as differences arise. Ancient heritages conflict behind closed doors. Even people who feel they've rejected their family's traditions in the name of modernity discover that their ethno-religious backgrounds affect the work they do, the way they think about education and food, sex and money. Many couples learn that they have far more powerful feelings about their heritages than they realized when they met.[1]

The authors continue their discussion of ethnic differences by highlighting the false assumptions often created in melting pot cultures, namely that all faiths are essentially the same at heart or, at the very least, the rejection of faith will lead to a rejection of all the behaviors that faith implicitly brings with it. For many individuals within inter-faith families it is a surprise to discover how much the ethnic aspects of their upbringing correspond to and impact the peoplehood equation. This often emerges most strongly within a marriage if an individual begins to revisit his or her childhood associations when contemplating having children, at the death of a parent, or during another trauma that may bring a personal need for faith and community into fuller focus.

> Just as many Jews who marry gentiles are often surprised to dis-cover that they feel an inexplicably powerful commitment to Jewish survival, so many Christians who wed Jews come to the sudden, unexpected realization that they care more than they had thought about Jesus, about the church, about the meaning of Christmas and Easter…. Often, these religious and cultural feelings are suppressed when a Jewish-Christian couple fall in love. They come to the surface as marriage approaches or when children are born. We call these feelings time bombs in an inter-faith relationship.[2]

Time bomb is a loaded, powerful expression that implies explosive argu-ments or fiery debates, and often it is only a matter of time before such differences do implode. They are time bombs not because couples are so deeply entrenched in their faith or ethnic commitments but precisely because they are not. They do not realize the power of what they always considered an invisible or imperceptible hold on their personal identi-ties. They did not necessarily enter a relationship consciously aware of the strains of peoplehood.

> When Jews and Christians first fall in love, they usually regard themselves as individualists who will be able to transcend the specific cultural demands of the pasts that shaped their beliefs and laid claims on their loyalties. But that is a more difficult task than they imagine, for at some profound level of self and psyche, most will always be attached to the religious and ethnic tribes in which they were raised…. If couples don't acknowledge

such assumptions ... they can damage the ecology of an intermarriage. If a struggle over religion does begin, it often takes
couples by surprise, thrusting them into confusing, seemingly
endless discussions. For suddenly, they discover that they are not
interchangeable parts of an American whole, but two people
whose different pasts have endowed them with a distinct set of
feelings.[3]

*Every month I write a brief letter to my community to share, as the
chief executive officer of our federation, my thoughts on a recent
trip to Israel or an upcoming holiday. Sometimes I discuss a contemporary piece of research that I've read or a trend that has been
brought to my attention. The letter is distributed to more than
15,000 people on our list-serve. As in all matters of cyberspace, I
have no idea who reads it and how it gets shared with others unless
someone presses the reply button. I am always grateful to respon-
dents, even those who disagree vehemently with something I have
said. They care. In response to one of my first letters—called
Misha's Musings—I heard from a woman who is the non-Jew in an
interfaith marriage. My musings that month had to do with being a
welcoming community. Research on our community indicates that
many people find our institutions not accessible or warm enough.
First-line receptionists can often be unhelpful or unfriendly. I was
profoundly disturbed by this finding and implemented a number of
customer service initiatives in addition to bringing it to the attention
to the heads of all of our agencies. I wrote my musings about being
a welcoming community, not anticipating all the depth of feeling
that this would stir in readers. The woman who wrote to me made
herself surprisingly vulnerable. She felt spurned by the Jewish community and any foray in was just met with abrasive dismissals. She
was profoundly hurt that she could not easily become a part of the
Jewish community but that since her husband was Jewish, he was
welcome simply because he was born Jewish. Her experiences con-
firmed her abiding feeling that Jews are insular and proud of being
insiders with each other. I acknowledged her hurt and validated it.*

But there was little else I could say. The psychologist in me under-
stood her alienation. The Jewish community leader in me recog-
nized the urgency of a welcoming campaign while knowing that the
signs of peoplehood are sometimes inevitable.

—MISHA GALPERIN

Institutional Responses to Intermarriage

No matter where you currently stand on the intermarriage debate as an institution or an individual—to include actively or to focus on in-marrieds—the issue may be much more complex than outreach or education alone can solve. After all, Jewish beliefs, history, and culture can be taught. Can peoplehood be taught? Non-Jewish individuals may be invited to serve on Jewish boards or welcomed as parents in Jewish schools, and this may still never achieve the sense of inclusion that the non-Jew in such a relationship seeks. And the belonging that is sought may never be able—even with all the institutional outreach and good-will in the world—to be felt because of the ethnic barriers that are an inevitable claim of peoplehood. This may be attributed, in part, to the *failures* of assimilation.

Assimilation, the great historic equalizer, has another side; it ironically flattens intensity. The neutralization that multiculturalism brings—"I am not one of anything, but neither am I strongly any-thing"—has its own costs. Individuals try to neutralize differences in order to stay in relationships. We all do. But there are times when this neutralization fails us because we want to feel emotions passionately. We want to feel connected. We long to be part of something that is not always dampening our stronger emotions but harnessing or elevating them. Assimilation may communicate acceptance, but it rarely gener-ates passion.

Peoplehood is not neutral. It involves a strong sense of loyalty, allegiance, and—for lack of a better word—emotional tribalism. Many who are intermarried are fine with faith and ritual; ironically, they struggle profoundly with peoplehood because expressions of tribalism can feel good and bad at the same time. These expressions offer belonging and attachment but can also spell out betrayal or simulate low-level racism against one's partner. It's like joining a club that won't accept your best friend as a member. It makes you question the spoken and unspoken rules of the club. Through interviewing more than three-hundred interfaith couples, Paul and Rachel Cowan concluded that there is asymmetry as far as intermarried Jews are concerned:

> Usually, even the most disaffected Jews want to raise their children as Jews.... Even though they themselves are intermarrying, they often are afraid that their children will be assimilated into Christian culture. They fear that if they don't insist on maintaining Judaism in their homes they will betray more than four thousand years of proud history and deprive their children of a valued legacy.... It is often impossible for their gentile partners to understand the intensity of these feelings. They wonder why so many Jews who marry Christians insist on celebrating Jewish holidays and ignoring Christmas; on sending children to Hebrew school and keeping them out of churches. Why are they so insensitive to some of the deepest feelings of the gentiles they say they love? Why, the Christians wonder, are Jews so stubborn? Why, some Jews respond, are the gentiles unable to understand the depth of their loyalty to their heritage and their people?[4]

Partners that began marriage in a religiously neutral or indifferent place can surprise themselves with this cognitive dissonance. When the spouse argues, "Hey, wait a minute, when did religion become so important to you?" or "This isn't you," they fail to recognize the changes and developments that individuals within a marriage undergo in their personal search for meaning. The failure to accept these changes can lead to a crisis of identity with another person in tow. In such a situation, a person may ask himself, "Do I stay true to myself or true to what this relationship has always been? Why does something meaningful to me have to compromise *us*? Why do I have to make such choices?" Personal growth in marriage is the capacity to say that who I am is not who I will always be. Nevertheless, that freedom of self-determination looks different when it compromises relationships of commitment.

Usually, the peoplehood problem in intermarriage does not arise when Judaism is still regarded as a private, personal spiritual affirmation. The problem emerges when somewhere along the lone journey of faith, the individual discovers the Jewish community and begins to realize that community is not a side dish in Judaism but the central, energizing life force of Judaism. As this sense of belonging—inclusion—grows, it often generates the fear of exclusion from a non-Jewish spouse. Sometimes this gnawing sense of exclusion is articulated; sometimes it is withheld. Sometimes it is a suspicion; sometimes it is read as a sign of rejection.

Sometimes, the quest for belonging is not expressed by the Jewish partner in an interfaith relationship but by the non-Jewish member who is curious and interested in the Jewish faith, Israel, or Jewish culture. Zvi Zohar, a professor at Bar-Ilan University, observed that "while marrying out was once an expression of a Jew's intent to abandon the Jewish tradition and adopt a lifestyle of his or her non-Jewish spouse, today it is often the non-Jewish spouse who seeks to become a part of the Jewish world."[5] This desire, which may lead to conversion, is not necessarily to live a halakhically observant lifestyle but to be part of a people. Zohar's research into the Talmud and post-Talmudic legal sources led him to assert a position of inclusion even if such converts do not live observant Jewish lives after conversion. He cites a Talmudic opinion that even if a convert regrets his or her decision and reverts to a former lifestyle, he or she is still considered legally Jewish, just as an apostate is.[6] In other words, the act of conversion is considered an entrance into peoplehood, not only into a life of faith and ritual. Once made, this covenantal bond is irrevocable from a legal perspective. But this boundedness is only a reality for the spouse that converts.

The complexity of intermarriage today may mean that Jewish communal institutions may not be doing outreach or "managing" intermarriage in a sufficiently compelling way. Because intermarriage today is largely not perceived as a personal statement against Judaism (and can open up interest in Judaism when an interfaith couple begins to explore their cultural and faith differences), the possibilities for enhancing a peoplehood commitment are enormous. The price of neglecting the impact of intermarriage on peoplehood will have personal and statistical consequences we dare not even approach.

Because of easier admission and participation of intermarried families in synagogues and community centers, many such unions are able to have a home that still reflects Jewish choices and even raise children with Jewish institutional support. This also means an added level of sensitivity to the language that we use, which can communicate exclusion. A young woman reflecting with a group of educators and community activists on her experiences as the daughter of an interfaith couple shared some disturbing encounters. She once asked the rabbi of her synagogue a question. He dismissed her. "He said he did not have time for me because he had to use his time to address families where there was a chance of Jewish continuity. How was that supposed to make me feel about being Jewish?" She now, understandably, bristles every time she hears the word *continuity*.

And yet, there is still understandable uneasiness and ambivalence about low-barrier admission and participation and its eventual cost to Jewish life. Jewish leaders have taken strong and often controversial positions about reaching out to intermarried families versus allocating, supporting, and facilitating the involvement of those who have made more mainstream choices to live Jewishly. Steven Cohen has described the growing abyss between the in-married and the intermarried in "A Tale of Two Jewries" and observes "The gaps between the in-married and the intermarried are so large and persistent that it seems that we are developing into two distinct populations."[7] This leads him to conclude that "intermarriage does indeed constitute the greatest single threat to Jewish continuity today."[8]

This is in sharp contrast to the view of Rabbi Kerry M. Olitzky, the director of the Jewish Outreach Institute, who views the prevalence of intermarriage as an opportunity to bring more people to the table and, with the nurturing created by inclusivity, have more children raised Jewishly. Olitzky is supported in his position by a recent study on the impact of intermarriage. The conclusion of "It's Not Just Who Stands under the *Chuppah:* Intermarriage and Engagement" posits that the impact of intermarriage largely depends on whether or not we are able to educate and transmit Judaism to the next generation and less on the rate of intermarriage: "It depends less on whom young Jews marry than their capacity to find meaning in Judaism and the ability of parents to be role models in this endeavor."[9] Our concern should not be limited to who stands under the bridal canopy but on the variety of meaningful encounters with Judaism after the wedding ceremony.

The current debate on the impact of intermarriage is heated and consequential. Our task is not to rehash these arguments or to wait until we have a firmer statistical grasp on the consequences of intermarriage beyond the academic wars taking place. However, it would be impossible to have a discussion about peoplehood and membership without mentioning the challenges and opportunities that intermarriage poses.

Many of my childhood years were spent in Deal, New Jersey, a mecca for Syrian Jews on the Jersey Shore. We were one of the few outlying Ashkenazi families living there at the time. Much of what I learned about community came from the experience of watching this remarkable network of Jews up close, not as a participant but as a curious observer. Syrians socialize together, do business together, run their extensive charitable safety net together, and create mechanisms for continuity within the Syrian Jewish community together. They also have an active herem, *or excommunication, in force for those who intermarry. When a Syrian Jew intermarries, it is understood as a total rejection of the community. An announcement is made in the synagogue; the person's name is mentioned along with a whole list of prohibitions. People cannot invite the said person and new family to any religious gatherings. The person is not permitted in the synagogue, cannot attend Syrian schools, or be buried in Syrian cemeteries. The community is strongly advised not to socialize or do business with this person. All of this applies even to women who intermarry whose children are still considered Jewish by Orthodox standards. An Ashkenazi rabbi who once witnessed such an announcement called over the Syrian rabbi after services. "How can you be so uncompromising? The woman's children will be Jewish." The Syrian rabbi turned to his colleague: "What is the rate of intermarriage among Ashkenazim?" The Ashkenazi rabbi sheepishly replied, "About one in every two couples." "In my community," the rabbi said triumphantly, "we have only one intermarriage every few years." This dialogue may have lacked demographic backing, but it was packed with emotion.*

—ERICA BROWN

Intermarriage as Normative

For institutional Judaism to confront the reality and possibilities presented by intermarriage is to join the two distinct populations that emerge in Cohen's study. Instead of funding projects for the intermarried, Cohen recommends strengthening in-married couples by having greater linkage between Jewish formal and informal Jewish identity-building experiences and greater funding for Jewish cultural, social, and religious initiatives for young adults and by training more rabbis to focus on conversion. Sociologist Sylvia Barack Fishman, author of *The Way Into the Varieties of Jewishness* (Jewish Lights), adds that high school behavior is very important in later family formation patterns and recommends that educational programs for this age group be a top priority for community organizers.[10]

Many scholars support Cohen's thesis and his practical recommendations. Others argue that Cohen's conclusions are deleterious for the work that currently needs to be done with intermarried families where investment of resources has proven successful. In another recent study, Leonard Saxe at Brandeis's Cohen Center claims that nearly 60 percent of children from intermarried homes are being raised Jewishly in Boston as a result of the communal investment in this population. Some say this is an aberration from the norm.

Fishman looks at the historic changes in the once relatively low intermarriage rate in the post–World War II years up until the 1970s. Since then, Fishman contends

American Jews today are intermarrying in a fluid cultural context characterized by porous boundaries. The majority of American Jews, like non-Jews in their socioeconomic and educational cohorts, regard intermarriage as part of the American lifestyle. American Jewish resistance to intermarriage has been replaced in recent years by the view that intermarriage is normative. The great majority of American Jews believe that intermarriage is inevitable in an open society, and fewer than half actively oppose such marriages among their children.[11]

Intermarriage may be more normative than in previous decades because, as a community, we may have created more mechanisms to educate and include non-Jewish partners in the fabric of Jewish communal life. This does not mean that on an individual level we will ever surmount the peoplehood dilemma.

For Jews, a Christmas tree or a cross may always carry the uncomfortable overtones of millennia of Christian anti-Semitism in a way that the Hanukkah menorah may not. For Christians, the contents of the Passover Haggadah may make them feel excluded and alone at a family Seder. These sentiments are not only natural; they are also a consequence of Judaism being far more of an ethnic identity than a belief system alone. As a Jew, you may reject belief in God, but you are still a product of history. You may not join a Jewish institution as an adult but still be very attached to the Jewish foods, songs, and friends of your childhood. You may disagree with some of Israel's military policies and yet find yourself slightly weepy every time you hear "*Hatikvah.*" Being Jewish is still a strong contributor to Jewish identity, even when Judaism is not practiced in a ritual sense. As a culture, an ethnic identity, a system of faith, and a nationality, being Jewish does not represent only one aspect of identity. It is a layered identity, and negating or minimizing some aspects of this layered identity does not mean that its impact on other aspects of identity is unfelt.

Some Jewish communal leaders support active outreach to the intermarried on what they claim are authentically Jewish grounds, looking for precedents from Jewish history or Jewish texts, specifically those that emphasize inclusivity. Fishman, borrowing historian Eric Hobswam's term, calls this the search for a usable past in her book, *Double or Nothing*. The idea that the Bible encourages kindness to the stranger and care for the vulnerable can lead to an Americanization of Jewish values that is not authentic to our textual tradition:

> The blurring of boundaries between insider and outsider, creating the image of a biblical inclusivist utopia, reflects the fact that American Jews like to think of themselves as inclusive—and included!—because so much of historical Jewish experience has been marked by exclusiveness.... The particularly American nature of this Judaism-as-inclusiveness construct is especially evident when examined in light of Jewish and Christian scholarship suggesting that biblical, ancient, and medieval Jewish societies each had strongly defined boundaries between insiders and outsiders, although they shifted over time.[12]

The desire to make American values into Jewish values generates a powerful emotional claim on its adherents. They are able, through this blurring of values, to avoid bifurcating two traditions to which they are deeply attached. But this need to simplify and streamline different values by manipulating them to be seamless is rarely authentic to traditional Jewish thought and law, nor does it promote peoplehood. Are we willing to risk honesty and integrity? Are we so enamored with the American values of tolerance and multiculturalism that we miscommunicate or misunderstand tradition in order to suit particular lifestyle choices?

A more authentic communal approach is articulated in Gary Tobin and Katherine Simon's book, *Rabbis Talk about Intermarriage*. They argue that on a communal level, we have to create standards that are explainable and consistent and train rabbis and others appropriately from all denominations. Their focus is not only on the policy that individual institutions set but also on the sensitivity to language and rejection that rabbis or other leaders use in explaining their policies. Rabbis, they posit, are often woefully underprepared to handle the complexity of intermarriage from an emotional point of view.

> [R]abbis cannot be effective leaders if they are acting only on their own personal philosophy and belief. Their beliefs and actions must be tied to a greater set of laws and guidelines that have both theological and communal roots and support. The leadership that comes from setting standards must be accompanied by leadership in explaining those standards. American Jews are highly educated. They need to understand the historical and religious antecedents to any particular approach to dealing with intermarriage. Rabbis can exert leadership by explaining their ideology and its roots in either traditional or evolving Judaism. Indeed, rabbis will earn more respect and exert more influence by being well grounded and having the ability to explain and translate that grounding to the Jewish public.[13]

The authors claim that Americans who grow up within a democratic tradition understand that different denominations have different standards. While couples may initially want to be accepted by any institution no matter what decisions they make, they will appreciate and respect those who have comprehensible standards that are well explained within their framework of interpretation and communicated with tenderness and sensitivity. Tobin and Simon continue:

> The presentation of standards must be accompanied, however, through teaching and counseling, and not through rejection.... Leadership comes primarily through education, compassion and integrity, not threats or unusual use of power.[14]

This approach has another important component to it; reasons for *in-marriage* also have to be carefully explained and not assumed. This value, not just the rejection of this value, must be well articulated as foundational to Jewish tradition with a coherent rationale and not simply a guilt-induced practice that makes little sense in a pluralistic environment.

Intermarriage and the Categorical Imperative

Many intermarried individuals who care about Judaism understand that their personal choices—while clear to them—do not make sense on a communal level and are destructive to the peoplehood equation. They understand that if every couple made the same decision that they did, it would dilute Judaism beyond recognition within only a few generations. The issue of peoplehood would certainly be at stake. After all, what ethnic identity would the grandchild of an American Jewish father and an Italian Catholic mother have if their son married an Asian-American female? All of this is possible and probable in America, but it does not, as is often promoted, contribute to a celebration of multiculturalism as much as a diminution in the ethnic strength of any one of these potentially strong ethnicities.

In thinking about intermarriage, we turn to a famous philosopher, Immanuel Kant. In his masterwork, *Groundwork for the Metaphysics of Morals*, Kant argued for a categorical imperative. A categorical imperative is an absolute, unconditional requirement that applies in all circumstances. As harsh as it sounds, it makes a great deal of sense. In making personal choices, we must consider the larger consequences were everyone to make the same choices we make. In Kant's words: "Act only according to that maxim whereby you can at the same time will that it should become a universal law." For example, imagine that each time you littered, you asked yourself, "What would the world look like if everyone did the same thing I just did?" No one would want that outcome, and thus, our litterbug is a transformed man; not only does he deposit all of his garbage in the proper receptacle, but he also smirks and even experiences momentary rage when he sees others litter.

Kant asks us to take to the extreme any one personal position to assess whether it can pass the test of being a universal demand. If not, then it is not worthy of us individually. If we asked ourselves, for example, what Judaism would look like if everyone were to engage in the same Jewish behaviors that characterize our own behavior, we may arrive at a very different-looking Judaism. We may convince ourselves that illiteracy is not personally significant, but few of us would agree that an entire people could thrive let alone survive if every member were ignorant. The same would be true of ritual observance, intermarriage, and a host of other issues. The slippage, assimilation, or ignorance of some members can be tolerated within any group, but *en masse* it would be a recipe for communal disappearance. Often, we find that people are honest about their lack of observance or knowledge but are happy to know that someone *else* is keeping the faith because they believe that Judaism should exist; they are just not prepared personally to make sacrifices for that existence. Again, if everyone in a group were to take this approach, then who would keep the flame of Jewish faith or culture alive?

If we use Kant's notion of an ethical imperative to explain the impact of intermarriage on peoplehood, we can distinguish between individual choices and communal positions. In Kant's formulation, individuals cannot behave in personal ways that would imperil communal values. In other words, their individual choices should be informed at the outset by a communal set of ethics. If I think it is wrong for people to murder, then I cannot murder. If I can imagine the moral catastrophe were everyone to steal from one another, then I can understand that my personal thievery has contributed to the breakdown of ethics generally. If we invert the terms, then an individual who intermarries but still values Judaism can understand that on a communal level, if we were to permit, encourage, or negate the significance of intermarriage, it would eventually lead to the nonexistence of our people. No one who values Judaism, on any level, would want that consequence.

The categorical imperative reminds us that our personal preferences translate into communal responsibilities. Are there categorical imperatives of peoplehood? We believe that there are. Individual behaviors are not always productive for the Jewish community; consequently, communal institutions and leaders cannot accommodate all individual behaviors. What they must do in thinking about intermarriage and making policy decisions is balance American tolerance with American Jewish intelligence and present clear, unambiguous, well-articulated positions with thoughtfulness and sensitivity.

QUESTIONS FOR CONSIDERATION

1. What is your personal position on intermarriage?
2. Now think of people you know who are in interfaith relationships. What challenges do they face and how do they handle them?
3. Think of a few Jewish institutions with which you are affiliated. What position do they have regarding acceptance of intermarried couples in terms of membership, board service, and acceptance of children?
4. How are these policies articulated? What kind of language is used?
5. In your opinion, how are notions of peoplehood affected by intermarriage?

7

JEWISH LITERACY AND THE PEOPLEHOOD PREROGATIVE

It's funny that in Russia we did not have religious books, but every home of a Jewish Russian intellectual contained a copy of something Jewish or something connected to Jewish life and culture. It might be Thomas Mann's Joseph and His Brothers, *a book of enormous significance for me. I remember reading Simon Dubnow's* History of the Jewish People *in my teens. The book was special, but the fact that my grandfather had preserved this very old copy for generations as a family treasure was just as special as whatever was to be found between its covers. Our common language as Jews was taken from whatever books we could obtain under communism. We were thirsty for knowledge and would take it from whatever we could get our hands on. It pains me that in a time when books are so easy to buy today—you don't have to leave your office chair to buy an entire library—that Jewish homes are not stocked with Jewish books.*

—Misha Galperin

Thus far, we have explored two barriers to peoplehood: the personalization of religion and the way in which boundaries limit membership. Our third obstacle is Jewish illiteracy. To become a citizen in the United States, you have to take a test that demonstrates a more than basic understanding of government and civic laws. To become a driver in this country and any other, you have to pass a test that demonstrates your skills and understanding of the rules of the road. Because citizenship bestows privileges and responsibilities, it requires some measurable means of knowledge. Because driving involves a degree of danger to yourself and others, you have to prove yourself worthy of a license. Being Jewish is a bit of an anomaly. You are a member of a family simply by birth. Your existence in that family is not a matter of knowledge, nor does it present any threat to others that requires rule setting. And yet, peoplehood is a combination of membership *and* purpose. To be a member on the most basic level requires nothing more than birth or conversion; to have a mission or purpose requires some degree of knowledge.

In *Ethics of the Fathers*, we encounter an aphorism that sums up the Jewish commitment to education: "An ignorant person cannot be pious."[1] It is as simple as that. Jewish literacy is not only one desideratum of a peoplehood agenda; in many ways, it *is* the peoplehood agenda. It is the unapologetic assumption that being Jewish means knowing something about your tradition. Spirituality is assumed to emerge out of knowledge. Anything of meaning and substance must be rooted in understanding, not ignorance. And Jewish learning, unlike other kinds of study, is premised on an educational ideal. We learn for the sake of learning, for the engagement in something sacred and transcendent, for the conversation that takes place between individuals who study together, and for the intellectual beauty that we encounter in the process.

The mandate of education is nestled in the first paragraph of the Shema, Judaism's central prayer taken straight from the pages of Deuteronomy. There, we find the imperative to teach our children. The command is not that our children should know, but that we must be active participants in their acquisition of knowledge. Study binds families to God and to each other. The seminal place that study occupies in the lives of Jews has very much influenced the contemporary Jewish emphasis on education. And yet today, there seems to be a troubling disconnect between study and Jewish literacy. Study is correlated with academic achievement and professional success. We would find it hard to imagine a Jewish parent allowing his or her Jewish child to forego college and graduate school; we find it totally credible that Jewish children are allowed to forgo Jewish education, often deciding on their own at bar and bat mitzvah ages to give up on whatever meager offerings they had in supplemental education. Strangely, Jewish literacy is regarded as ancient and out of step with modernity. And yet, the professors and lawyers, the businesspeople and physicians of today still live in the potent shadow of the Jewish push to become more knowledgeable, more ambitious, and more accomplished, yet they may have lost touch with the origins of this drive for literacy.

Literacy in the ancient world was connected with piety. We might read this statement of old from *Ethics of the Fathers* and conclude that piety is not a personal goal. Why be knowledgeable if the spiritual outcome promised is not something of worth or value to the reader? Answers to this question will be suggested in this chapter. To begin the process, we turn to one of the most articulate voices for Jewish education today: Leon Wieseltier in Abigail Pogrebin's book *Stars of David: Prominent Jews Talk about Being Jewish*. The citation is long but allows Wieseltier to express an idea with a level of depth:

> I think the great historical failing of American Jewry is not its rate of intermarriage but its rate of illiteracy. I can go on for many long hours about this. The amount of Judaism and the Jewish tradition that is slipping through the fingers of American Jewry in times of peace and security and prosperity is greater than anything that has ever happened in the modern period anywhere. It is a *scandal*. Now what I'm not saying is that there should be more believing or more belonging Jews; this is a free country. We believe in freedom; people can think and do what they want. The problem is that most American Jews make their decisions about their Jewish identity knowing nothing or next to nothing about the tradition they are accepting or rejecting. And a lot of American Jews *accept* things out of ignorance, too. The magnitude of American Jewish ignorance is so staggering that they don't even *know* that they're ignorant ... we have no

right to allow our passivity to destroy this tradition that miracu-lously has made it across two thousand years of hardship right into our laps. I think we have no right to do that. Like it or not, we are stewards of something precious; we are custodians, trustees, guarantors. We inherit the language in which we think, we inherit most of the concepts that we use, we inherit all kinds of habits, and one of the things we inherited is this thing called Jewish tradition.[2]

We might compare Jewish literacy, in Wieseltier's sense, to the American right to vote. It is a basic right of an American citizen to vote for his or her leadership; voting is both a choice and an expression of the freedoms that we are given in this country. There are those who do not take advantage of this freedom because they care little about leadership or issues of local, national, and international importance. Alternatively, there are those who go to the polls because they believe in principle that people should be given the right to vote, but they have no studied opin-ion on who the candidates are and what the issues are that require their judgment. They believe in the principle but do not take the time to edu-cate themselves each time about the particulars. One might say that such individuals are not dramatically different than the first group, and in some instances, the first group is preferable in protecting a citizen's right to vote. If you cast your ballot out of ignorance, you may be doing more harm than not voting at all. We know that today an enormous amount of media attention is paid to a candidate's clothing, hobbies, and family life, and consequently, many individuals vote for "personalities" and not posi-tions. The first group is apathetic. The second is often misguided.

I was asked to address a board meeting of an area JCC about our new engagement agenda, our local attempt to open more doors and create low barriers for involvement of the unaffiliated. Washington, like other large American cities, has an unaffiliation rate of more than 50 percent. I have made it a special campaign to attend to this number and change it significantly in the years ahead. As I spoke to this group about the importance of Jewish belonging, a woman raised her hand and asked, "What's so important about Jewish values? My kids want to know. I thought Jewish values were just humanistic values." I proceeded to get passionate about the importance of study as a way into Judaism. I am not talking about commitment per se, but about real engagement with the language, assumptions, and discussions of Jewish importance over the centuries. Basic Jewish literacy is more than knowing texts. It's also about being able to negotiate a modern world with values that have been tested over time.

The woman who asked the question was committed to Jewish institutions and was sitting on this board. The legacy she received from her parents was a commitment to volunteerism, and she was continuing it. But we have to be wary of a commitment to cultural or organizational Judaism that is only surface deep. It's okay to come to a JCC and use it as a portal into the Jewish community, but we need to make sure that it does not stay the only "Jewish" experience a person has. Exercise equipment may help a Jewish person stay fit, but it does not provide an authentic Jewish experience. Having literacy at the center—even when disagreeing with its conclusions—means having a language that is both meaningful and flexible over time. You can reject Jewish values and Jewish texts but do so from a place of knowledge. You can only really reject that which you know.

—MISHA GALPERIN

Education and Language

Moshe Halbertal, in his book *The People of the Book*, analyzes the role that the canonization of various Jewish texts has had on Jewish identity.[3] His book explores the process of canonization and how closing a book allows the process of commentary to begin in earnest. Although Jews were called the people of the book by Muslims, who created a special status for adherents of religions that possessed sacred texts, Jews internalized this epithet as a means of self-understanding and identification. In other words, Jews were not the only ones to have sacred texts, but they were the only ones who took the title that an outside body gave them and internalized it as a badge of pride. Jews, throughout history, have distinguished themselves by being bookish and intellectual. Halbertal argues, as his book comes to a close, that in all periods of Jewish history Jews saw themselves as defined by texts or defined by their opposition to a text. Opposition also implies a relationship, one that is reactive and responsive. Today, Halbertal contends, Jews do not have texts to claim as their common language and general culture has done much to strip away the collective in favor of the personal voice. These individualized voices that lead to personal choices may provide a high degree of autonomy but offer little by way of common cultural norms, expectations, or assumptions. If you take away a language that binds, what replaces it?

Another contemporary scholar, Barry Holtz, formulates the question in another way, a way that searches for some practical conclusions:

> Once upon a time ... in the intact world of medieval Jewry the connection between text and life was clear and the *authority* of the classic sources to influence, indeed to determine, the destiny of one's life was beyond question. But here we now stand, no longer part of that reality, confronted by a new unfamiliar literature once as close to us as our skins.... We cannot go back in time; we cannot really know what it means to see the world as our ancestors did.... What previously defined us as a people now both literally and figuratively feels like a foreign language. So what are we to do about the library?[4]

One response to the closed library problem of literacy is to open the library by creating more and better adult educational services in local Jewish communities. Give people the keys to this library by making education more attractive, personally meaningful, and engaging. In addition, create curricula that don't dabble in a dilettantish way in obscure or curious topics of Jewish interest. Help people fill in the gaps with a solid taste of Jewish history, Jewish texts, philosophy, and a sense of the great Jewish thinkers who have shaped a religion and a culture. In addition to cerebral approaches, help adults find meaning in shared

Jewish experiences that have a textual basis, such as volunteer opportunities preceded by group study of a range of sources on social activism, *tikkun olam* (repairing the world), and *hesed* (acts of kindness). Such a mingling of the intellectual and practical can give literacy a real leveraging power in framing experience.

A number of communal entities across North America (as opposed to synagogue-based study options, which generally assume a level of institutional commitment) have done just that with striking results. But not enough communities have thought about adult education in terms of communal infrastructure. Philanthropic non-profits have not invested enough in making sure their donors are Jewishly knowledgeable. Classes are offered in a largely unstrategic fashion based on the whims, agendas, or interests of the instructors or institutions. Infrastructures generally exist for social services, but opportunities for Jewish literacy are almost regarded as a luxury for the elite rather than the right of every Jewish adult. They may be by invitation only, come with a high price tag, or not exist at all. This vacuum of educational opportunities, not surprisingly, often correlates with the level of congregational or Hebrew school success. In areas where Jewish education for adults is thriving and has become a communal norm, the standards for both day and Hebrew school education are on the increase. Why? Because an adult who has been exposed to a transformative educational Jewish experience will not be satisfied with a substandard educational opportunity for his or her child.

This discussion has been largely practical in nature. It has presented Jewish illiteracy as a fact and the enhancement of community-wide adult study opportunities as a solution. But the conversation—and it is not an original one—ignores the most basic question. Why not be illiterate?

Isn't Ignorance Bliss?

To tackle the "why" problem, we have to survey some of the standard justifications for Jewish literacy that have been articulated. Some have argued that ancient Jewish literature should be regarded with the same status as any other classic of literary or philosophical note. Texts of ancient wisdom have offered great depth and personal relevance to those who have been patient and studious. Why not add Jewish texts to the mix? And yet, compelling as it is to make this comparison— that struggling with texts generally adds to our level of insight into the human condition and is itself a pleasurable act—it assumes a level of intellectual drive that is hard to muster in an age of consumerism. This may be a satisfactory approach for those with a strong idea-centered focus but may not work on a more universal plane.

Wieseltier made the case that we should be literate because of a responsibility to a tradition much older than ourselves. We are stewards and custodians of a treasure whether we like it or not, and we cannot turn our backs on it. The problem with this approach is not unlike the problem with the first. Some people will feel an obligation to tradition and its language because they are responsible people in general and because they have a sense of history. The first reason to study assumes a literary or an intellectual sensibility. The second assumes a historical sensibility. For those who have these sensibilities, a reasonable case can be made that, if you are prepared to study Shakespeare or the French Revolution, then Maimonides and the Italian Jewish Renaissance make equally good, if not better, study material.

But in making the case for literacy, we cannot be naive. How many among us care deeply for literature, philosophy, and history? Outside mandatory university courses or even desired courses within our respective majors, the pleasures of study are self-exclusionary and not a draw for the majority of illiterate Jews. In this regard, brushing up on the positions of candidates in preparation for the vote is a lot easier than jumping into the black hole of Jewish texts, which include but are not exhausted by thirty-nine biblical books, the multivolume Talmud, the Hebrew language, encyclopedic works on Jewish law, dense medieval philosophical tomes, sixteenth-century mystical literature, responsa literature, Yiddish plays, Israeli novels, and contemporary American Jewish literature. The sheer scope alone is intimidating.

Some have made the case for Jewish literacy on practical terms and for a limited group: Jewish leaders. Involvement in the Jewish community on a board or leadership level should require Jewish literacy, partly as an intellectual companion to "institutional" memory and also in order to inform an organization's mission within the framework of the larger mission of the Jewish people throughout history. There is also a powerful component of Jewish ethics that can shape and guide institutions, particularly during morally ambiguous times or through ethically troubling issues that institutions may, on occasion, confront. Joseph Telushkin attempted to respond precisely to this point in his influential work called *Jewish Literacy*:

> At a time when Jewish life in the United States is flourishing, Jewish ignorance is too. Tens, if not hundreds of thousands of teenage and adult Jews are seeking Jewish involvements—even Jewish leadership positions—all the while hoping no one will find out their unhappy little secret: *They are Jewishly illiterate.* The most basic terms in Judaism, the most significant facts in Jewish history and contemporary Jewish life, are vaguely familiar or unknown to most modern Jews. They can tell you the three components of the trinity but have an infinitely harder time explaining *mitzvah*. They know what happened to Columbus in 1492 but not what momentous event shattered the whole Jewish world that year.[5]

Telushkin tells us with a tinge of embarrassment the dirty secret of Jewish illiteracy without offering any reasons why literacy is important to leadership. Its significance is almost assumed. But we cannot afford to make such assumptions, and we have to connect peoplehood to literacy so that a sense of a shared notion of *klal Yisrael* remains an idea that undergirds education.

> *One of the most surprising outcomes of our course in Jewish leadership is the thrill that people get in studying ancient Jewish wisdom; it's a taste that they thought they had to acquire. Yet the foray into this relatively unknown world of Jewish texts turns around negative associations they've carried with them since childhood. This has*

meaning. This speaks to me. In their own words, let's listen to what our participants told us about literacy and leadership from a recent evaluation:

- *"The use of Jewish literacy throughout the class resonated by grounding leadership in the origins of Judaism."*
- *"It wasn't so much that I learned 'what would a Jewish leader do'; rather, it was an opportunity for me to learn what I would/should do in a leadership situation by leveraging my own Jewish identity that was apparently more suppressed than I realized."*
- *"This course made me more aware of the qualities to look for in leaders of Jewish organizations."*

No one really expected a biblical text, a Talmudic passage, or a contemporary Jewish philosopher to speak directly to them about their own leadership. And yet, each time the texts did speak to their personal experiences in astoundingly helpful ways. The one observation that dozens of people have shared with me upon completing our course—which is a combination of business literature on leadership, Jewish texts, personal reflections, case studies, and exercises—is that they thought they could lead without literacy and now are embarrassed that they ever deluded themselves into thinking that Jewish leadership requires no Jewish knowledge. It is nearly impossible to say why it was unimportant to them before they studied, but now they could not imagine their own current leadership devoid of a textual anchor. Literacy became a personal compass for their own decision making and sense of mission.

—ERICA BROWN

We, as a Jewish public, have not made Jewish literacy a prerequisite for Jewish leadership, so we can hardly fault Jewish leaders for not being better educated. As the vignette demonstrated, many Jewish leaders realize the value of literacy only after they have engaged in text study; fewer feel an urgent need to be knowledgeable to do their jobs beforehand. The value of literacy comes with retrospect; it is not yet a communal norm supported by well-advanced reasoning. And even if we were to overcome these obstacles, this argument only makes the case for educated leaders, not an educated Jewish community generally.

Compelling arguments have been made for the personal journey that Jewish literacy provides. Rather than be a tourist in our own faith, snapping sentimental photo-quality moments at life-cycle events and then walking away, we are encouraged to be seekers. Tourists know that their trip is of a limited duration and will provide only a superficial, often nostalgically familiar, or too foreign, exposure to some place. They have little interest in knowing the geography or language well. There is simply no need. Seekers, on the other hand, prepare for such trips. They read and inquire; they try the local food. They immerse themselves in new environments and even imagine themselves as residents of this new, changed place. Seekers do not have to go far to take this kind of journey, although a change of place often stimulates some of the ways in which a seeker begins to question his or her current surroundings.

Today, many people are seeking out this kind of relationship with Judaism. It is more intense and personal; it is a journey of meaning that has no set destination or hidden agendas. Although it is true that such personal journeys of meaning can take place within multiple faiths or on multiple paths, there is something touching or even logical in beginning the trip in your own backyard. Approach the culture and religion you know somewhat as a lodestone or a touchstone to a deeper experience.

For some, their familiarity with Judaism has had the opposite effect. They will try anything but the faith of their parents. They see no need to revisit something that has possibly negative associations or even no neutral associations. They find the Far East more compelling than the Near East. These seekers, whatever path they are on, know that literacy is a key ingredient in enlightenment. They do not expect that their personal spiritual journeys will require no labor, no change, and no new education. If they are seeking transformation, then they understand that work must be done to get there. In this sense, Judaism becomes a method for reaching a spiritual plane. Wieseltier argues that, within this framework, Judaism is useful for achieving universalism in a very particular way.

> You take this highly specific, highly particular thing, this concrete tradition, and you use it to break open the universal questions. That's what our tradition is for. It's not there to be smugly particular or to keep one in love with oneself. If the Jewish tradition is beautiful, it's not because it's *my* tradition. It's a great human tool. And everyone needs a tool.[6]

That literacy is the backbone for spiritual journeys of substance can be a motivation for people to seek knowledge, but it is not a motivation that requires any notion of peoplehood. And when it comes to personal journeying, Judaism is just one of many possible portals. It competes but does not always win when it comes to the avenue of choice for such journeys. Not only is this reason for literacy not necessarily connected to peoplehood, but, at times, the personal is also at uncomfortable odds with the communal. People in this seeker category are not looking for a joint experience that involves acknowledgment and responsibility to the other. There has been criticism that such seekers engage in spiritual narcissism because their faith is so self-absorbed and self-centered. But we are not here to find fault with what anyone finds meaningful. Our task is to connect literacy to peoplehood. Personal journeys may end with spirituality and literacy well twinned (because it is hard to present Judaism authentically without teaching about its emphasis on education), but such personal journeys rarely start with that as a desired outcome.

There are other personal reasons to become Jewishly literate that are not simply about creating a spiritual path for oneself. The vacuum of communal living and the loss of shared ethical norms has driven many to seek in the major Western faiths an affirmation of morality and a guide for living that sometimes feels alien to American culture. People are searching for a moral guide in a society that has largely backed away from such notions, and it is natural to begin that search within familiar territory. If it is Christianity for some, then they may turn to the church or to the New Testament. For those brought up Jewish, they might try what feels like home first to see whether it can provide them with what they are looking for. Many people seek out this spiritual foundation when they get married, have children, or face the death of a parent, because they feel bereft of the rituals that will bring meaning and solace. They want rituals that offer a framework of continuity, and often in the search for rituals, such individuals inevitably end up getting a Jewish education of sorts. Although this is more about family spirituality than the personal seeker approach, it is just as "unreliable" in its commitment to a peoplehood agenda; it may be stumbled upon or avoided altogether.

What's In It for Me?

No one will come to the Jewish classroom unless there is a compelling reason, and research has provided us with many. Roberta Louis Goodman and Betsy Dolgin Katz, in *The Adult Jewish Education Handbook*, discuss some very basic and compelling reasons to educate Jewish adults about their traditions:

> Learning is a way of strengthening one's Jewish identity and connection to our tradition. Additionally, since much of Jewish learning is done with others, it augments community building. Through studying together, people get to know one another in a personal, often deep and meaningful way. These study experiences can lead to friendships as well as the formation of *chavurot* that gather for celebrations, holiday observances, and the doing of *ma'asim tovim*—righteous deeds.
>
> Learning can provide the skills and knowledge that augment an adult's feelings of confidence as a Jew. Adults used to feeling competent in their work, relationships, special interests, volunteer roles, and family life want likewise to be confident in performing rituals in the home or synagogue, in prayer, in answering questions of non-Jewish friends or colleagues, and in grappling with difficult questions about life and death, good and evil, and purpose and direction. They want to be able to find resources and to use the tools that can help then access answers. Unfamiliar often with the vocabulary of Jewish life, and even less adept at understanding Hebrew or translating Hebrew texts, they still want to know enough to feel included in the Jewish venture.[7]

In addition to the practical, social, and spiritual importance of adult study, we might add the psychological aspects that the thinkers Erik Erikson and Martin Buber identified. According to Erikson, there are eight stages of human development, three of which take place during adulthood. In short, adults develop as a result of conflict and the resolution of conflict. Their full maturity at each stage is dependent on their ability to hold two conflicting notions of identity at the same time, such as intimacy and isolation or integrity and despair. Wisdom, Erikson's final stage of development, arises as a positive outcome of living within these dynamic tensions.

Diane Tickton Schuster, in her study of Jewish adult education, *Jewish Lives, Jewish Learning*, contends that many adults come to class for the first time in the wake of some personal upset, crisis, or change in life stage. Following Erikson's insights, adults find that the classroom environment and the analytical and spiritual process of learning helps them better manage and understand their own stage in human development.

> When Jewish adults have disruptive or "disorienting" experiences that challenge previously held worldviews, they sometimes wonder if Judaism can help them to "understand" their situation in new ways. When these adults embark on new meaning-making, new learning can transform their view of themselves as Jews.... As Jewish adults mature and grapple with pressing questions and ambiguities, they discover paradoxes in their thinking about Judaism and their lives as Jews.... When Jewish adults are grappling with questions of meaning, they find it beneficial to engage in learning and discourse with other learners.[8]

Adults who have already completed their formal educations, chosen professions, and established families invest so much time and energy in these endeavors that their own emotional and moral growth can become arrested. Once some of the major life decisions have been settled, adults have greater mental and psychic freedom to explore character development. In addition to the ordinary passage of time, crisis can stimulate growth and movement to the next stage of maturity, perhaps captured best in Gail Sheehy's popular book, *Passages.*

Buber believed that adulthood was precisely the time that individuals experience character development, because the questions and ambiguities that preoccupy young adults during adolescence and early professional development are distracting.

Recent research has also helped us understand that adult education has an important role to play in the formation of Jewish identity through the personal search for meaning: "[A]dults are looking for meaning: about themselves, their values, their religious commitments, and what gives them a sense of place and connection in a world characterized by upheaval and change."[9] If this search for meaning takes place within a positive Jewish context, then Jewish identity becomes strengthened.

QUESTIONS FOR CONVERSATION

1. How would you describe your own Jewish literacy?
2. Can you recall a moment of Jewish education that was transformative for you? Describe it.
3. Do you have positive or negative associations with Jewish study? Explain.
4. How do you think education impacts identity?
5. Collectively, how could we enhance Jewish literacy today?

8

IRRECONCILABLE DIFFERENCES? JEWISH AND ISRAELI IDENTITY

For many people, the 1967 war represented a turning point in their relationship to Israel. It did for me too, but my story is a little different. When I was nine years old, during the 1967 war, I came home from school and told my father that I was angry at the Israeli aggressors who were hurting our Arab socialist friends. That was the message in school that I had absorbed from my teachers in the former Soviet Union. That's when my father realized it was time to tell me our story. He sat me down and described the relationship of Jews to Israel and tied my identity forever with the identity of the Jewish State.
—MISHA GALPERIN

In May 2006, A. B. Yehoshua, the prominent Israeli novelist, imploded the issue of the American/Israeli Jewish divide. He was asked to speak at the American Jewish Committee's conference marking their hundredth anniversary, and he used the platform to question American Jewish identity, claiming that American Jews were playing with their identity. Later, he told a reporter from *The Jerusalem Post* that he was surprised by the uproar his comments created: "It seems to me obvious that our Jewish life in Israel is more total than anywhere outside Israel. I think this is common sense. If they were *goyim*, they would understand it right away."[1] Yehoshua implied that authentic Jewishness is only possible in Israel and that the American Jewish failure to understand this had to do with the lack of objective distance American Jews have. Others—those on the outside—would no doubt understand.

Later, in a more formal response, Yehoshua tried to explain himself again in an article of his own in the Israeli newspaper, *Ha'aretz*. He first took on the misunderstanding his comments generated:

> All of the reports suggesting that I said there can be no Jewishness except in Israel are utterly preposterous. No one would ever think of saying such an absurd thing. It is Israel and not the Diaspora that could be a passing episode in Jewish history.[2]

Yehoshua then explained what he meant about Israeli Jewish identity that has to

> contend with all the elements of life via the bonding and sovereign framework of a territorially defined state. And therefore the extent of its reach into life is immeasurably fuller and broader and more meaningful than the Jewishness of an American Jew, whose important and meaningful life decisions are made within the framework of his American nationality or citizenship. His Jewishness is voluntary and deliberate, and he may calibrate its pitch in accordance with his needs.[3]

Yehoshua was incensed at the thought that the study of Jewish texts or involvement in the organized Jewish community could have the same significance for Jewish identity as the spectrum of commitments that a Jew has living in the Jewish State. Yehoshua called this kind of portable identity that would be shaped by personal preferences and the social mores of a host country a "garment that is removed and replaced with another garment in times of trouble." A garment is too easy to put on and take off. "If Israeliness is just a garment and not a test of moral responsibility, for better or worse, of Jewish values, then it's no wonder that poverty is spreading, that the social gaps are widening and that cruelty towards an occupied people is perpetrated easily and without pangs of conscience."[4]

Yehoshua worried that being Israeli would become just as much a garment as the identity of being Jewish is to American Jews. He was not prepared for that reality, so he tried to provoke controversy to have people engage in this question of identity. One of those he provoked was Natan Sharansky, former Soviet refusnik and current Israeli politician and writer. Sharansky felt that Yehoshua's emphasis on being Israeli trumped all other forms of Jewish identity and will have grave consequences. Sharansky was less concerned with Yehoshua's remarks about Israeli/Diaspora relations than about Yehoshua's own identity claims: "My identity is Israeli. The Jewish religion does not play a role in my life; it is the territory and the language that build my identity." Sharansky retorted with a strong criticism of this narrow definition of identity:

> This definition of identity grants a bill of divorcement to the Jewish people, to the Jewish heritage, to 3,000 years of culture, creativity, prayer, rituals, tradition and everything that is subsumed in the term Judaism and shows a preference for the Israeli "nation," which "arose form the sea" 100 years ago. For Yehoshua—and many, many others in Israel—the only thing that is important, existential and relevant from the Jewish perspective is what happens here, in Israel; everything outside Israel is obsolete and its fate is to be lost. In making this claim, Yehoshua undermines and weakens the justification for the State of Israel.[5]

Sharansky challenged a Jewish identity connected to land and language alone. An American Jewish writer gave less thought to Yehoshua's personal Jewish identity and instead stridently questioned Yehoshua's assumptions about the Diaspora: "Numerous Jewish institutions of learning, culture and social action flourish all over the world. There is nothing in Jewish law or history to support the proposition that you have to have an Israeli address in order to have a Jewish identity."[6] The same writer claimed that at least Yehoshua gave some time to the question, whereas very few Israelis think about it at all. His claim that "millions of dollars and rivers of ink" are spent on figuring out Jewish identity may be exaggerated, but his suggestion that "every budget cycle adds new increments" to institutions preoccupied with this question is probably true. It is as if some important voices in this conversation never speak, while some do not stop talking.

In these situations of conflict and debate, it may be worth taking a nuanced approach rather than siding somewhere on the dramatic divide created between thinkers such as Yehoshua and Sharansky. Robert Putnam's distinction between "bonding" and "bridging" is helpful. We have to create bonds with those who share similar identity markers and with whom we feel connected to in significant ways. In the absence of certain bonds or common denominators, it behooves us to create bridges. Certainly Israeli and Diaspora Jews have many bonds with which to strengthen connections. We are also highly invested in creating bridges rather than lengthening and widening differences until an uncrossable abyss is created that cannot be bridged.

The Impact of These Differences on Peoplehood

We have laid out this book in terms of definitions and challenges, what peoplehood means, and what gets in the way of achieving it. Few would have the chutzpah to say that Israel gets in the way of Jewish identity; if anything, it is one of the most important mechanisms and foci of constructing Jewish identity. One of the major ways in which Jewish identity is enhanced in North America is by taking individuals and groups on missions to Israel, be they free trips for college students, family-based synagogue missions, or federation-sponsored community tours. Israel, in many ways, has become the great case study and joint project of Jewish peoplehood. Israel still has the power to unite us. Its celebrations are our celebrations; its emergencies are our emergencies and evoke sincere concern and support. Israel is still the destination that most inspires immersive, Jewish identity-building experiences, which enable people to feel that they are "home," part of an extended family suffused with purpose.

Ironically, Israelis are also having Jewish identity-building experiences in North America and getting to know its institutions and its

Jewish culture of inclusivity. These cross-cultural experiences make it impossible to imagine a Jewish identity without a relationship to Israel. And yet, with all of this travel designed to intensify positive Jewish immersion experiences, we find an unsettling trend that is getting in the way of a global sense of peoplehood. Jewish identity for Americans and for Israelis is just not the same thing and, at times, conflicts in profound ways.

> I was living in Boston and working for their federation, the Combined Jewish Philanthropies. Our twin city was Haifa, and the Boston community made an incredible effort to make this more than a nostalgic relationship. I had participated in several missions to Haifa and gotten to know many of our partners there. It was always gratifying to watch real human connections form and a lot of misperceptions melt away as our Boston Jews sat in the living rooms of their new Haifa friends. One year, we funded a reverse mission to Boston and took a group of Haifa Israelis all over the city. In addition to tourist sites, they visited day schools of multiple denominations and met with rabbis from every segment of Jewish life. Many had not been in a synagogue in decades, nor would they readily enter one back in Israel. For so many of that group, living in Israel was enough of a Jewish identity. To borrow from A. B. Yehoshua, Judaism was their garment, and it was sitting deep in a closet untouched. The group was highly receptive to what they were taking in. One evening, doing a text study in a Boston living room, one member of the group choked up and then laughed: "Matzati Elohim b'Boston"—"I have found God in Boston." Free from the sticky patina of politics and coercion in Israel, religion and Jewish communal norms can be more welcoming to Israelis visiting or living in North America.
>
> —ERICA BROWN

The title of this chapter is borrowed from the title of a book considering the "end" of the American Jewish love affair with Israel. Such an end or even its contemplation impacts Jewish identity and Jewish notions of peoplehood immeasurably. Just as Jews of the first decades of the twentieth century could not have imagined the actual existence of a Jewish

State, Jews of the twenty-first century cannot contemplate Jewish peoplehood *without* the presence of a Jewish homeland and refuge. Israel has become inextricably woven into a life of meaning, national pride, and Jewish self-determination. The impact Israel has on Jewish identity, however, can only be fully understood by creating a historical context in which to understand the delicate and changing relationship of Jews inside and outside this homeland.

To reconcile differences and ameliorate the weakening ties between American Jews and Israel, we must begin with the beginning of the relationship between Israel and Diaspora Jewry, specifically American Jewry. After a brief survey of this relationship, we can outline the troubling issues that create divisions and examine the measures necessary to bridge this divide. The creation of the State of Israel in the twentieth century has had an enormous impact on Jewish identity, both for those who see Israel as the ultimate Jewish destination and for those who wrestle with its politics, policies, and Zionism as a philosophy of Jewish interaction with the world. Jewish identity and its connection to a Jewish homeland often embodies one of two attitudes. There are Jewish attitudes mined in the Diaspora that have taken extreme forms of positive, unquestioning support and loyalty and those who have questioned Israel's very right to exist. There is much literature that examines the waxing and waning of American Jewish attitudes toward Israel, and we will survey some of these developments. But there is also a growing body of literature that emerged with the early precursors of Zionism who questioned the legitimacy and existence of a Diaspora culture at all. This literature is less well known but critical to an understanding of what happens to Jewish peoplehood when Israelis question the value of Jews and Judaism outside Israel's borders. Each community has different narratives, and without a real and profound inquiry into those narratives, it becomes virtually impossible to cross the abyss.[7]

American Jewish Attitudes to Israel

Some have argued that the 1967 war represented a turning point in American attitudes to Israel. No longer viewed as the weak cousin or the pesky brother-in-law, Israel suddenly reawakened Jewish identity for

Jews worldwide.[8] It was deemed worthy of American Jewish support, both politically and financially. Chaim Waxman has argued, however, that a distinction must be made between the American Jewish community and the American Jewish population.[9] Institutionally, American Jews in past decades have offered broad support for Israel and have created an undeniable presence in Israel via financial support; the creation of institutions, missions, travel opportunities; and political advocacy. Yet, as individuals, Waxman finds that many baby boomers have little connection with institutional American Judaism, and therefore, their relationship to Israel is weak as a marker of Jewish identity. The Jews of this generation often live close to other Jews, but their neighborhoods are not characterized by anything overtly Jewish. Thus, rituals or symbols of Israel are not important to this segment of the Jewish population.

Waxman cites a sociologist who makes an important distinction between traditional ethnicity and symbolic ethnicity.[10] In traditional ethnicity, individuals subordinate their personal identities to a powerful group identity, which can shape and form who they are, what they think, where they live, and how they make decisions. The group exerts social control. In symbolic ethnicity, the group has no such power. Ties exist on a purely emotional level. It is, in Waxman's words, "a psychological community but not a sociological one."[11] In other words, individuals pick and choose aspects of group identity that conform to their personal tastes and proclivities. They are not wedded to rules and regulations that would stymie their personal movement and decision making. Their Jewishness may consist in living or socializing with other Jews or conducting business with other members of the "tribe," but all of these ties exist in a limited or symbolic fashion. Such individuals do not need this group identity for self-determination. They are drawn to it because it resonates emotionally with them, but it does not constitute a serious basis of meaning or content. Waxman understands the relationship of Jews to Israel along these lines.

> Although there may be sporadic and short-lived surges of manifestations of "symbolic Judaism," especially with respect to episodic

American Jewish attention to Israel, there has been a decline in attachments that are socially meaningful and significant—that is, involving the individual for any length of time in ways that can be empirically demonstrated. An important question then becomes whether those weakening ties will strengthen those in Israel who already wish to distance themselves from the American Jewish community and what impact such a trend may have on both the American Jewish community and Israel.[12]

Israel's frequent appearance in the media as an embattled nation in crisis and political turmoil and an "occupier" only pushes away intimacy with Israel in the symbolic ethnicity model. If the connection to Israel is primarily emotional and not based on actual experiences or knowledge, then when negative emotions are generated, the connections become even looser.

Israeli Attitudes to Diaspora Jewry

In *Irreconcilable Differences?*, author Steven Rosenthal traces the roots of the American/Israeli relationship to the precursors of Zionism. Long before there was a Jewish State, there were potent writings on a philosophy of Zionism that saw it as more than a dream of a geographic homeland. Zionism presented a way for Jews to act autonomously and creatively in a homeland and in the world. Naturally, in this scheme, there was little purpose in a Jewish Diaspora culture other than its practical support of the fledgling state. There were early Zionist thinkers who went so far as to believe that with the emergence of Israel, the Diaspora would cease to exist, or its existence would only be a "sickly manifestation" of mistaken residual ties to host countries. Rosenthal quotes Jacob Klatzkin, an important Zionist figure in both the Jewish National Fund and the World Zionist Organization:

> Galut [exile] can only drag out the disgrace of our people and sustain the existence of a people disfigured in both body and soul—in a word, of a horror.... Such a life, even if it continues

to exist, will represent no more than a rootless and restless wandering between two worlds. It will cause rent and broken human beings to persist—individuals diseased by ambivalence, consumed by contradictions, and spent by restless inner conflict.[13]

Klatzkin boldly contends that the lack of a homeland is the cause of Jewish wandering and restlessness. There can be little doubt that using words such as *diseased, ambivalent,* and *conflict* creates a portrait of an impotent Judaism outside Israel.

Klatzkin mirrors many of the sentiments that emerged much later in the world of Israeli politics and literature. A former Israel deputy foreign minister, Yossi Beilin, for example, argued that with Israel's developing economy and its place on the modern and vital stage of world politics, it no longer required America's aid.[14] Views like this are ostensibly meant to help American/Israeli relations achieve a degree of equality as partners, but rather than view this statement as a much-needed admission of independence, American leaders were irate at the assumption that Israel does not require America's support; dozens of pro-Israel organizations in the United States were created to finance Israeli initiatives, lobby on Israel's behalf, and advocate for her security.

A less extreme picture than negation of the Diaspora entirely is a general ignorance and lack of curiosity about Diaspora Jewry. Jewish communities outside Israel's borders are not regarded as models of collective responsibility or institutional or charitable vitality; they are places of mistaken location. There is little desire among many Israelis to learn how other Jewish communities organize themselves or promote Jewish identity. If Israel is not at the center of Jewish identity construction in the Diaspora, then many Israelis feel disdain or a simple lack of comprehension for their brothers and sisters on the other side of the sea.

Perception as Reality

What are the perceptions about Judaism that Israeli and American Jews have? In *Two Worlds of Judaism,* authors Charles Liebman and Steven Cohen write that at least among American Jews,

[t]here is a widespread belief that the Judaism of Americans and that of Israelis are essentially the same: notwithstanding the differences of interpretation between the modernist, secularist left and the traditionalist, religious right, the Jewish beliefs, practices, symbols and myths of the American Jews and Israeli Jews are identical. Recent events in Israel may erode this belief ... most American Jews continue to subscribe to the slogan "We Are One" and take it for granted that being Jewish means the same things to Israelis as it does to Americans. Israelis, on the other hand, believe that their own Jewish existence is fundamentally richer, fuller, more stable, and ultimately more significant than that of any Diaspora community, including the one in the United States. But the primary distinction that Israelis draw between American and Israeli Judaism can be cast in qualitative terms: Israelis believe that the commitment of American Jews to Judaism is more fragile than their own and that most American Jews are likely to succumb to the allures of assimilation. In other words, Israelis believe that American Jews are the same kind of Jews they are, only less so—less firmly committed to Judaism and the Jewish people, less knowledgeable, and less proud, but not essentially different.[15]

Liebman and Cohen believe that both American and Israeli identities are key components of peoplehood, and their differences lie chiefly in symbols, motifs, and a different interpretation of certain historical events or their significance:

Both American and Israeli Jews construct their sense of what it means to be a Jew from the common perspective of historical familism. In each society Jews see themselves as part of an extended family, with a common descent and destiny and a special obligation and responsibility towards each other. In addition they use the memory of their collective past to draw lessons about the present....[16]

Not only have two Judaisms failed to emerge, but we do not see the possibility of their emergence in the near future.

> That Israeli Jews and American Jews interpret the tradition in
> significantly different ways is not only to be expected but is in
> many respects healthy.[17]

The authors, while not seeing a serious split in Jewish identity, do,
however, believe that American Jews have become overly universal-
ist in orientation and Israelis have become too particularistic and
parochial. American Jews are not faithful enough to tradition, while
Israelis have not created sufficiently meaningful structures of personal Judaism that are authentic for those who are not traditional.
These problems, as they have identified them, would benefit from
cross-cultural dialogue but do not indicate an abyss that cannot be
crossed.

What is the familism to which both Israel and American Jews
ascribe? It has been given two distinct qualities:

> The first is that of ascription: a family is a group into which a
> person is born and of which the person remains a part regardless
> of what he or she does. The second element is a sense of mutual
> responsibility: the members of a family care about each other.
> These feelings are suffused with a sense of compulsion, obliga-
> tion, and permanence that characterized the relationship
> of Jews.[18]

The authors point out an important anomaly in this sense of familism
that is at the heart of peoplehood. Jews often regard themselves as a
people with a purpose—ethical, activist, or religious. This implies
that the bonds among fellow Jews are linked not only to being members of an extended family but also to being unified by particular
goals or outlooks. As mentioned earlier, families are constructed of
individuals whose often sole connection is birth, not purpose.
People's family is not of their choosing; it is a fact. Conscious decisions about purpose and meaning, however, are of an individual's
choosing. These two factors—familism and purpose—do not have to
be mutually exclusive.

In certain ways, Israelis have embraced familism as a component of peoplehood with greater intensity than American Jews have. Being part of a small and progressive nation often under siege and the only democracy in the Middle East has created a degree of isolation from Israel's geographic neighbors that mimics the ties that exist in families. Every triumph is shared; every loss is grieved. Everyone is counted. American Jews, however, have "compensated" for the lack of a geographic locus of Jewish identity through bonds of Jewish meaning created by institutional memberships, expressions of Judaism through the arts and culture, and an exploration of faith and spirituality. Broadly speaking, these represent peoplehood as an expression of purpose. One side pulls toward familism. One side pulls toward purpose. Yet no piece of this identity is complete without the other.

Jews without Land

Many chapters ago, we discussed Haman's prime characterization of the Jews as a people "scattered and dispersed"—an essential definition of Diaspora. Nationhood without land, in Haman's scheme, was regarded with curiosity and even disdain. And yet the epithet of the Jewish people as wanderers speaks directly to the reality of a nation without the trappings of land. In many ways, issues of Zionism and peoplehood are profoundly related to the role that land plays within Jewish history and identity.

One of the great curiosities of life in Russia is the little-known experiment that Stalin conducted with the Jews. Stalin also believed in the notion of a Jewish homeland. He created a place on the fringes of Siberia called Birobodzhan, which was regarded as an autonomous Jewish republic. Stalin defined nationality as having a common language, history, culture, and land. Land was an essential and defining characteristic of nationhood. He believed that the Jews as a nation were entitled to live as a nation. There are still Jews who live there today, not far from the collective farms of China. It has not been a seat of Jewish culture or creativity. It is largely just a land mass with no special religious importance or national flavor. Ironically, it was Stalin who taught me that land is never enough to create peoplehood.

—MISHA GALPERIN

Abraham, as the first Jew, is called upon to leave his native land and go to a land that God will determine. Once he arrives there, in Genesis 12, it does not take him long to leave. Within fewer than ten verses of his arrival, he is already seeking food elsewhere because of famine. Famine will overshadow a Jewish presence in Canaan, prompting our patriarchs and matriarchs to sustain themselves outside the land and ultimately bring our fledgling tribe to Egypt for hundreds of years. It is fair to say that in the biblical history of the first Five Books of Moses, the Jewish people spend virtually their entire national existence outside Israel, except for a few brief stints in Genesis. The fact that the Torah is revealed at Sinai, outside Israel proper, is also intriguing. What does all of this mean in terms of our relationship to land as a marker of Jewish identity?

No one would argue that not having land is better than having it. However Israel is viewed—as home, refuge, fulfillment of divine promise, place of distinctive culture and collective Jewish achievement—there is no question that having a homeland is a distinct advantage in creating and sustaining a Jewish presence in the world at large and a Jewish identity at home. How then are we to explain how we have survived so long as a nation outside a homeland?

The French poet and thinker Edouard Valdman claims that Abraham wandered, as did other Jewish leaders after him, to teach the Israelites the value of not *primarily* being landowners.

Abraham suddenly gives their lives a different meaning. No longer are they bound to a particular territory or delimited by landmarks, repetitions or the seasons' unchanging timeless rhythms.... Suddenly life, so accustomed to its daily round in the repetitive cycle of nature, becomes tension, action, direction ...

Man alters himself and the world around him by wandering. The world outside him opens up even as man travels towards the other world inside himself…. By walking, Abraham realizes that man is not merely this quest outside himself but first and foremost an inward quest.[19]

Valdman believes that the Israelites wandered the desert for two generations in order to internalize the values of impermanence, of searching, and of being a people who are not defined exclusively by land. They needed the freedom to become rather than merely to exist. The act of journeying—Abraham's first calling—is an essential component of Jewish peoplehood that transcends a connection to any particular place.

Even when Abraham lives in the Land of Israel, he sees himself as both part and not part of the place. When he loses his wife, Sarah, in Genesis 22, he speaks to a tribal people there and identifies himself as a *ger ve'toshav*, a resident alien who needs to purchase land to bury her. He is aware that he is not wholly a resident of the land as much as a sojourner. Abraham raises flocks, digs wells, and creates alliances—all acts that show residency. But even when all of those acts are complete, he still describes himself as a stranger.

The idea of being part of a journey—both as individuals and as a nation—as Abraham and as the Exodus indicates, represents, in symbolic terms, the notion of heading toward promise rather than actually accomplishing it. This notion of peoplehood inspires a collective existence as an ongoing developmental quest rather than a state of arrival. The Diaspora is not only about the existence of a scattered and dispersed people; it also reminds us of an essential quality of being Jewish. We *are* proud landowners, but more than ownership of a place is a yearning and restlessness that transcends physicality. This yearning is perhaps best expressed in a song of Jewish national identity, Israel's national anthem, "*Hatikvah*" or "The Hope":

> As long as within our hearts
> The Jewish soul sings,
> As long as forward to the East

> To Zion, looks the eye—
> Our hope is not yet lost,
> It is two thousand years old,
> To be a free people in our land;
> The land of Zion and Jerusalem.

These words remind us of the longing for homeland, even once in it. It is a song attached to human freedoms and hopes. It also assumes that our enduring optimism will not be lost as long as our collective eye still looks toward a future *together*. In the words of Edouard Valdman, the act of longing itself has value. "To achieve anything, man needs true solitude, a true question, a true desert, a true pain, a true quest towards the Promised Land, a true tension, a true despair."[20]

QUESTIONS FOR CONVERSATION

1. How does the existence of Israel influence your Jewish identity?
2. How could Israeli Jews be positively influenced in their own Jewish identity through their relationship to Diaspora Jewry?
3. Do you think that being an Israeli is a different expression of Jewishness or a different category of identity altogether?
4. In your opinion, what would enhance the bridging of Israeli and Diaspora identities?
5. What stands in the way?

9

STEPPING ACROSS THE GENERATIONAL DIVIDE

One of my students that I study with regularly talked with criticism about his father's Judaism. This is the flavor of what he shared: "My father cared about fitting in. That's all. Fitting in. He changed his name to be less Jewish. My parents made a bar mitzvah for me, but it was one of those horrible bar mitzvahs where you don't understand anything you are saying or doing. Now I'm coming back to Judaism, just exploring it because I want to know what Jewish purpose is in the world. I am looking for a personal sense of meaning. What does it mean to be Jewish in a real way? In my own way. I am not interested in my father's Judaism."

—Erica Brown

The generational divide among Jews is not new. Arguably, it is as old as Judaism itself. With every generation, Judaism confronts new challenges. One of those generational challenges is the difference in attitudes about peoplehood that have been studied across a range of ages. You may not want your father's Judaism (and he may not want yours), but, as a people, what kind of common denominators can we expect to find in research on Jewish identity? Having explored peoplehood and the challenges of choice, membership and boundaries, illiteracy, and the Israeli/American divide, we now turn our attention to ageism: how do generational differences enhance or get in the way of a communal conversation about peoplehood?

In 1889, Ahad Ha'am, the Jewish writer and Israeli statesman, wrote an essay called "The Wrong Way." In it, he made the case for a chain of Jewish tradition that was able to adapt and change in each generation without losing its commitment to continuity.

> One long chain unites all the generations, from Abraham, Isaac, and Jacob to the end of time; the covenant which God made with the Patriarchs he keeps with their descendants, and if the fathers eat sour grapes, the teeth of the children will be set on edge. For the people is one people throughout all its generations, and the individuals, who come and go in each generation, are but as those minute parts of the living body which change every day, without affecting in any degree the character of that organic unity which is the whole body.[1]

This desire to capture the imagination of the next generation was a burning issue in the early days of Israeli statehood. All depended on the animation, excitement, and efforts of the young fed by the ideology of those who came before them. Ha'am understood the power of the garment that Yehoshua mentioned in the last chapter; identity for the young today comes in multiple guises and is put on and taken off in distinctive ways. Ha'am understood that Jewish identity comes in all forms, not just an original, recognizable form. Today, the level of experimentation with Jewish identity among the millennial generation is astounding. A recent research paper produced by the Hillel Foundation drives home the point that the majority of Jewish college students today are not complacent about Judaism, but they are not sure how to express their identity either.

> Even while they celebrate multiple aspects of their identities, students value their Jewishness. Many of them, though, do not know how to express their commitment, or do not choose to express their Jewish connection in normative ways. They seem

to see religion in its traditional sense as separating them, and so they observe few rituals and participate in prayer services infrequently. Yet, they are proud of being Jewish; many want Jewish children and many have Jewish friends, even while they downplay the importance of marrying other Jews and claim that having Jewish friends is not important to them. Their Jewishness reflects a tension, concurrent universalism and particularism, pride without isolation. What pulls them to Jewishness, finally, is not guilt, fear or inherent obligation but Jewish meaning and the opportunity to celebrate that meaning with their Jewish and non-Jewish friends.[2]

There is a lot to digest in this passage. Let's take the first assumption: generation Y or the millennials do not express their Jewish connection in normative ways. To illustrate, Bryan Fogel and Sam Wolfson are shown lighting cigarettes from a Hanukkah menorah on the cover of their book *Jewtopia: The Chosen Book for the Chosen People*. The cover is not the only act of irreverence. In between the covers of this book, based on their play of the same name, the authors have a fictive grandson of Adolf Hitler write the foreword, show you how to use a piece of matzo as a roof shingle or coaster, and record phone conversations with their respective mothers. The book is full of sexual innuendoes between Golda Meir and David Ben-Gurion, fake notes in the Wailing Wall, and themed bar mitzvahs featuring pig luaus. Talk about letting go of your father's Judaism. *Jewtopia* is only one of many such initiatives. There are salons across the country where young Jews are raising difficult questions about culture and identity. Controversial publications such as *Heeb* and *Guilt and Pleasure* are pushing the envelope on traditional Jewish notions of family and community. This is an all-out retooling of whatever is sacred, a sometimes humorous, sometimes painful, questioning of standard assumptions.

For the crowd whom it is designed to appeal to, it works. Generation Y does not hide from ethnic roots. They proudly flaunt their Jewishness; it, however, does not demand more commitment from them than any of the multiple identities that have shaped a complex generation weaned on technology and multiculturalism. One magazine called this generation of new Jews "edgy Jewish tastemakers" who have been fearless in capturing popular trends in music, arts, and intellectual activity and offering them a distinctively Jewish orientation in an atmosphere of casual encounter rather than formal attendance and membership. Steven Cohen and Ari Kelman have watched these developments and brought us an informative and provocative paper, "The Continuity of Discontinuity: How Young Jews Are Connecting, Creating, and Organizing Their Own Jewish Lives," and claim that what everyone thought was a passing phase is really here to stay. This has presented an enormous challenge to organizational Jewish life in America, best expressed by the authors:

> From a philanthropist's perspective, this established new reality in the new Jewish world presents a set of unique challenges. We are caught in a generational hex, knowing the traditional Jewish organizations we love are not engaging young Jews despite our most steadfast support, yet these new forms of Jewish organizing are not in our vernacular and many of us find them borderline uncomfortable. Which path are we to pursue? Do we fund what we understand even though we know it does not work? Or fund what works, even though we don't fully understand it?[3]

The discomfort is understandable. Since when has Judaism been cool? Even knowing that it worked, would Jewish communal institutions take limited resources that fund education and social welfare for the elderly and vulnerable and invest in Jewish reggae if it had a following? It is not only about money. The debate is also about commitment.

There are also some practical questions that have to be asked. Naturally, organizations like to fund programs and initiatives that work, which leaves open the question that Cohen and Kelman have yet to answer from a long-range perspective: does this approach work? What are the desired outcomes and who determines them? If the "establishment" is or becomes more committed to funding such hip Jewish experiments, are there metrics we could create to assess success? And how would we define success? Success may be about recruitment, attendance, and participation on the one hand, which may show these examples as enormously successful. On the other hand, objectives such as greater commitment, knowledge, or loyalty to the Jewish community over time may be desired outcomes that have yet to be determined.

As an example, the founders of JDub records, cutting-edge music producers on the Jewish scene, are undoubtedly affiliated: "It's very clear that we are Jewish and that these artists define themselves as Jewish." And yet, their goal is not to create community but "moments of community" that make other young Jews feel proud.[4] They prefer events and concerts to anything long term because they are interested in gathering and identification. This theme of providing social networking opportunities under a minimal Jewish guise—from Jewish happy hours to Jewish Facebook groups—has often been a goal of mainstream Jewish organizations that may once have hosted dances and balls for the same reason. What's the difference now?

In this question lies the essential paradox. It seems that one of the main differences is that these events are both overtly more Jewish and often more substantial in content and spiritual overtones than the purely social opportunities created by generations past. They are also more irreverent than the more innocent gatherings of years past, potentially undermining the very traditions with which they are playing. Jews and tattoos, Jews and plays on anti-Semitism, Jews and music that may use foul, sexually loaded language. It is this very paradox that makes older generations unsure of the lasting power and validity of such trends. It also raises the problematic issue of whether this "movement" is about satisfying rather specific, individual interests or whether it is about community building. Some may argue that we should not care about this question at all. If we're creating Jewish programs that actually bring in a segment of the Jewish population who feel disenfranchised, then who cares what the long-term goals are?

> *I first sit in a college classroom and then in a synagogue classroom.*
> *I ask both groups of generation Y Jews the same set of questions.*

- *What are five issues your generation cares about?*
- *Name five human iconic figures.*
- *Name five products that have come to symbolize your era.*
- *Name five movies and songs that sum up your lives.*
- *Name five Jewish issues that you care about.*

Beloit College in Wisconsin produces the Beloit Mindset *annually. The* Mindset, *written by faculty members, describes the worldview of the incoming freshman class: which world events, leaders, celebrities, and objects did and did not shape their lives; what they know and what they do not know. I invite you to look at Beloit College's website and see* The Mindset *for yourself. I reproduced it for my students. They didn't like it. They felt it was inaccurate and a bit condescending. They wondered how faculty members could write such a description without the guidance of students. Where is the voice of the generation itself?*

So I asked them the questions above and wrote their answers on the board. Through their answers, they discovered they were actually mad at themselves. They looked at a board that contained words such as Iraq War, Global Warming, Sept. 11/Fear, Terrorism, No Child Left Behind, *and* Economy *but had a hard time situating themselves within these issues as activists. They added to these issues the two words that one young woman felt summed up her generation:* Apathy *and* Disillusionment. *This was followed by another two words offered by someone else:* Instant Gratification. *Two of their icons were Osama bin Laden and Saddam Hussein, since these two tyrants have had an enormous impact on their world. And yet, they struggled to identify heroes among all the celebrities and politicians that litter the media. Can Jon Stewart be considered a hero? Michael Jordan? They debated these questions. The products of their generation affirmed the instant gratification one student mentioned earlier: iPods, PlayStations, laptops, BlackBerries, cell phones, and hybrid cars tell the story of their concern with the environment but also their ability to have access to information and to each other instantly. Theirs is a generation that never knew a world without technology and reality TV.*

On the board were also words of Jewish identity, such as Intermarriage, Israel, Intifada, Jdate, Celebrity Judaism, Hebrew School, Post-Denominationalism, *and the* Decline in Holocaust Survivors. *They are the generation of multiculturalism and birthright. Then there were the words I've come to expect:* Disillusionment with Institutional Judaism, Decline in Membership and Activism, Individual Spirituality, and Lack of Theology. *They looked at the board, saw that their Jewish identity was sandwiched between words that described their generational identity and came to the conclusion that their generation was decidedly in need of more meaning and activism. We looked at the songs of my generation that stirred harmony, such as "Ebony and Ivory" and "We Are the World." Then we talked about a recent song by John Mayer, "Waiting for the World to Change." What a difference in approach. Is it our world to take ownership of, or do we wait for someone else to do the work?*

—ERICA BROWN

The desire to take Judaism out of institutions and make it fresh, inviting, and personal is not new. Again, the *chavurah* movement, popularized by Reconstructionist Judaism, felt secure enough to allow practice and worship in living rooms instead of traditional sanctuaries. Rather than threaten a movement, it made it more meaningful and lasting for many; the movement often bridged the distance between formal worship and fellowship. In a study of the *chavurah* movement conducted in the late 1970s, one of the compelling reasons for joining such social clusters was precisely to fill the void of social networking and meaning that individuals and families were not experiencing within traditional Jewish prayer structures: "The *chavurah* becomes a surrogate extended family by providing a sense of belonging to its member families. It does so partly by responding to the adult social needs of the husband and wife and partly by meeting their needs as parents rearing a family."[5] But these smaller clusters were never meant to be stand-alone social structures; they were designed to "have an invigorating effect on the life of the synagogue,"[6] because it was assumed that the more active individuals became in the *chavurah*, the more likely it was for the individuals to translate that participation into synagogue life. In addition, the idea of such groups was never to be simply social; the success of a group was measured by whether or not it provided a "substantive Jewish experience."[7] Returning to our earlier summation of peoplehood as a sense of belonging to an extended family with a mission, *chavurot* were designed to communicate just those feelings. This objective and measure of success may be increasingly important in evaluating and funding programs and initiatives emerging out of generation Y, because many of the same reasons that spurred the *chavurah* movement are reappearing in this new generation of "dissatisfied customers."

Cohen and Kelman claim that Judaism for many of today's young people feels "socially exclusionary and overly bounded," just as stiff as synagogue worship did for those in the *chavurah* movement. It is the suit-and-tie religion rather than the socially acceptable casual Friday. These Jews are also not interested in toeing the ideological line that has separated Jews from non-Jews in the same way as former generations. Again, Cohen and Kelman offer us their language:

> Younger adults also resist and reject the normative conformism or normative advocacy that they see as widely characterizing the Jewish institutional world and culture. They speak of Jewish institutions as having an "agenda," referring to their interest in advocating specific beliefs and behaviors, in particular those centered on matters of "Jewish continuity" or group survival. Agendas, by their nature, are not subtle, and younger adults are savvy consumers, able to spot an agenda at a distance, especially that in which they are the prime targets and are being told to marry (each other) and the contemporary version of "be fruitful and multiply" for the good of the Jewish People. Consequently, they prefer not to be subject to those, who, in effect, represent their parents.[8]

Institutions, however, do have agendas, and they cannot be faulted for having particular missions and sticking to them. In order for institutions to communicate meaning effectively, they have to have missions or convey a sense of overarching purpose. In that sense, the Jewish people also has an agenda, and it is not only an agenda about survival but about a meaningful survival that has translated into a rich history of communal compassion for each other and the world at large. Mission rather than agenda communicates a positive, purpose-driven enterprise. Perhaps *agenda* is too loose a word, and it needs fine-tuning. We need to understand what kind of mission and vision is acceptable or repellent to this generation and why. In the words of one young and idealistic Jewish woman, "I'm not interested in agendas. I'm looking for causes."

The Generational Divide

Today, we are giving the generational divide more and more attention because the assumptions various generations make about Jewish identity can be vastly different. Just to make sure that we are all on the same timeline, the following is a loose guide to age brackets that carry with them different associations about life and about Judaism.

Traditionalists (1900–1945)

Baby Boomers (1946–1964)

Generation Xers (1965–1980)

Millennials or Generation Y (1981–1999)

Some have argued that within Jewish tradition, these age blocks are not accurate enough because they fail to account for major events in the life of the Jewish people, such as the Holocaust, the creation of the State of Israel, and the 1967 war, which are all strong Jewish identity markers not captured by these somewhat arbitrary divisions. Nevertheless, we have chosen dating that has become more universally accepted.

What seems to be the problem? Lynne Lancaster and David Stillman jointly wrote a book, *When Generations Collide*, about age differences in the workplace and the impact they are having on work life generally.[9] Lisa Belkin, a *New York Times* writer, tried to encapsulate some of the problems of this generation in the workforce in her article on a young man who, unsure of a future career path, decided to take a different job for every week of the year. In the words of Sean Aiken, the restless career seeker, "I like changing tasks. I enjoy continual change. And it should be something interactive. With people."[10] A French psychologist commenting on Sean's blog remarked that Sean represents the "vocation-searcher"; "It is a job that only one applicant can fit and is made up of all the skills and talents of Sean. The best way to involve all your skills in your job is to create a job made of all your skills—instead of trying to fit in an existing and traditional one. Sean is now the hero of a quest turned into an adventure."[11] Sean may represent a hero of sorts; his behavior is certainly intriguing, if not extreme, but we can hardly imagine that Sean is a hero to his boss or bosses, who must have found this experiment rather frustrating. And this restless need to personalize and find some sense of ultimate happiness or move on has become emblematic of criticisms laid on this generation in the workforce and also in the Jewish community.

We have distilled some of the major findings in *When Generations Collide* to show the overlap in sentiments and tensions the Jewish community is experiencing that have an impact on Jewish identity, and we have added some common refrains from the work of Jewish communal professionals and lay leaders. Rather than present each side at length, we have abbreviated the comments to show their diverse and competitive aspects. Remember that these are generalizations, not facts.

COMPLAINTS OF TRADITIONALISTS AND BABY BOOMERS

The younger generation feels more entitled.

They expect more but give less of themselves.

They use lots of filler words in language and speak immaturely.

They prefer technology over cultivating face-to-face relationships.

They are difficult to manage at work because they feel superior and more educated.

They are less committed to long-term relationships and to staying with an organization.

They don't get involved.

They don't pay their dues.

They don't value family and community as much as older generations do.

They don't value the age and maturity of older coworkers.

COMPLAINTS OF GENERATION XERS

Older generations always point to age as a sign of immaturity.

Older generations don't value irreverence and sarcasm as part of my culture.

There is too much emphasis on loyalty in the general culture, even at the expense of personal happiness.

Older generations don't fully appreciate fun and the importance of liking what you do.

Older generations are uncomfortable with hyphenated-identity, where each piece of my life is equally important and does not consist of a hierarchy of values.

Older generations are too judgmental.

Older generations don't appreciate that it is more expensive to live now, so there are more financial pressures.

Younger people are expected to live longer and work longer without the same benefits or commitments from companies that older generations enjoyed.

Older generations don't understand that there is more turnover in younger people's work lives and less financial security.

Reviewing these lists and trying to understand their significance, we find that certain assumptions breed particular behaviors and psychic obstacles in bridging many of these understandable conflicts. Traditionalists and baby boomers complain that it is more difficult to recruit gen-Xers and millennials to Jewish institutions, and it is harder to get funding for established institutions and membership dues from this population. Gen-Xers and millennials have grown up with such diverse multiculturalism that they may not value being Jewish over other commitments, and this can show up in inconsistent participation or leadership in Jewish organizations or in the lack of interest in Jewish organizations altogether. Older generations question whether their notions of long-term communal living have become impaired in the fast-paced technological pull of today's lifestyles. This has left many lay and professional leaders to question whether or not they will be able to pass down tradition and their own shared language to those who may not embody or value it.

On the positive side, gen-Xers and millennials have brought in fresh blood and new approaches to older, institutional thinking that can sometimes turn stale. New trends force us to stay on top of technology and use it to enhance relationship building and social networking. While the trend among millennials is to challenge institutional Judaism, that very challenge has come from a place of deep idealism that has created a shakeup for many organizations. Traditionalists and baby boomers should show rather than tell why their values work to build community in an age when people are searching for belonging. Organizations need to make room for these important voices of change, while younger generations need to make some mental room for the wealth of experience and commitment that has been demonstrated in the generations before them.

We need to capitalize on a Jewish identity that is very idealistic while at the same time more humanitarian than that of generations past. The change in Hillel's vision from "to maximize the number of Jews doing Jewish with more Jews" to the title of its most recent research, "Distinctively Jewish, Universally Human," shows a sea change in attitude. Generation Y may feel ethnic pride, but it is not particularistic in the way it reaches out and integrates with the world at large. One of the challenges is to tap into this idealism and offer it Jewish flavor by providing the Jewish social and textual underpinnings for social activism and by channeling some of this vital energy and enthusiasm back into the Jewish community through volunteerism and leadership. Judaism should not be disconnected from our idealism but an essential animus for it.

In looking at Jewish identity and peoplehood from this universal lens, the Swiss developmental psychologist Jean Piaget (1896–1980) provides a helpful distinction between accommodation and assimilation in his developmental cognitive schemata. How do we organize knowledge and process it? In the mode of assimilation, we develop a unique and personal way of understanding the world. New information that we glean is absorbed into this worldview: augmenting it, affirming it, or challenging it. In assimilation, our worldview stays essentially the same over time. In accommodation, we take new information or knowledge and change ourselves in accordance with that information. Accommodation is an actual modification of a belief system or can be a paradigmatic shift in worldview.

What we are actually finding is that generationally our perceptions are all shaped by experience, even though younger generations generally use more accommodation than assimilation. This makes perfect sense; at certain ages—while our views of the world are still in flux—we may be open and mentally flexible enough to adapt and reformulate the way we view our universe of discourse and action. Older generations value assimilation because they have made many of their important life decisions already and feel more settled about their values and orientation. The generational divide that exists now within the Jewish world—and that has always existed through time—must incorporate both assimilation and accommodation to be enriched and meaningful. Older generations need not fear accommodation; younger generations need not spurn assimilation. The balancing of values that create anchor experiences informed by new approaches can create a sense of peoplehood that reaches and touches more people in more ways.

Translating these changes into the subculture of American Jews, we find a new term for Jewish identity that bridges the generational divide: the remix Jew. *Remix culture* is a term employed by Lawrence Lessig, founder of Stanford Law School's Center for Internet and

Society, to describe a society that allows and encourages derivative works. Such a culture would be, by default, permissive of efforts to improve upon, change, integrate, or otherwise remix the work of copyright holders. Lessig presents this as a desirable ideal and argues, among other things, that the health, progress, and wealth creation of a culture is fundamentally tied to this participatory remix process. Lessig's definition of remix may be applicable to the current state of American Jewry. With the increased ability to travel—both physically and virtually—we have greater access to other cultures' music, writing, and experience than ever before. We live in a time when remixing fashion, thoughts, food, and other cultural expressions is the norm. This influences our experiences and has produced individuals who are comfortable living on the cultural borders of various ethnic identities.[12]

In music, a remix is the taking and changing of a song so that it has some sense of adherence to the original tempo, lyrics, playing time, or any defining characteristics but is a unique alternative. An individual may like a song but want to adapt it somewhat so that it stays true to the original while reflecting some degree of personalization. A remix is not a simple copy; it requires a degree of ownership by the listener. A remix identity has two components: a core identity and a portable identity. The core identity in our metaphor is what makes the remixed song identifiable with the original and will generate resonance from multiple listeners. The portable identity is the unique piece of customization that adds something different to what already exists. This remix takes effort, creativity, and a desire to make someone else's interpretation of a song work for an individual listener. A remix identity is a commentary on an existing identity.

Rather than bemoan the presence of such customized identities, we need to recognize the beauty of remix identities among younger generations of Jews who respect the "original" enough to take hold of it and make it their own. The issue in this metaphor that requires the most attention is the original or core identity. Who determines it, and how recognizable is it? Is it like a well-known song that virtually anyone can hum so that slight variations will still be discerned by others, or is the original itself obscure?

Take, for example, Slingshot, the brainchild of a group of twelve individuals ages eighteen to twenty-eight, who got together for a weekend to consider innovation and change in the Jewish community. They formed an association called Grand Street that took upon itself the challenge of identifying the way forward for Jewish identity through innovation. They set themselves the task of identifying fifty of the most innovative projects in the Jewish community for special, targeted funding and created metrics to arrive at certain outcomes. They identified four measures of success: innovation, impact, strong leadership, and organizational effectiveness. Organizations that achieved these characteristics with high impact were profiled together in a brochure and online as worthy of philanthropic attention, and they specifically targeted a number of these organizations and offered their own generous funding. Each year, since its inception in 2002, Grand Street has added twelve young individuals to their growing pool of funders and strategists.

Slingshot modeled itself, on one level, on the network of Jewish philanthropies in the United States, and it funds projects that have emerged out of many well-established Jewish institutions. But the idea of owning and promoting the funding by a young cohort who often are marginalized in larger, well-established charities made this a remix project of very significant proportions, perhaps unimaginable a decade earlier. In the 1980s, we might have expected that young Jews uncomfortable with the current state of Jewish giving would have turned away from Judaism and their perception of it as a dinosaur. Instead, young leaders are taking hold of charity, music, Jewish study, writing, and social networking and creating some of the most radical, shattering, and interesting projects that Jewish modernity has ever witnessed. Far from discouraging these innovations, many leaders of the baby boom and traditionalist generations have begun to embrace these developments and have seen them as a sign of good health in the present and a good omen for the future.

One of the most significant questions in determining the Jewish future is our ability to bridge the emerging age gap that comes loaded with assumptions of membership, identity, and responsibility. A senior professional of an important Jewish philanthropic foundation has arrived at a striking conclusion: "I have started to comprehend that the question isn't whether the next generation is prepared for its communal responsibilities. The question is whether the community is prepared for the next generation."[13] Clearly, Jewish identity stretches across the age divide and is not owned by any one generation. That one generation must care deeply and prepare the way for the next is not new to Jewish tradition; it is at the essence of Jewish peoplehood.

In the traditional Jewish prayer *U'va Letzion*, we read,

> My spirit which is upon you and My words which I have put in your mouth shall not depart from your mouth, nor from the mouth of your children, nor from your children's children … from now to eternity.

This prayer, in many ways, articulates a mouth-to-mouth resuscitation of Judaism, the passing of a treasure or something of worth from generation to generation. It does not imply that this object of worth stays the same as it travels through time, only that it maintains its importance for each generation that holds it.

QUESTIONS FOR CONVERSATION

1. Which age category do you fall under?
2. Given the category, how has your age and the concerns of your generation influenced Jewish living?
3. What do you think can be done to create more intergenerational ties in the organized Jewish community?
4. Do you believe that generational issues have always challenged the Jewish community, or is this a relatively new problem?
5. What do you think will characterize the generation that follows generation Y?

10

DREAMS, DESIRED OUTCOMES, AND THE JEWISH FUTURE

In Russia, the popular doll when I was growing up was not a Barbie doll with her slim waist and impossible American figure. We had the matroishka, nesting dolls who wore peasant clothes and had wide hips. Even today, these dolls bring joy. Every time you open one doll, another smaller version comes out. Just when you think it's impossible to make a doll smaller, you find a miniature gift inside the last one. I have a Jewish matroishka; each layer has a Jewish face and distinguishing symbol. For me, this simple folk art symbolizes continuity. It's not that we keep getting smaller or that we all look the same, but that each generation produces the generation that comes after it. Each new generation is a surprise and a source of delight. We keep becoming larger, not smaller. We keep growing in influence, not shrinking.

—Misha Galperin

We have discussed the importance of a shared language of Jewish commitment and defined peoplehood as an extended family with a mission, or a people with a purpose. We have looked at the ways that collective and personal identities are constructed and have looked at some of the obstacles that stand in the way of achieving a shared language of peoplehood. These ruminations have been psychological, sociological and philosophical in orientation. They have not been practical. And yet without a conversation on the practical ways to strengthen peoplehood, these ideas will remain on paper and not in the hearts and minds of Jews across the world, who yearn to belong to something larger than themselves but do not have the vocabulary of community to do so.

It is possible and necessary to create general desired outcomes for peoplehood that serve as a template for the work individual leaders and Jewish communal institutions do. The following seven overarching suggestions are mechanisms for strengthening Jewish peoplehood:

- Connect more Jews to other Jews, both as individuals and as communities.
- Engender the feeling of belonging, specifically through attachment to a community.
- Provide venues for discovering meaning in Judaism that raises the threshold of Jewish intensity.
- Inject Jewish literacy that demonstrates relevance wherever possible.
- Advance the notion of responsibility to one's family, community, people, and world.
- Experience Judaism through the lens of a commitment unlike your own.
- Model and strengthen warm and inclusive Jewish leadership.

The shared thread in these seven recommendations is that each should bring individuals to Judaism through a meaningful experience of community. Far beyond a personal, spiritual experience of Judaism, peoplehood mandates an inspiring encounter with Judaism that is shared and demonstrates warmth and responsibility to others. It also involves experiencing Judaism differently than one's accustomed practice. Personal growth is often triggered by an experience that takes us out of our own comfort zone. Many Jews today have never had an experience of Judaism radically different than the one they grew up with and have not had their assumptions challenged. For peoplehood to be substantial and not a lowest-common-denominator approach to Judaism, it has to move people beyond the familiar to the uncertain. Institutions need to provide experiences of Judaism that are new, different, and significantly more intense. To transform our culture of tolerance that can lead to blandness, we have to create opportunities that challenge assumptions.

None of these are programmatic suggestions. They are a very general rubric to strengthen peoplehood that provides a guide to consider how and why we provide programming, what should inform our institutional cultures, and what kinds of experiences generate these desired outcomes. From an institutional point of view, Jewish organizations should think through their mission, mandate, services, staffing, and image through these seven lenses. Ideally, these outcomes are presented or provided in combination so that programs that are funded or supported advance all seven objectives simultaneously.

Some may argue that our seven recommendations for a peoplehood agenda are nothing new or original. We were not seeking originality in writing this book. We were trying to frame a conversation on group identity and the challenges and obstacles that are currently getting in the way. Nonetheless, we are recommending changes that represent not a difference in kind but in *degree*. We know through demographic studies throughout North America that institutional affiliation is remarkably low. Whatever we are doing, we are not doing enough of it, or with sufficient quality or the required intentionality, to make a difference. We are recommending a more user-friendly approach with low barriers to entry and high content, a more *strategic* way for Jewish institutions to go about the business of generating peoplehood, and a more value-laden approach to inclusion. Inclusion is only as valuable as the meaning that a person accrues once inside any given institution or Jewish framework.

We are not suggesting that we merely offer more of what we have already made available. We hear a great number of complaints about mediocrity and oversaturation. "That event was so boring." "There are so many programs in the Jewish community. I'm out every night of the week." "How many dinners can one person go to? I've gained ten pounds this year!" The number of programs and offerings has not necessarily enhanced Jewish peoplehood as much as it has given institutions a justification for existing. Rather than *do* more, we have to *think* more.

We have to ensure that whatever we do, or plan, or create is suffused with the seven aspects or objectives of peoplehood mentioned above. In the words of a contemporary professor of social policy and research, strengthening peoplehood requires us to provide "educational experiences that are cognitively rich, emotionally stimulating and behaviorally engaging."[1]

Living in the Big Tent

Earlier we spoke of big tent Judaism, a term used by Rabbi Kerry M. Olitzky and others, to engage more people. Now, we would like to focus less on just getting people in the tent and more about what it means to live in the tent, not merely to enter freely and exit just as freely. We believe in encouraging universal participation in Jewish life using any entry point or portal available. We want to create the welcoming house with open doors and windows that we mentioned in chapter one.

However—and this is a big however—an entry point is only the threshold of a Jewish experience. The entry point should not be confused with the destination. An entry is a way into deeper engagement, and it is often at this point of moving people beyond the threshold that we fail institutionally. In the words of a successful CEO in the for-profit sector: "How is it that the Jewish community manages to lose the same customer four times?" Marginally affiliated Jews often seek a Jewish communal experience or a personal experience of Judaism at different life stages. They might walk into a local JCC for a preschool experience, or think about a synagogue membership a year before the bar mitzvah of a child; they may register a kid for Hebrew school or consider a Jewish home for the aged for an elderly parent. Their sole contact with the Jewish community may be a call from a Jewish institution at a dial-a-thon. Rather than have multiple *positive* touch points across a Jewish life span, each experience may reinforce a sense of mediocrity or lack of professionalism, warmth, or inclusion. What is remarkable is that people give us another chance.

When we make it easy and friendly to enter, we have to follow up with future encounters that layer and intensify the experience of peoplehood in the following ways:

- They should strengthen Jewish literacy and meaning.
- They should be inspiring.
- They should involve and affirm the beauty and necessity of community.
- They should support, teach, and demonstrate Jewish ethics and values.
- They should reflect warmth and enhanced intimacy with other Jews.
- They should reinforce mutual responsibility rather than passive involvement.
- They should demonstrate a concern for the world's betterment through *tikkun olam* or social activism.
- They should create contexts where Jews of different walks of life and orientations can come together and cross the boundaries of difference.
- They should promote outreach to the community at large informed by Jewish particularism.

This last point is counterintuitive to some. Why must outreach and the repair of the world emerge from a distinctly Jewish approach to peoplehood? It does not have to, but it can be more mission driven and powerful when it is. Here we take a lesson from Isaac Bashevis Singer in his observations about writing from a particular worldview to capture a universal truth or sentiment: "[T]he more a writer belongs to his own people, the more he belongs to all people. A great artist is always part of his nation, its culture, its history, its aspirations."[2] Writers are routinely advised to write what they know. Work from a well-known vantage point, because your writing will be stronger, more well informed, more passionate, and more credible. If this is true of writing, how much more so is it true of living, volunteerism, education, and giving back to the world that has nurtured us? Informed by a set of particular values, we embrace our universalism from a place of genuine self-knowledge and strength.

Natan Sharansky, in his latest book, *Defending Identity*, makes this very point about his personal fight for freedom and for the freedoms of others. It is one of the lessons he took from his nine-year prison sentence:

> I discovered that only by embracing who I am—by going back to the *shtetl*, by connecting to my own people, by building my own particular identity—could I also stand with others. Far from negating freedom, identity gave me both inner freedom and the strength to help others. When Jews abandon identity in the pursuit of universal freedom, they end up with neither. Yet when they embrace identity in the name of freedom, as Soviet Jews did in the 1970s, they end up securing both. When freedom and identity are separated, both are weakened.[3]

Sharansky believes that his ability to help in the humanitarian quest for freedom emerged from his own discovery of Judaism. The passion for universalism was inspired by Sharansky's particularism. Sharansky also challenges today's democracy without strong identity and asks what kind of communities we are creating if they are void of meaningful particularism.

> Democracy offers a vision of opportunity, self-determination, and peace. But without a particular way of life and a set of commitments to live for, the democratic vision inevitably loses force, becoming empty and abstract. Without identity, a democracy becomes incapable of defending the values it holds most dear.[4]

Strengthening identity is another way of enhancing the threshold of intensity; it is critical for a notion of peoplehood that is genuinely substantial and not diluted. If this is to be the case, then peoplehood must also push the issue of diversity further than it has been pushed thus far. We speak about the importance of diversity, but how many of us in our daily lives really encounter the other and invite the experience of Jewish otherness into our lives? Usually, we affirm our life choices by creating relatively homogeneous social, cultural, religious, and professional circles. It is hard to intensify your experience of Judaism if everywhere you turn is never markedly different from where you currently are. The provocation of difference gives us a chance to transcend our normal boundaries and experience Judaism from other places of interest and intensity.

Think of a synagogue on a normal Shabbat morning. In the interest of choice and accommodation, there may be a family service, a youth *minyan*, a tot Shabbat, and a senior lunch. Most of the people there will at least have a loose denominational affiliation that joins them. They will cluster in groups that affirm their place in the life span and confirm their denominational choice. They may never have an experience of Judaism that pushes them radically out of this comfort zone and expands their notion of community, stretching it to contain a more expansive view of peoplehood. After all, peoplehood goes beyond the people who are the usual suspects in our lives to encompass a collective sense of family in the largest possible way.

The job of a Jewish leader in this scenario is to create clusters of belonging that enable people to comprehend and validate their existence within a particular circle while creating intersecting circles that continuously expand these clusters and connect more people to each other in more innovative ways. The leader orchestrates and facilitates this process of entry, identification, and expansion. In other words, the leader helps us cement our identity with the closest circle of membership—the family—and then stimulates us to work outward to include community in ever-increasing numbers and with enhanced diversity. Rabbi Abraham Kook, first chief rabbi of Palestine, writes lyrically of this notion of expansion: "The love for Israel implies the love for humanity.... There is a person who sings the song of his own soul ... there is one who sings the song of his people ... there is one whose soul expands until it spreads beyond the limits of Israel and sings the song of humanity."[5] The notion of an ever-expanding community is not impossible, but it is challenged by a number of potential obstructions.

Stopped at the Door

Just as we need to create greater intentionality about low barriers and intensified experiences beyond the threshold, we must be acutely aware of what happens to people who get stopped at the door. There are individuals who, for whatever reason, do not make it to the door or are turned away at the point of entry. Among the obstacles to the desired outcomes expressed above are two perceptions of Jews as a people who turn people away, rather than strengthen their commitments to each other and a life of Jewish values and meaning. They are:

1. Jews are not warm and friendly people. Why strengthen ties to a people who don't want you anyway?
2. Jews are critical, fatalistic, or nihilistic. Why strengthen ties to a people who are always on the verge of crisis or ravaged by guilt? People are drawn to success, not distress.

Our institutions can feel cold and unwelcoming. Our marketing and fund-raising can read as if we are on the brink of extinction. We regularly hear from people who feel disenfranchised by the Jewish community, who feel left out of synagogues and schools, or who feel sought after only by Jewish fund-raisers. They get one call a year from the Jewish community or one piece of mail, and it is a solicitation. We have to understand the impact that this has on peoplehood when we fail to create real avenues of substantial meaning and community building.

As we read about in an earlier chapter, there are formal conversations about boundaries, and then there are the invisible boundaries created by a general lack of openness and welcoming that seem to be inherent in many Jewish institutions, which can translate into the behavior of their members. Such institutions fail to see the invisible wall of alienation that they have created. Some institutions have taken steps to reach out and welcome people but do so with such formality that it can feel staged. Having a welcoming or hospitality committee is tasking people with a level of friendliness that every member of an institution should ideally possess.

The word *welcoming* connotes an initial greeting, like a welcome mat or salutation. It needs to extend beyond greeting to treating people warmly throughout sustained interactions. A South African woman who moved to the Washington, D.C., area reported that she went to four synagogues. In each, people said hello and even asked some initial questions. But greetings never became deeper encounters. She still has not found a synagogue to call home. When we are friendly to someone, not only are we being polite and breaking down superficial boundaries, we may also be accomplishing much more psychically by creating a direct route to peoplehood. The following quotation from Rabbi Joseph Soloveitchik, an influential scholor of the last century, illustrates the alienation and self-recovery that a simple act of friendliness generates:

> Quite often a man finds himself in a crowd of strangers. He feels lonely. No one knows him. No one cares for him, no one is concerned about him. It is an existential experience. He begins to doubt his own ontological worth. This leads to alienation from the crowd surrounding him. Suddenly someone taps him on the shoulder and says, "Aren't you Mr. So-and-so? I have heard so much about you." In a fraction of a second his awareness changes. What brought about the change? The recognition by someone, the word![6]

We have spent so much time arguing about the principles of exclusion and inclusion that it seems, at times, we have ignored the human dimension of boundary setting—of the wonder of acceptance and the pain of rejection. The above quotation illustrates that being friendly is not really a matter of politeness; it is ultimately about giving someone a sense of self-worth by valuing and respecting individual humanity, dignity, and divinity.

In order to feel this, members of institutions have to be genuinely inclusive, and leaders of organizations have to be exemplars of personal warmth and inclusivity. And here, we state something obvious but sorely problematic in Jewish communities all over North America and arguably the world. We are not always friendly. Centuries of otherness have created suspicion and even a questioning of the stranger, an approach to unfamiliar people that makes them enemies before friends, outsiders before insiders. In a family, you give some kind of preferential

treatment to those close to you; you certainly do not ignore their existence or shun them, even if you are meeting a second cousin for the first
time.

> *I have two experiences that happen repeatedly that confirm the mag-*
> *nitude of this problem—our lack of friendliness. One of them hap-*
> *pens to others; one, to myself. I often teach groups of students who*
> *do not know each other. My goal, in addition to content and*
> *instruction, is always to create a community of learners who speak*
> *to each other and can make themselves vulnerable in the presence of*
> *others. I hear time and again the complaint. "I've been living in*
> *Washington for _____ (fill in the blank; it's usually more than ten*
> *years), and I don't feel connected to the Jewish community at all."*
> *Although our demographic study tells us that our community is not*
> *all that transient (the average time given for living in the D.C. area*
> *is sixteen years), it does not report on how well situated individuals*
> *feel within our community. There is loneliness and rejection and,*
> *sometimes, simply no Jewish place that feels friendly to outsiders. A*
> *friend who is intermarried quipped that when he brings his wife to*
> *synagogue, few people outside their social circles say hello. When he*
> *goes to her church, everyone is friendly.*
>
> *For my part, I speak several times a year in synagogues around*
> *the country for Shabbat. I have uncovered a phenomenon I would*
> *rather not share. On Friday night, when I go to services, hardly a*
> *person says hello. Possibly a "Shabbat Shalom" in passing. Rarely a*
> *full conversation. After I speak on Shabbat morning, many people*
> *approach me, and I am not alone for the rest of the day. On Friday*
> *night I am an outsider. On Shabbat morning—because the presi-*
> *dent or rabbi introduces me—I become an insider, even temporar-*
> *ily. But the problem is that I should never be an outsider in a Jewish*
> *institution. Every Jewish institution should treat its members and*
> *visitors as insiders. The narrative of suspicion is not serving us well.*
> *If we really are an extended family, then we have to treat everyone*
> *like family. It's time.*
>
> —ERICA BROWN

Nixing Fatalism

What about our fatalism? How does that get in the way of peoplehood? Years ago, a famous essay on Jewish history both shaped and ridiculed assessments of the Jewish future. The article is called "Israel: The Ever-Dying People," and it suggests that readings of Jewish history and the present regularly alarm us with their ominous predictions for a bleak Jewish future.[7] Intermarriage and assimilation statistics make us cower and are often distorted or read in an unbalanced fashion, as if to suggest that we are on the precipice of extinction in every generation. Instead, we have found the opposite to be true. We seem to be the ever-living people, continually growing in influence and achievement the world over. The article continues:

> Jews a century ago thought they would be the last surviving generation. They were not. We are witnesses to the continuity of Jews as a community and as a people. The notion that contemporary Jewish communities are in the process of decline and disintegration is a powerful myth but, in the case of the United States, a poor and distorted description of the reality of Jewish life.[8]

Why is the myth of extinction so popular? Do we really need the myth of a Jewish life that is lean, difficult, and decreasing in size and scope to keep our institutions alive and our sense of purpose ignited? These myths have pernicious consequences that we are not always honest enough to confront. People today are no longer drawn to crisis in the way they once were. It is hard in a culture of positive affirmation and self-esteem to appeal and attract people to a vision of extermination and extinction. Why would anyone want to be part of a failed project of peoplehood?

Instead of bemoaning the declining numbers offered by pessimistic scholars, it is time to ask questions about qualitative Jewish life and how to leverage our *success* to build a more collective and expansive vision of Jewish peoplehood. As the article states,

[I]f you look for the negative you will find it, and you will have the numbers to back you up. But you will miss the positive, which shows that the negative numbers do not tell the complete story. If you look at the whole, you will see a balance, a trans-formed American Jewish community that is both encouraging and challenging for the future. In this sense, both the views about decline and those about renewal are correct. They are simply referring to different parts of the community and to dif-ferent indicators of group cohesion.[9]

If our conversation feels too American in orientation or too generous, Norman Solomon, an English scholar of Judaism at Oxford, enlightens us on Jewish identity across the Atlantic and the perils of trying too hard to control the future.

No one can know what forms Jewish identity will take when the dust has settled on the New Europe and if and when lasting peace comes in Israel and the Middle East. New and distinctive forms of Judaism and Jewish identity will doubtless emerge. Fools may predict what this Judaism will be; they may be proved wrong, but there is no great harm in that. Knaves who seek power will try to impose their own patterns on the future; they will probably fail, and will certainly do great damage in the attempt.[10]

Solomon concludes his thoughts on a note of profound optimism: "Never—certainly not since the days of Late Antiquity—has the Jewish world experienced such intellectual and emotional turbulence. Yet never has it produced such vigorous responses." There is great energy in the turbulence. The current state of uncertainty about Jewish identity has generated many and varied attempts to craft shared identity. Perhaps these attempts themselves signal desperation and pathos, a last resort at defining the terms of an entity in a state of such rapid change that the moment we give it a name it will require another. There is a Talmudic principle that in the event of doubt and in the presence of certainty, always stick with a sure thing. Choose what is solid, stable, and present rather than risk all on the whim of possibility. It is easy to understand the popularity of such a gamble. Choosing the well-trodden, secure path of certainty is always safer. And yet, when it comes to collective Jewish identity, it is unclear what is certain and what is not, what is a risk and what is not.

One of the reasons that leaders within the Jewish community predict, pontificate, or present images about the health, vibrancy, or decline of the Jewish future is to distract us from an engaging conversation about the Jewish present. It is always easier to paint a picture of what will be without knowing what it is than to do the kind of research and penetrating analysis that will help us understand our current milieu. In fact, it would appear from some who do study the future professionally that the best advice on offer is to be well acquainted with the present before trying to shape the past.[11] Any educated predictions must derive from this understanding. The trouble with our Jewish present is that it seems to elude comprehension. Why?

The Dreamer Identity

Remember the story of Joseph from the Bible and Andrew Lloyd Webber fame? If you recall, Joseph became the second in command in Egypt as a result of one act: he interpreted Pharaoh's dreams. In days of old—long before Freud told us that dreams were disguised wish fulfillment—dreams were taken very seriously. The Jewish court in existence during the times of the Talmud, the *Sanhedrin*, employed many dream interpreters, and one chapter of the Talmud is devoted almost exclusively to dream interpretation.[12] The significance of dreaming in Jewish tradition did not emerge in rabbinic writings. It came out of a biblical tradition so strong that the lives of many of our biblical patriarchs were shaped and molded by their dreams. From Jacob's first dream of a heavenly ladder reaching from earth to heaven and mounted by moving angels, the latter half of Genesis is dominated by dreamscapes.

Joseph is propelled by his own dreams of superiority to his brothers that seem to end in the bottom of a pit but eventually become true.

Other sheaves of wheat do bow to his when his brothers come down to Egypt to seek respite from the famine, and Joseph's clever, entrepreneurial spirit enables them to get sustenance. They see Joseph and bow in subordination, not knowing that the minister in charge of their future existence is actually the "dreamer" that they threw into a pit years before. In that earlier scene, the brothers were shepherding sheep and saw Joseph arriving at a distance. At the point of vision, they call him the *ba'al ha-halamot*; the literal translation of this strange expression is not merely "the dreamer" but "the owner of dreams," the one who possesses visions. Ironically, in their sarcasm, they are the ones who identify Joseph's true essence. They label him not just because of one dream, but because he embraced the act of vision.

Vision plays a key role in the unraveling of the Joseph story and the salvation of both the Egyptians and the Israelites. Pharaoh's dreams of fat corn and fat cows and lean corn and lean cows puzzled his ministers. They saw before them two distinct dreams and could not understand their relationship. Only Joseph interpreted what Pharaoh thought were two dreams to be only one dream, a continuous narrative of the future of Pharaoh's people. They would experience seven years of plenty followed by seven years of famine. Joseph, being wise and understanding, figured out that the future for the Egyptians lay in using the good times ahead to prepare carefully for the predicted lean times. Later, he gathered and put away food for the years ahead to protect Egypt and sustain the people during difficult times. It requires a great deal of discipline to realize that there are lean years ahead and to measure out stock at a time of abundance. Our natural tendency is to exploit abundance and live to the hilt, woefully unconcerned about the days when we will have to live on the edge.

> *I am watching a production of* Joseph and the Amazing Technicolor Dreamcoat *that I am told is remarkable. It is an all-woman cast, and the performance was created during the Second Intifada to offer some light, creativity, and hope to residents living under constant gunfire. The musical begins with an announcement of how many women have been injured during the production, but their commitment to the show*

stayed firm throughout. One of the "brothers" lost a son who was in the army during the war, and the atmosphere is heavy and freighted with meaning. She asks the audience to rise for a recitation of psalms before the play begins to ask for God's protection at this time of great vulnerability. The play proceeds with color and verve, until Joseph sits isolated in jail and begins to sing quietly, "The Children of Israel Are Never Alone." I hear the murmur in the audience of those who join in the song and watch as one spectator after another begins to cry. This is not just some song that Broadway made famous. It is a theme song of a people who need its reassurance again. It is a solace and a unifying moment of faith that the music can somehow carry all of us to a better place. We are not alone—not then, and not now.

—ERICA BROWN

The Joseph story is one of enormous significance for us today. We are living in the wake of years of abundance: material, spiritual, and educational. We have more financial resources and more Jewish institutions than ever. Spiritual seekers have a plethora of options before them today; this is coupled by the presence of more Jewish day schools and congregational schools than at any other time in Jewish history. We might even fool ourselves into a comfortable picture of smugness. It cannot get better than this.

It is precisely at this time that we need the vision to see hard times ahead and prepare for them appropriately. Overabundance can create its own problems, and only those with vision and honesty can see that. Joseph's gift was not only the interpretation of dreams; it was first and foremost his capacity to dream ambitiously and to act on the interpretation of his dreams to prepare for a future only visible in his imagination.[13] There are many studies available today on the Jewish community. It would appear that we have taken the Joseph story to heart. But what does it mean to study the Jewish future? Calvin Goldscheider asks this very question in his book, *Studying the Jewish Future*. He arrives at the conclusion that:

Studying the Jewish future means to examine the ways scholars have envisioned it, to ask how they have used their conceptions of the future to interpret past and contemporary Jewish communities and to uncover ideological assumptions underlying these conceptions. Studying the future requires outlining an array of possibilities and identifying some futures that are more likely than others. We cannot know with certainty the direction in which the Jewish community is going.... Yet Jews can steer a little better if they know where they would like to go and what hazards may be waiting during the passage.[14]

Goldscheider reminds us that we cannot know the future with certainty; we can only make educated predictions based on assumptions about the past and comparative studies of how others have fared in similar circumstances. He lets us know that there is not just one possible outcome, but instead presents us with the excitement and the terror of multiple possibilities, many different futures. He also leaves these predictions in the hands of scholars, stimulating some open-ended questions. Do we change every challenge into an opportunity and believe that the change in language will represent an actual change in reality? Or do we invest more in the survival of particular institutions than in the long-term continuity of our people?

Joseph not only predicted a future based on dreams; he carried out a program of activities that would respond to and complement his vision and shape the future. Joseph was also an interpreter of his past. When his brothers fear for their lives after Joseph's stunning self-revelation, Joseph tells them then, and reminds them again later, that he forgives them for their earlier hatred and cruelty. He understood that had they not thrown him into a pit, then the other events and circumstances that followed would never have taken place. Ironically, those events brought him to a position of prestige and influence that allowed him to save and redeem thousands. Vision is not only a forward-thinking process, rife with uncertainties and hopeful assumptions. Vision must translate into practical changes. Vision is also a means of assessing the past with clarity and objectivity.

In assessing the past and considering the future of Jewish peoplehood, Jewish institutions today must ask the right questions rather than only the expedient or practical ones. In the words of Barry Shrage, president of Combined Jewish Philanthropies of Greater Boston, strategic thinking has to go well beyond an institutional mentality. He asks the following question of his organization, and in so doing, asks us to consider it as well: "Is the purpose of this enterprise to survive? Or is the purpose to do God's work in the world and to create meaningful communities for human beings?"[15]

Using Joseph's model, we need to use these past years of abundance to prepare for a future that might not be as rich in human and financial resources. Like Joseph, we need leaders with big ambitions who dream the impossible. Like Joseph, we need to make peace with the past and believe that the future can be different. Like Joseph's reconciliation with his brothers, we need to find a shared language of Jewish identity that bridges financial and generational gaps. We need a shared language of peoplehood that prevents our Israeli brothers and sisters from floating away over time like the projected separations of continents, slowly, incrementally, but also irrevocably. We need a language of peoplehood that creates an authentic feeling of belonging, meaning, and purpose. The landscape of change is inescapable. So is the language of separate identities. But all of these strains make us genetically stronger, not weaker. They enhance, enrich, and dynamically shape any conversation on who we are as a people.

Being part of an extended family with a mission gives support and strength to each member while being a driving force for the organism as a whole. Peoplehood is not racist or limiting or too particularistic. It is a way to view an expansive world from a specific ethnic, cultural, and spiritual place that presents an opportunity *and* a responsibility to care and nurture the world at large. Peoplehood reminds us that we as Jews cannot be afraid of being too much in the world, only of being too little.

Our early discussion of peoplehood began with Jacob, the patriarch who wrestled with an angel for the name that we all carry: Israel. His life was one of blessing and suffering, of triumph and struggle. He gave that gift to his son Joseph, who also struggled with fate but eventually turned his dreams into a powerful reality of success beyond measure. Jacob was devastated when he thought Joseph was dead. He says time and again that without Joseph his life is not worth living. But a miracle occurs.

Toward the end of Genesis, Jacob is reunited with Joseph in what seems like an impossible encounter. When Jacob's days are numbered, he calls for Joseph in order to bless him, his son, and his grandsons. He says words that haunt us with their sense of majesty: "And Israel said to Joseph, 'I never expected to see you again, and here God has let me see your children as well.'"[16] This is not only the man Jacob speaking in an intimate family encounter. It is Israel, the man representing the nation, who speaks to his family through time immemorial. At so many points in Jewish history, we thought we faced our last generation. Time and again we have proven history wrong. We have become a people who accomplish impossible things because we have created so much possibility. We are still the recipients of Jacob's blessing; we are still the children of impossibility who defy expectation. We are forever linked in this same family of impossibility. We are joined by the bonds of peoplehood that have given us a community of meaning throughout our history. It is our responsibility to ensure the future of Jewish peoplehood. Continuity is not only about survival. It is about *meaningful* survival within a constellation of caring and community. It is about membership in an extended family with a purpose. It is about embracing both possibility and impossibility. "I never expected to see you again, and here God has let me see your children as well."

QUESTIONS FOR CONVERSATION

1. What's in your remix identity?
2. How should we shape a vision for the Jewish future?
3. What do you think we can do to popularize and spread the notion of peoplehood?
4. Do you think we are in the lean years or in the fat years? Substantiate your answer with examples.
5. What vision do you have of a meaningful and collective Jewish future?

Notes

Introduction: Jews in the 'Hood

1. Eli Valley, "Jewish Peoplehood: What Does It Mean?," *Contact* (Spring 2008): 2.
2. We would like to thank Alan Hoffmann for sharing the expression "threshold of intensity" with us in regard to peoplehood. It captures so much of what we are trying to say.
3. We are grateful to Dyonna Ginsburg for her comments on the difference between peoplehood as a means and as an end.
4. Jonathan Woocher, *Sacred Survival: The Civil Religion of American Jews* (Bloomington: Indiana University Press, 1986).
5. Robert Seltzer, "Sustaining Jewish Belief in a Secular or Christian America," *Secularism, Spirituality, and the Future of American Jewry*, eds. Elliott Abrams and David G. Dalin (Washington, D.C.: Ethics and Public Policy Center, 1999), 39.

1. Defining Peoplehood

1. This information was provided by Margot Charlton, an employee of the Oxford English Dictionary, on January 2, 2008, in e-mail correspondence. *Peoplehood* will appear in the third edition of the dictionary but currently only appears in Oxford's online dictionary.
2. Dan Ehrenkrantz, "The Primacy of Peoplehood," *Contact* (Spring 2008): 3.
3. Alan Hoffmann and Susan Berrin, "Challenging Peoplehood," *Sh'ma* 37 (2006), www.shma.com/oct_06/challenging_peoplehood.htm.
4. Ibid.
5. Ibid.
6. Jonathan Ariel, "Your People Shall Be My People: Notes on Nurturing Jewish Peoplehood," *The Peoplehood Papers* (New York: United Jewish Communities, 2007), 34.
7. Leon Wieseltier, *Kaddish* (New York: Vintage, 2000), 259.

8. Steven M. Cohen, "A Tale of Two Jewries: The 'Inconvenient Truth' for American Jews" (Waltham, MA: The Steinhardt Foundation for Jewish Life, 2006).
9. Ibid.
10. David Gedzelman, "The Idea of the Jewish People," *Contact* (Spring 2008): 7.
11. Steven M. Cohen and Jack Wertheimer, "Whatever Happened to the Jewish People?," *Commentary* (June 2006): 34.
12. Leo Rosten, *The Joys of Yiddish* (New York: McGraw-Hill, 1968), 248.
13. Kenneth Feinberg, *What Is Life Worth?* (New York: PublicAffairs, 2006).
14. Michael Wex, *Born to Kvetch* (New York: Harper, 2005), 19.
15. Andrew Silow-Carroll, "The Way We Do the Things We Do," *New Jersey Jewish News Online* (March 2008), www.NJJewishnews.com/NJJN.com/080207/edco (accessed August 2, 2007).
16. Ariel, *The Peoplehood Papers*, 29.
17. Jay Michaelson, "Peoplehood: There's No There There," *The Peoplehood Papers*, 10.
18. Neil Gillman, "Sustaining Jewish Belief," *Secularism, Spirituality, and the Future of American Jewry*, 43.
19. Jonathan Sacks, *The Home We Build Together* (London: Continuum, 2007), 23.

2. Collective Jewish Identity

1. Cohen, "A Tale of Two Jewries."
2. Philip Roth, *Operation Shylock* (New York: Simon and Schuster, 1993), 334.
3. As told by Dvorah Telushkin in her wonderful memoir, *Master of Dreams* (New York: William Morrow, 1997), 96.
4. Tiffany Schlain, "Guide from the Perplexed: The Tribe," a guide to the film *The Tribe*, produced by Tiffany Schlain and Carlton Evans, 2005.
5. Genesis 32:25.
6. Genesis 32:29.
7. Michael Walzer, "The Anomalies of Jewish Political Identity," *Judaism and the Challenges of Modern Life*, eds. Moshe Halbertal and Donniel Hartman (New York: Continuum, 2007), 134.
8. Roberta Rosenberg Farber and Chaim I. Waxman, "Post-Modernity and the Jews: Identity, Identification and Community," *Jews in America: A Contemporary Reader*, eds. by Roberta Rosenberg Farber and Chaim I. Waxman (Hanover, NH: Brandeis University Press, 1999), 398.
9. Jonathan Sacks, "The Politics of Memory," *Covenant and Conversation* (August 3, 2007), the website of Chief Rabbi, United Hebrew Congregations of the Commonwealth, www.chiefrabbi.org/thoughts/index/html (accessed June 2008).
10. Steven M. Cohen and Gabriel Horenczyk, *National Variations in Jewish Identity* (Albany: State University of New York Press, 1999), 24.

11. Jonathan D. Sarna, *American Judaism* (New Haven: Yale University Press, 2004), 373.

12. Abigail Pogrebin, "Leon Wieseltier," *Stars of David: Prominent Jews Talk about Being Jewish* (New York: Broadway Books, 2005), 159.

13. Esther 3:8.

14. Daniel Elazar, "The Organization of the American Jewish Community," *Jews in America*, 117.

15. Sylvia Barack Fishman, *Jewish Life and American Culture* (New York: State University of New York Press, 2000), 153.

16. Elazar, *Jews in America*, 96.

17. Ibid., 98.

18. Calvin Goldscheider, *Studying the Jewish Future* (Seattle: University of Washington Press, 2004), 6.

19. Walzer, *Judaism and the Challenges of Modern Life*, 136–7.

3. Constructing a Personal Jewish Identity

1. Perry London and Barry Chazan, *Psychology and Jewish Identity Education* (New York: American Jewish Committee, 1990), 13.

2. Charles Taylor, *Sources of the Self: The Making of the Modern Identity* (Cambridge: Harvard University Press, 1989).

3. Aaron Lansky, *Outwitting History* (Chapel Hill: Algonquin Books, 2005), 308.

4. Haym Soloveitchik observed that the Orthodox community today is experiencing a crisis as a result of losing some of its mimetic aspects. See his article "Rupture and Reconstruction: The Transformation of Contemporary Orthodoxy," *Tradition* 28, no. 4 (Summer 1994): 64–133.

5. Leon Wieseltier, *Against Identity* (New York: William Drenttel, 1996), 23.

6. Ibid., 18.

7. Genesis 18:19.

8. Sid Schwarz, *Judaism and Justice* (Woodstock, VT: Jewish Lights, 2006), 5.

9. Ibid., 8.

10. Wieseltier, *Against Identity*, 33.

11. Aimee Landman, American University student in her final essay (Fall 2007).

4. Pro-Choice Judaism: Are There Too Many Identity Options?

1. Jonathan Sacks, *The Dignity of Difference* (London: Continuum, 2002), 13.

2. Ibid., 40.

3. Barry Schwartz, *The Paradox of Choice* (New York: Harper Perennial, 2004), 4.

4. Rabbi Irving Greenberg quoted by Peter Steinfels, "Beliefs," *New York Times*, August 7, 1993.

5. Neela Banerjee, "Challenging Tradition, Young Jews Worship on Their Terms," *New York Times*, November 28, 2007, A18.

6. Ibid.

7. Steven M. Cohen and Arnold Eisen, *The Jew Within* (Bloomington: Indiana University Press, 2000).

8. Ibid., 39.

9. Jonathan Woocher, "Building Community and Peoplehood in a Time of Personalism" (remarks, General Assembly, Nashville, TN, November 2007).

10. Charles Taylor, *The Ethics of Authenticity* (Cambridge: Harvard University Press, 2001), 2.

11. Ibid., 5.

12. Charles Liebman, "Post-War American Jewry: From Ethnic to Privatized Judaism," *Secularism, Spirituality, and the Future of American Jewry*, 11.

13. Einat Wilf, "The Mitzvot of Peoplehood," *The Peoplehood Papers*, 12–13.

14. Ibid., 13.

15. See Gary Tobin, "Jewish Federations Matter but They Need to Adapt," *Reimagining Federated Philanthropy*, Jewish Telegraphic Association (November 5, 2007), www.jta.org/cgi-bin/iowa/news/article/20071105GTobinoped.html (accessed February 2008).

16. Jonathan Woocher, "Spirituality and the Civil Religion," *Secularism, Spirituality, and the Future of American Jewry*, 24–25.

5. Membership and Boundaries

1. Donniel Hartman, *The Boundaries of Judaism* (New York: Continuum, 2007), 15, citing Isaiah Berlin, "Two Concepts of Liberty," in *Four Essays on Liberty* (Oxford: Oxford University Press, 1969), 171.

2. Benedict Anderson, *Imagined Communities* (London: Verso, 1993), 164.

3. Peter Novick, *The Holocaust in American Life* (New York: Mariner Books, 1999), 170.

4. Yosef Hayim Yerushalmi, *Zakhor: Jewish History and Jewish Memory* (Seattle: University of Washington Press, 1982), 5.

5. Hartman, *The Boundaries of Judaism*, 16.

6. Ibid., 6.

6. Peoplehood and Intermarriage

1. Paul and Rachel Cowan, *Mixed Blessings* (New York: Penguin Books, 1988), 31.

2. Ibid., 128.

3. Ibid.

4. Ibid., x.

5. Zvi Zohar, "'Like a Newborn Baby': Intermarriage and Conversion," Shalom Hartman Institute website (February 7, 2008), www.hartmaninstitute.com/opinion-C_view_eng.asp?article_10=J (accessed May 2008).

6. BT, Yevamot 47b.

7. Cohen, "A Tale of Two Jewries," 10.

8. Ibid., 11.

9. Fern Chertok, Benjamin Phillips, and Leonard Saxe, "It's Not Just Who Stands under the *Chuppah*: Intermarriage and Engagement" (Waltham, MA: Steinhardt Social Research Institute, 2008), 25.

10. Sylvia Barack Fishman, "Transformations in the Composition of American Jewish Households," *Changing Jewish Communities*, Jerusalem Center for Public Affairs website, www.jcpa.org/cjc/cjc-Fishman-F05.htm (accessed May 2008).

11. Ibid. Fishman quotes from the 2000 American Jewish Committee Public Opinion Survey.

12. Sylvia Barack Fishman, *Double or Nothing* (Hanover, NH: New England University Press, 2004), 136.

13. Gary Tobin and Katherine Simon, *Rabbis Talk about Intermarriage* (San Francisco: Institute for Jewish and Community Research, 1999), 160.

14. Ibid.

7. Jewish Literacy and the Peoplehood Prerogative

1. *Ethics of the Fathers* 2:6.

2. Leon Wieseltier interview in *Stars of David*, 155.

3. Moshe Halbertal, *The People of the Book* (Cambridge: Harvard University Press, 1997).

4. Barry Holtz, *Finding Our Way* (Philadelphia: Jewish Publication Society, 2005), 7.

5. Joseph Telushkin, *Jewish Literacy* (New York: William Morrow and Co., 1991), 9.

6. Leon Wieseltier interview in *Stars of David*, 159.

7. Roberta Louis Goodman and Betsy Dolgin Katz, *The Adult Jewish Education Handbook* (Denver: A.R.E. Publishing, 2004), xi–xii.

8. Diane Tickton Schuster, *Jewish Lives, Jewish Learning* (New York: UAHC Press, 2003), 115.

9. Lisa Grant et al., *A Journey of the Heart and Mind: Transformative Jewish Learning in Adulthood* (New York: The Jewish Theological Seminary of New York, 2004), 4.

8. Irreconcilable Differences? Jewish and Israeli Identity

1. Nathan Guttman, "A. B. Yehoshua Sparks Uproar in U.S.," *The Jerusalem Post*, May 4, 2006.

2. A. B. Yehoshua, "People without a Land," trans. Ann Pace, *Ha'aretz* (May 13, 2006), www.ajc.org/site/appsn/net/content2.aspx?c=ijitizphkog8b=17003738oct=2489063.

3. Ibid.
4. Ibid.
5. Natan Sharansky, "There Is No Zionism without Judaism," *Ha'aretz*, May 5, 2006.
6. David Chinitz, "Next Time Invite American Olim Instead of A. B. Yehoshua," *The Forward*, May 19, 2006.
7. Donniel Hartman articulated the fantasies that American and Israeli Jews have created about each other that do not correspond to reality and that prevent real understanding in "Leadership and Israel: The New Paradigm" (lecture, Congregation Beth Sholom, Potomac, MD, December 19, 2007).
8. See Arthur Hertzberg, "Israel and American Jewry," *Commentary* 44, no. 2 (August 1967): 69–73.
9. Chaim J. Waxman, "Center and Periphery: Israel in American Jewish Life," *Jews in America*, 212–25.
10. See Herbert J. Gans, "Symbolic Ethnicity: The Future of Ethnic Groups and Culture in America," *On the Making of Americans: Essays in Honor of David Riesman*, eds. Herbert J. Gans, Nathan Glazer, Joseph R. Gusfeld, and Christopher Jencks (Philadelphia: University of Pennsylvania Press, 1979), 193–220.
11. Waxman, *Jews in America*, 221.
12. Ibid., 223.
13. Steven Rosenthal, *Irreconcilable Differences?* (Hanover, NH: Brandeis University Press, 2001).
14. His remarks are from the *Long Island Jewish World*, February 11–17, 1994, 2.
15. Charles Liebman and Steven Cohen, *Two Worlds of Judaism* (New Haven: Yale University Press, 1990), 1–2.
16. Ibid., 157.
17. Ibid., 174.
18. Ibid., 17.
19. Edouard Valdman, *Jews and Money* (Rockville, MD: Schreiber Publishing, 2000), 15–16.
20. Ibid., 95.

9. Stepping Across the Generational Divide

1. Ahad Ha'am, "The Wrong Way" (1889), *Essential Texts of Zionism*, trans. Leon Simon (Philadelphia: Jewish Publication Society of America, 1912).
2. Beth Cousens, "Hillel's Journey: Distinctively Jewish, Universally Human" (Washington, D.C.: Hillel: The Foundation for Jewish Campus Life, 2007), 7.
3. Steven M. Cohen and Ari Kelman, "The Continuity of Discontinuity: How Young Jews Are Connecting, Creating, and Organizing Their Own Jewish Lives," Andrea and Charles Bronfman Philanthropies, 21/64 Division (2007), www.acbp.net/about/PDF/continuity%20of%20discontinued.PDF (accessed January 2008).

4. Ibid., 14.

5. Bernard Reisman, *The Chavurah: A Contemporary Jewish Experience* (New York: Union of American Hebrew Congregations, 1977), 135.

6. Ibid., 48.

7. Cohen and Kelman, "The Continuity of Discontinuity."

8. Ibid.

9. Lynn Lancaster and David Stillman, *When Generations Collide* (New York: Collins, 2003).

10. Lisa Belkin, "What Do I Do? Depends on What Week It Is," *New York Times*, November, 29, 2007, G–2.

11. Ibid.

12. Schlain, "Guide from the Perplexed," 56–57.

13. Sharna Goldseker, "Engaging Young Philanthropists," *Reimagining Federated Philanthropy*.

10. Dreams, Desired Outcomes, and the Jewish Future

1. Leonard Saxe, "Jewish Peoplehood and Young Adults," *Contact* (Spring 2008): 5.

2. Telushkin, *Master of Dreams*, 94.

3. Natan Sharansky, *Defending Identity* (New York: PublicAffairs, 2008), 15.

4. Ibid., 6.

5. Rabbi Abraham Kook, *Orot Ha-Kodesh* (Jerusalem: Mossad HaRav Kook, 1961), 2:444.

6. Rabbi Joseph Soloveitchik, "The Community," *Tradition* 17, no. 2 (1978): 7–83.

7. Simon Rawidowicz, *Israel: The Ever-Dying People and Other Essays* (Rutherford, NJ: Fairleigh Dickenson University, 1986).

8. Ibid., 15.

9. Ibid., 19.

10. Norman Solomon, *Judaism: A Very Short Introduction* (Oxford: Oxford University Press, 2000), 17.

11. See, for example, Mark Penn and Kinney Zelesne in *Microtrends: The Small Forces Behind Tomorrow's Big Changes* (New York: Twelve, 2007).

12. BT, Brakhot, ch. 9.

13. We are grateful to Amira Rosenberg for sharing her reading of the Joseph story with us.

14. Goldscheider, *Studying the Jewish Future*, 4.

15. Barry Shrage, "The Rabbi, the Synagogue and the Community" *Secularism, Spirituality, and the Future of American Jewry*, 51.

16. Genesis 48:11.

NOTES

NOTES

NOTES

NOTES

Bar/Bat Mitzvah

The JGirl's Guide: The Young Jewish Woman's Handbook for Coming of Age
By Penina Adelman, Ali Feldman, and Shulamit Reinharz
This inspirational, interactive guidebook helps pre-teen Jewish girls address the many issues surrounding coming of age. 6 x 9, 240 pp, Quality PB, 978-1-58023-215-9 **$14.99**
  Also Available: **The JGirl's Teacher's and Parent's Guide**
  8½ x 11, 56 pp, PB, 978-1-58023-225-8 **$8.99**
Bar/Bat Mitzvah Basics: A Practical Family Guide to Coming of Age Together
Edited by Cantor Helen Leneman 6 x 9, 240 pp, Quality PB, 978-1-58023-151-0 **$18.95**
The Bar/Bat Mitzvah Memory Book, 2nd Edition: An Album for Treasuring the
Spiritual Celebration *By Rabbi Jeffrey K. Salkin and Nina Salkin*
8 x 10, 48 pp, Deluxe HC, 2-color text, ribbon marker, 978-1-58023-263-0 **$19.99**

For Kids—Putting God on Your Guest List, 2nd Edition: How to Claim the
Spiritual Meaning of Your Bar or Bat Mitzvah *By Rabbi Jeffrey K. Salkin*
6 x 9, 144 pp, Quality PB, 978-1-58023-308-8 **$15.99** *For ages 11–13*
Putting God on the Guest List, 3rd Edition: How to Reclaim the Spiritual
Meaning of Your Child's Bar or Bat Mitzvah *By Rabbi Jeffrey K. Salkin*
6 x 9, 224 pp, Quality PB, 978-1-58023-222-7 **$16.99**; HC, 978-1-58023-260-9 **$24.99**
  Also Available: **Putting God on the Guest List Teacher's Guide**
  8½ x 11, 48 pp, PB, 978-1-58023-226-5 **$8.99**
Tough Questions Jews Ask: A Young Adult's Guide to Building a Jewish Life
By Rabbi Edward Feinstein 6 x 9, 160 pp, Quality PB, 978-1-58023-139-8 **$14.99** *For ages 12 & up*
  Also Available: **Tough Questions Jews Ask Teacher's Guide**
  8½ x 11, 72 pp, PB, 978-1-58023-187-9 **$8.95**

Bible Study/Midrash

**Abraham's Bind & Other Bible Tales of Trickery, Folly, Mercy
and Love** *By Michael J. Caduto*
Re-imagines many biblical characters, retelling their stories.
6 x 9, 224 pp, HC, 978-1-59473-186-0 **$19.99** *(A book from SkyLight Paths, Jewish Lights' sister imprint)*
Ancient Secrets: Using the Stories of the Bible to Improve Our Everyday Lives
By Rabbi Levi Meier, PhD 5½ x 8½, 288 pp, Quality PB, 978-1-58023-064-3 **$16.95**

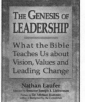

The Genesis of Leadership: What the Bible Teaches Us about Vision,
Values and Leading Change *By Rabbi Nathan Laufer; Foreword by Senator Joseph I. Lieberman*
Unlike other books on leadership, this one is rooted in the stories of the Bible.
6 x 9, 288 pp, Quality PB, 978-1-58023-352-1 **$18.99**; HC, 978-1-58023-241-8 **$24.99**
Hineini in Our Lives: Learning How to Respond to Others through 14 Biblical Texts
and Personal Stories *By Norman J. Cohen* 6 x 9, 240 pp, Quality PB, 978-1-58023-274-6 **$16.99**
Moses and the Journey to Leadership: Timeless Lessons of Effective Management from
the Bible and Today's Leaders *By Dr. Norman J. Cohen*
6 x 9, 240 pp, Quality PB, 978-1-58023-351-4 **$18.99**; HC, 978-1-58023-227-2 **$21.99**
Self, Struggle & Change: Family Conflict Stories in Genesis and Their Healing Insights for
Our Lives *By Norman J. Cohen* 6 x 9, 224 pp, Quality PB, 978-1-879045-66-8 **$18.99**
The Triumph of Eve & Other Subversive Bible Tales *By Matt Biers-Ariel*
5½ x 8½, 192 pp, Quality PB, 978-1-59473-176-1 **$14.99**; HC, 978-1-59473-040-5 **$19.99**
(A book from SkyLight Paths, Jewish Lights' sister imprint)

The Wisdom of Judaism: An Introduction to the Values of the Talmud
By Rabbi Dov Peretz Elkins
Explores the essence of Judaism. 6 x 9, 192 pp, Quality PB, 978-1-58023-327-9 **$16.99**
  Also Available: **The Wisdom of Judaism Teacher's Guide**
  8½ x 11, 18 pp, PB, 978-1-58023-350-7 **$8.99**

Or phone, fax, mail or e-mail to: **JEWISH LIGHTS Publishing**
Sunset Farm Offices, Route 4 • P.O. Box 237 • Woodstock, Vermont 05091
Tel: (802) 457-4000 • Fax: (802) 457-4004 • www.jewishlights.com
Credit card orders: (800) 962-4544 (8:30AM–5:30PM ET Monday–Friday)
Generous discounts on quantity orders. SATISFACTION GUARANTEED. Prices subject to change.

Judaism / Christianity / Interfaith

Talking about God: Exploring the Meaning of Religious Life with Kierkegaard, Buber, Tillich and Heschel *by Daniel F. Polish, PhD*
Examines the meaning of the human religious experience with the greatest theologians of modern times.   6 x 9, 176 pp, HC, 978-1-59473-230-0 **$21.99**
(A book from SkyLight Paths, Jewish Lights' sister imprint)

Interactive Faith: The Essential Interreligious Community-Building Handbook
Edited by Rev. Bud Heckman with Rori Picker Neiss
A guide to the key methods and resources of the interfaith movement.
6 x 9, 320 pp, HC, 978-1-59473-237-9 **$29.99**
(A book from SkyLight Paths, Jewish Lights' sister imprint)

The Jewish Approach to Repairing the World (*Tikkun Olam*)
A Brief Introduction for Christians *by Rabbi Elliot N. Dorff, PhD, with Reverend Cory Willson*
A window into the Jewish idea of responsibility to care for the world.
5½ x 8½, 256 pp, Quality PB, 978-1-58023-349-1 **$16.99**

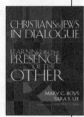

Modern Jews Engage the New Testament: Enhancing Jewish Well-Being in a Christian Environment *by Rabbi Michael J. Cook, PhD*
A look at the dynamics of the New Testament.
6 x 9, 416 pp, HC, 978-1-58023-313-2 **$29.99**

Disaster Spiritual Care: Practical Clergy Responses to Community, Regional and National Tragedy
Edited by Rabbi Stephen B. Roberts, BCJC, & Rev. Willard W.C. Ashley, Sr., DMin, DH
The definitive reference for pastoral caregivers of all faiths involved in disaster response.
6 x 9, 384 pp, HC, 978-1-59473-240-9 **$40.00** *(A book from SkyLight Paths, Jewish Lights' sister imprint)*

The Changing Christian World: A Brief Introduction for Jews
by Rabbi Leonard A. Schoolman 5½ x 8½, 176 pp, Quality PB, 978-1-58023-344-6 **$16.99**

The Jewish Connection to Israel, the Promised Land: A Brief Introduction for Christians *by Rabbi Eugene Korn, PhD* 5½ x 8½, 192 pp, Quality PB, 978-1-58023-318-7 **$14.99**

Christians and Jews in Dialogue: Learning in the Presence of the Other
by Mary C. Boys and Sara S. Lee; Foreword by Dorothy C. Bass
Inspires renewed commitment to dialogue between religious traditions.
6 x 9, 240 pp, Quality PB, 978-1-59473-254-6 **$18.99**; HC, 978-1-59473-144-0 **$21.99**
(A book from SkyLight Paths, Jewish Lights' sister imprint)

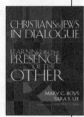

Healing the Jewish-Christian Rift: Growing Beyond Our Wounded History
by Ron Miller and Laura Bernstein; Foreword by Dr. Beatrice Bruteau
6 x 9, 288 pp, Quality PB, 978-1-59473-139-6 **$18.99**
(A book from SkyLight Paths, Jewish Lights' sister imprint)

Introducing My Faith and My Community
The Jewish Outreach Institute Guide for the Christian in a Jewish Interfaith Relationship
by Rabbi Kerry M. Olitzky 6 x 9, 176 pp, Quality PB, 978-1-58023-192-3 **$16.99**

The Jewish Approach to God: A Brief Introduction for Christians
by Rabbi Neil Gillman 5½ x 8½, 192 pp, Quality PB, Original 978-1-58023-190-9 **$16.95**

Jewish Holidays: A Brief Introduction for Christians *by Rabbi Kerry M. Olitzky and Rabbi Daniel Judson* 5½ x 8½, 176 pp, Quality PB Original, 978-1-58023-302-6 **$16.99**

Jewish Ritual: A Brief Introduction for Christians *by Rabbi Kerry M. Olitzky and Rabbi Daniel Judson* 5½ x 8½, 144 pp, Quality PB Original, 978-1-58023-210-4 **$14.99**

Jewish Spirituality: A Brief Introduction for Christians *by Rabbi Lawrence Kushner*
5½ x 8½, 112 pp, Quality PB Original, 978-1-58023-150-3 **$12.95**

A Jewish Understanding of the New Testament
by Rabbi Samuel Sandmel; new Preface by Rabbi David Sandmel 5½ x 8½, 368 pp, Quality PB,
978-1-59473-048-1 **$19.99** *(A book from SkyLight Paths, Jewish Lights' sister imprint)*

We Jews and Jesus: Exploring Theological Differences for Mutual Understanding
by Rabbi Samuel Sandmel; new Preface by Rabbi David Sandmel A Classic Reprint
6 x 9, 192 pp, Quality PB, 978-1-59473-208-9 **$16.99**
(A book from SkyLight Paths, Jewish Lights' sister imprint)

Show Me Your Way: The Complete Guide to Exploring Interfaith Spiritual Direction
by Howard A. Addison 5½ x 8½, 240 pp, Quality PB, 978-1-893361-41-6 **$16.95**
(A book from SkyLight Paths, Jewish Lights' sister imprint)

Pastoral Care Resources
LifeLights/™אורות החיים

LifeLights/™אורות החיים are inspirational, information-al booklets about challenges to our emotional and spiritual lives and how to deal with them. Offering help for wholeness and healing, each *LifeLight* is written from a uniquely Jewish spiritual perspective by a wise and caring soul—someone who knows the inner territory of grief, doubt, confusion and longing.

In addition to providing wise words to light a diffi-cult path, each *LifeLight* booklet provides suggestions for additional resources for reading. Many list organi-zations, Jewish and secular, that can provide help, along with information on how to contact them.

> "Invaluable for those needing comfort and
> instruction in times of difficulty and loss."
> **Rabbi David Wolpe**, Sinai Temple, Los Angeles, CA

> "Particularly useful for hospital visits and shiva calls—and
> they enable me to help at those times when I feel helpless."
> **Rabbi Sally Priesand**, Monmouth Reform Temple,
> Tinton Falls, NJ

Categories/Topics:

Health & Healing

Abortion and Judaism: Rabbinic Opinion and Jewish Law
Caring for Your Aging Parents
Caring for Yourself/When Someone Is Ill
Facing and Recovering from Surgery
Facing Cancer as a Family
Finding Spiritual Strength in Pain or Illness
Jewish Response to Dementia: Honoring Broken Tablets
Living with Cancer, One Day at a Time
Recognizing a Loved One's Addiction, and Providing Help
When Madness Comes Home: Living in the Shadow of a Loved One's Mental Illness

Loss / Grief / Death & Dying

Coping with the Death of a Spouse
From Death through Shiva: A Guide to Jewish Grieving Practices
Jewish Hospice: To Live, to Hope, to Heal
Making Sacred Choices at the End of Life
Mourning a Miscarriage
Taking the Time You Need to Mourn Your Loss
Talking to Children about Death
When Someone You Love Is Dying
When Someone You Love Needs Long-Term Care

Categories/Topics continued:

Judaism / Living a Jewish Life

Bar and Bat Mitzvah's Meaning: Preparing Spiritually with Your Child

Choosing a Congregation That Is Right for You

Considering Judaism: Choosing a Faith, Joining a People

Do Jews Believe in the Soul's Survival?

Exploring Judaism as an Adult

Jewish Meditation: How to Begin Your Practice

There's a Place for Us: Gays and Lesbians in the Jewish Community

To Meet Your Soul Mate, You Must Meet Your Soul

Yearning for God

Family Issues

Jewish Adoption: Unique Issues, Practical Solutions

Are You Being Hurt by Someone You Love? Domestic Abuse in the Jewish Community

Grandparenting Interfaith Grandchildren

Healing Estrangement in Your Family Relationships

Interfaith Families Making Jewish Choices

Jewish Approaches to Parenting Teens

Looking Back on Divorce and Letting Go

Parenting through a Divorce

Raising a Child with Special Needs

Talking to Your Children about God

Spiritual Care / Personal Growth

Bringing Your Sadness to God

Doing Teshuvah: Undoing Mistakes, Repairing Relationships and Finding Inner Peace

Easing the Burden of Stress

Finding a Way to Forgive

Finding the Help You Need: Psychotherapy, Pastoral Counseling, and the Promise of Spiritual Direction

Praying in Hard Times: The Soul's Imaginings

Surviving a Crisis or a Tragedy

Now available in hundreds of congregations, health-care facilities, funeral homes, colleges and military installations, these helpful, comforting resources can be uniquely presented in *LifeLights* display racks, available from Jewish Lights. **Each *LifeLight* topic is sold in packs of twelve for $9.95.** General discounts are available for quantity purchases.

Visit us online at **www.jewishlights.com** for a complete list of titles, authors, prices and ordering information, or call us at (802) 457-4000 or toll free at (800) 962-4544.

Congregation Resources

Inspired Jewish Leadership: Practical Approaches to Building Strong Communities
By Dr. Erica Brown
6 x 9, 256 pp, HC, 978-1-58023-361-3 **$24.99**

Becoming a Congregation of Learners: Learning as a Key to Revitalizing
Congregational Life By Isa Aron, PhD; Foreword by Rabbi Lawrence A. Hoffman
6 x 9, 304 pp, Quality PB, 978-1-58023-089-6 **$19.95**

Finding a Spiritual Home: How a New Generation of Jews Can Transform the
American Synagogue By Rabbi Sidney Schwarz
6 x 9, 352 pp, Quality PB, 978-1-58023-185-5 **$19.95**

Jewish Pastoral Care, 2nd Edition: A Practical Handbook from Traditional &
Contemporary Sources Edited by Rabbi Dayle A. Friedman, MSW, MAJCS, BCC
6 x 9, 528 pp, HC, 978-1-58023-221-0 **$40.00**

Jewish Spiritual Direction: An Innovative Guide from Traditional and Contemporary
Sources Edited by Rabbi Howard A. Addison and Barbara Eve Breitman
6 x 9, 368 pp, HC, 978-1-58023-230-2 **$30.00**

The Self-Renewing Congregation: Organizational Strategies for Revitalizing
Congregational Life By Isa Aron, PhD; Foreword by Dr. Ron Wolfson
6 x 9, 304 pp, Quality PB, 978-1-58023-166-4 **$19.95**

Spiritual Community: The Power to Restore Hope, Commitment and Joy
By Rabbi David A. Teutsch, PhD 5½ x 8½, 144 pp, HC, 978-1-58023-270-8 **$19.99**

The Spirituality of Welcoming: How to Transform Your Congregation into a
Sacred Community By Dr. Ron Wolfson 6 x 9, 224 pp, Quality PB, 978-1-58023-244-9 **$19.99**

Rethinking Synagogues: A New Vocabulary for Congregational Life
By Rabbi Lawrence A. Hoffman 6 x 9, 240 pp, Quality PB, 978-1-58023-248-7 **$19.99**

Children's Books

What You Will See Inside a Synagogue
By Rabbi Lawrence A. Hoffman and Dr. Ron Wolfson; Full-color photos by Bill Aron
A colorful, fun-to-read introduction that explains the ways and whys of Jewish
worship and religious life. 8½ x 10¼, 32 pp, Full-color photos, Quality PB, 978-1-59473-256-0 **$8.99**
For ages 6 & up (A book from SkyLight Paths, Jewish Lights' sister imprint)

The Kids' Fun Book of Jewish Time
By Emily Sper 9 x 7½, 24 pp, Full-color illus., HC, 978-1-58023-311-8 **$16.99**

In God's Hands
By Lawrence Kushner and Gary Schmidt 9 x 12, 32 pp, HC, 978-1-58023-224-1 **$16.99**

Because Nothing Looks Like God
By Lawrence and Karen Kushner
Introduces children to the possibilities of spiritual life.
11 x 8½, 32 pp, Full-color illus., HC, 978-1-58023-092-6 **$17.99** *For ages 4 & up*

Board Book Companions to *Because Nothing Looks Like God*
5 x 5, 24 pp, Full-color illus., SkyLight Paths Board Books For ages 0–4

What Does God Look Like? 978-1-893361-23-2 **$7.99**

How Does God Make Things Happen? 978-1-893361-24-9 **$7.95**

Where Is God? 978-1-893361-17-1 **$7.99**

The Book of Miracles: A Young Person's Guide to Jewish Spiritual Awareness
By Lawrence Kushner. All-new illustrations by the author
6 x 9, 96 pp, 2-color illus., HC, 978-1-879045-78-1 **$16.95** *For ages 9 and up*

In Our Image: God's First Creatures
By Nancy Sohn Swartz 9 x 12, 32 pp, Full-color illus., HC, 978-1-879045-99-6 **$16.95**
For ages 4 & up

Also Available as a Board Book: **How Did the Animals Help God?**
5 x 5, 24 pp, Board, Full-color illus., 978-1-59473-044-3 **$7.99** *For ages 0–4*
(A book from SkyLight Paths, Jewish Lights' sister imprint)

What Makes Someone a Jew? By Lauren Seidman
Reflects the changing face of American Judaism.
10 x 8½, 32 pp, Full-color photos, Quality PB Original, 978-1-58023-321-7 **$8.99** *For ages 3–6*

Children's Books by Sandy Eisenberg Sasso

Adam & Eve's First Sunset: God's New Day
Engaging new story explores fear and hope, faith and gratitude in ways that will delight kids and adults—inspiring us to bless each of God's days and nights.
9 x 12, 32 pp, Full-color illus., HC, 978-1-58023-177-0 **$17.95** *For ages 4 & up*

Also Available as a Board Book: **Adam and Eve's New Day**
5 x 5, 24 pp, Full-color illus., Board, 978-1-59473-205-8 **$7.99** *For ages 0–4*
(A book from SkyLight Paths, Jewish Lights' sister imprint)

But God Remembered
Stories of Women from Creation to the Promised Land
Four different stories of women—Lillith, Serach, Bityah, and the Daughters of Z—teach us important values through their faith and actions.
9 x 12, 32 pp, Full-color illus., Quality PB, 978-1-58023-372-9 **$8.99**; HC, 978-1-879045-43-9 **$16.95** *For ages 8 & up*

Cain & Abel: Finding the Fruits of Peace
Shows children that we have the power to deal with anger in positive ways. Provides questions for kids and adults to explore together.
9 x 12, 32 pp, Full-color illus., HC, 978-1-58023-123-7 **$16.95** *For ages 5 & up*

God in Between
If you wanted to find God, where would you look? This magical, mythical tale teaches that God can be found where we are: within all of us and the relationships between us. 9 x 12, 32 pp, Full-color illus., HC, 978-1-879045-86-6 **$16.95** *For ages 4 & up*

God's Paintbrush: Special 10th Anniversary Edition
Wonderfully interactive, invites children of all faiths and backgrounds to encounter God through moments in their own lives. Provides questions adult and child can explore together. 11 x 8½, 32 pp, Full-color illus., HC, 978-1-58023-195-4 **$17.95** *For ages 4 & up*

Also Available: **God's Paintbrush Teacher's Guide**
8½ x 11, 32 pp, PB, 978-1-879045-57-6 **$8.95**

God's Paintbrush Celebration Kit
A Spiritual Activity Kit for Teachers and Students of All Faiths, All Backgrounds
Additional activity sheets available:
8-Student Activity Sheet Pack (40 sheets/5 sessions), 978-1-58023-058-2 **$19.95**
Single-Student Activity Sheet Pack (5 sessions), 978-1-58023-059-9 **$3.95**

In God's Name
Like an ancient myth in its poetic text and vibrant illustrations, this award-winning modern fable about the search for God's name celebrates the diversity and, at the same time, the unity of all people.
9 x 12, 32 pp, Full-color illus., HC, 978-1-879045-26-2 **$16.99** *For ages 4 & up*

Also Available as a Board Book: **What Is God's Name?**
5 x 5, 24 pp, Board, Full-color illus., 978-1-893361-10-2 **$7.99** *For ages 0–4*
(A book from SkyLight Paths, Jewish Lights' sister imprint)

Also Available: **In God's Name video and study guide**
Computer animation, original music, and children's voices. 18 min. **$29.99**

Also Available in Spanish: **El nombre de Dios**
9 x 12, 32 pp, Full-color illus., HC, 978-1-893361-63-8 **$16.95**
(A book from SkyLight Paths, Jewish Lights' sister imprint)

Noah's Wife: The Story of Naamah
When God tells Noah to bring the animals of the world onto the ark, God also calls on Naamah, Noah's wife, to save each plant on Earth. Based on an ancient text.
9 x 12, 32 pp, Full-color illus., HC, 978-1-58023-134-3 **$16.95** *For ages 4 & up*

Also Available as a Board Book: **Naamah, Noah's Wife**
5 x 5, 24 pp, Full-color illus., Board, 978-1-893361-56-0 **$7.95** *For ages 0–4*
(A book from SkyLight Paths, Jewish Lights' sister imprint)

For Heaven's Sake: Finding God in Unexpected Places
9 x 12, 32 pp, Full-color illus., HC, 978-1-58023-054-4 **$16.95** *For ages 4 & up*

God Said Amen: Finding the Answers to Our Prayers
9 x 12, 32 pp, Full-color illus., HC, 978-1-58023-080-3 **$16.95** *For ages 4 & up*

Holidays/Holy Days

Rosh Hashanah Readings: Inspiration, Information and Contemplation
Yom Kippur Readings: Inspiration, Information and Contemplation
Edited by Rabbi Dov Peretz Elkins with Section Introductions from Arthur Green's These Are the Words
An extraordinary collection of readings, prayers and insights that enable the modern worshiper to enter into the spirit of the High Holy Days in a personal and powerful way, permitting the meaning of the Jewish New Year to enter the heart.
RHR: 6 x 9, 400 pp, HC, 978-1-58023-239-5 **$24.99**
YKR: 6 x 9, 368 pp, HC, 978-1-58023-271-5 **$24.99**

Jewish Holidays: A Brief Introduction for Christians
By Rabbi Kerry M. Olitzky and Rabbi Daniel Judson
5½ x 8½, 144 pp, Quality PB, 978-1-58023-302-6 **$16.99**

Reclaiming Judaism as a Spiritual Practice: Holy Days and Shabbat
By Rabbi Goldie Milgram
7 x 9, 272 pp, Quality PB, 978-1-58023-205-0 **$19.99**

7th Heaven: Celebrating Shabbat with Rebbe Nachman of Breslov
By Moshe Mykoff with the Breslov Research Institute
5⅛ x 8¼, 224 pp, Deluxe PB w/flaps, 978-1-58023-175-6 **$18.95**

Shabbat, 2nd Edition: The Family Guide to Preparing for and Celebrating the Sabbath
By Dr. Ron Wolfson 7 x 9, 320 pp, illus., Quality PB, 978-1-58023-164-0 **$19.99**

Hanukkah, 2nd Edition: The Family Guide to Spiritual Celebration
By Dr. Ron Wolfson. Edited by Joel Lurie Grishaver.
7 x 9, 240 pp, illus., Quality PB, 978-1-58023-122-0 **$18.95**

The Jewish Family Fun Book, 2nd Edition: Holiday Projects, Everyday Activities, and Travel Ideas with Jewish Themes *By Danielle Dardashti and Roni Sarig. Illus. by Avi Katz.*
6 x 9, 304 pp, 70+ b/w illus. & diagrams, Quality PB, 978-1-58023-333-0 **$18.99**

The Jewish Lights Book of Fun Classroom Activities: Simple and Seasonal Projects for Teachers and Students *By Danielle Dardashti and Roni Sarig*
6 x 9, 240 pp, Quality PB, 978-1-58023-206-7 **$19.99**

Passover

My People's Passover Haggadah
Traditional Texts, Modern Commentaries
Edited by Rabbi Lawrence A. Hoffman, PhD, and David Arnow, PhD
A diverse and exciting collection of commentaries on the traditional Passover Haggadah—in two volumes!
Vol. 1: 7 x 10, 304 pp, HC, 978-1-58023-354-5 **$24.99**
Vol. 2: 7 x 10, 320 pp, HC, 978-1-58023-346-0 **$24.99**

Leading the Passover Journey
The Seder's Meaning Revealed, the Haggadah's Story Retold
By Rabbi Nathan Laufer
Uncovers the hidden meaning of the Seder's rituals and customs.
6 x 9, 224 pp, Quality PB, 978-1-58023-399-6 **$18.99**; HC, 978-1-58023-211-1 **$24.99**

The Women's Passover Companion: Women's Reflections on the Festival of Freedom
Edited by Rabbi Sharon Cohen Anisfeld, Tara Mohr, and Catherine Spector
6 x 9, 352 pp, Quality PB, 978-1-58023-231-9 **$19.99**

The Women's Seder Sourcebook: Rituals & Readings for Use at the Passover Seder
Edited by Rabbi Sharon Cohen Anisfeld, Tara Mohr, and Catherine Spector
6 x 9, 384 pp, Quality PB, 978-1-58023-232-6 **$19.99**

Creating Lively Passover Seders: A Sourcebook of Engaging Tales, Texts & Activities
By David Arnow, PhD 7 x 9, 416 pp, Quality PB, 978-1-58023-184-8 **$24.99**

Passover, 2nd Edition: The Family Guide to Spiritual Celebration
By Dr. Ron Wolfson with Joel Lurie Grishaver 7 x 9, 352 pp, Quality PB, 978-1-58023-174-9 **$19.95**

Life Cycle
Marriage / Parenting / Family / Aging

The New Jewish Baby Album: Creating and Celebrating the Beginning of a Spiritual Life—A Jewish Lights Companion
By the Editors at Jewish Lights. Foreword by Anita Diamant. Preface by Rabbi Sandy Eisenberg Sasso.
A spiritual keepsake that will be treasured for generations. More than just a memory book, *shows you how—and why it's important*—to create a Jewish home and a Jewish life. 8 x 10, 64 pp, Deluxe Padded HC, Full-color illus., 978-1-58023-138-1 **$19.95**

The Jewish Pregnancy Book: A Resource for the Soul, Body & Mind during Pregnancy, Birth & the First Three Months
By Sandy Falk, MD, and Rabbi Daniel Judson, with Steven A. Rapp
Includes medical information, prayers and rituals for each stage of pregnancy, from a liberal Jewish perspective. 7 x 10, 208 pp, Quality PB, b/w photos, 978-1-58023-178-7 **$16.95**

Celebrating Your New Jewish Daughter: Creating Jewish Ways to Welcome Baby Girls into the Covenant—New and Traditional Ceremonies *By Debra Nussbaum Cohen; Foreword by Rabbi Sandy Eisenberg Sasso* 6 x 9, 272 pp, Quality PB, 978-1-58023-090-2 **$18.95**

The New Jewish Baby Book, 2nd Edition: Names, Ceremonies & Customs—A Guide for Today's Families *By Anita Diamant* 6 x 9, 336 pp, Quality PB, 978-1-58023-251-7 **$19.99**

Parenting as a Spiritual Journey: Deepening Ordinary and Extraordinary Events into Sacred Occasions *By Rabbi Nancy Fuchs-Kreimer* 6 x 9, 224 pp, Quality PB, 978-1-58023-016-2 **$16.95**

Parenting Jewish Teens: A Guide for the Perplexed
By Joanne Doades
Explores the questions and issues that shape the world in which today's Jewish teenagers live. 6 x 9, 200 pp, Quality PB, 978-1-58023-305-7 **$16.99**

Judaism for Two: A Spiritual Guide for Strengthening and Celebrating Your Loving Relationship *By Rabbi Nancy Fuchs-Kreimer and Rabbi Nancy H. Wiener; Foreword by Rabbi Elliot N. Dorff* Addresses the ways Jewish teachings can enhance and strengthen committed relationships. 6 x 9, 224 pp, Quality PB, 978-1-58023-254-8 **$16.99**

Embracing the Covenant: Converts to Judaism Talk About Why & How *By Rabbi Allan Berkowitz and Patti Moskovitz* 6 x 9, 192 pp, Quality PB, 978-1-879045-50-7 **$16.95**

The Guide to Jewish Interfaith Family Life: An InterfaithFamily.com Handbook *Edited by Ronnie Friedland and Edmund Case* 6 x 9, 384 pp, Quality PB, 978-1-58023-153-4 **$18.95**

Introducing My Faith and My Community
The Jewish Outreach Institute Guide for the Christian in a Jewish Interfaith Relationship *By Rabbi Kerry M. Olitzky* 6 x 9, 176 pp, Quality PB, 978-1-58023-192-3 **$16.99**

Making a Successful Jewish Interfaith Marriage: The Jewish Outreach Institute Guide to Opportunities, Challenges and Resources *By Rabbi Kerry M. Olitzky with Joan Peterson Littman* 6 x 9, 176 pp, Quality PB, 978-1-58023-170-1 **$16.95**

The Creative Jewish Wedding Book: A Hands-On Guide to New & Old Traditions, Ceremonies & Celebrations *By Gabrielle Kaplan-Mayer* 9 x 9, 288 pp, b/w photos, Quality PB, 978-1-58023-194-7 **$19.99**

Divorce Is a Mitzvah: A Practical Guide to Finding Wholeness and Holiness When Your Marriage Dies *By Rabbi Perry Netter; Afterword by Rabbi Laura Geller.* 6 x 9, 224 pp, Quality PB, 978-1-58023-172-5 **$16.95**

A Heart of Wisdom: Making the Jewish Journey from Midlife through the Elder Years *Edited by Susan Berrin; Foreword by Harold Kushner* 6 x 9, 384 pp, Quality PB, 978-1-58023-051-3 **$18.95**

So That Your Values Live On: Ethical Wills and How to Prepare Them *Edited by Jack Riemer and Nathaniel Stampfer* 6 x 9, 272 pp, Quality PB, 978-1-879045-34-7 **$18.99**

Current Events/History

A Dream of Zion: American Jews Reflect on Why Israel Matters to Them
Edited by Rabbi Jeffrey K. Salkin Explores what Jewish people in America have to say
about Israel. 6 x 9, 304 pp, HC, 978-1-58023-340-8 **$24.99**
   Also Available: **A Dream of Zion Teacher's Guide** 8½ x 11, 32 pp, PB, 978-1-58023-356-9 **$8.99**

The Jewish Connection to Israel, the Promised Land: A Brief Introduction for
   Christians *By Rabbi Eugene Korn, PhD* 5½ x 8½, 192 pp, Quality PB, 978-1-58023-318-7 **$14.99**

The Story of the Jews: A 4,000-Year Adventure—A Graphic History Book
   Written & illustrated by Stan Mack 6 x 9, 288 pp, illus., Quality PB, 978-1-58023-155-8 **$16.99**

Hannah Senesh: Her Life and Diary, the First Complete Edition
   By Hannah Senesh; Foreword by Marge Piercy; Preface by Eitan Senesh; Afterword by Roberta Grossman
   6 x 9, 368 pp, b/w photos, Quality PB, 978-1-58023-342-2 **$19.99**

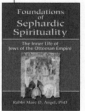

The Ethiopian Jews of Israel: Personal Stories of Life in the Promised
Land *By Len Lyons, PhD; Foreword by Alan Dershowitz; Photographs by Ilan Ossendryver*
Recounts, through photographs and words, stories of Ethiopian Jews.
10½ x 10, 240 pp, 100 full-color photos, HC, 978-1-58023-323-1 **$34.99**

Foundations of Sephardic Spirituality: The Inner Life of Jews of the Ottoman Empire
By Rabbi Marc D. Angel, PhD 6 x 9, 224 pp, HC, 978-1-58023-243-2 **$24.99**

Judaism and Justice: The Jewish Passion to Repair the World
By Rabbi Sidney Schwarz 6 x 9, 352 pp, Quality PB, 978-1-58023-353-8 **$19.99**

Ecology/Environment

A Wild Faith: Jewish Ways into Wilderness, Wilderness Ways into Judaism
By Rabbi Mike Comins; Foreword by Nigel Savage
Offers ways to enliven and deepen your spiritual life through wilderness experience.
6 x 9, 240 pp, Quality PB, 978-1-58023-316-3 **$16.99**

Ecology & the Jewish Spirit: Where Nature & the Sacred Meet
   Edited by Ellen Bernstein 6 x 9, 288 pp, Quality PB, 978-1-58023-082-7 **$18.99**

Torah of the Earth: Exploring 4,000 Years of Ecology in Jewish Thought
   Vol. 1: Biblical Israel: One Land, One People; Rabbinic Judaism: One People, Many Lands
   Vol. 2: Zionism: One Land, Two Peoples; Eco-Judaism: One Earth, Many Peoples
   Edited by Arthur Waskow Vol. 1: 6 x 9, 272 pp, Quality PB, 978-1-58023-086-5 **$19.95**
   Vol. 2: 6 x 9, 336 pp, Quality PB, 978-1-58023-087-2 **$19.95**

The Way Into Judaism and the Environment *By Jeremy Benstein, PhD*
   6 x 9, 288 pp, Quality PB, 978-1-58023-368-2 **$18.99**; HC, 978-1-58023-268-5 **$24.99**

Grief/Healing

Healing and the Jewish Imagination: Spiritual and Practical
Perspectives on Judaism and Health *Edited by Rabbi William Cutter, PhD*
Explores Judaism for comfort in times of illness and perspectives on suffering.
6 x 9, 240 pp, Quality PB, 978-1-58023-373-6 **$19.99**; HC, 978-1-58023-314-9 **$24.99**

Grief in Our Seasons: A Mourner's Kaddish Companion *By Rabbi Kerry M. Olitzky*
   4½ x 6½, 448 pp, Quality PB, 978-1-879045-55-2 **$15.95**

Healing of Soul, Healing of Body: Spiritual Leaders Unfold the Strength & Solace
   in Psalms *Edited by Rabbi Simkha Y. Weintraub, CSW*
   6 x 9, 128 pp, 2-color illus. text, Quality PB, 978-1-879045-31-6 **$14.99**

Mourning & Mitzvah, 2nd Edition: A Guided Journal for Walking the Mourner's
   Path through Grief to Healing *By Anne Brener, LCSW*
   7½ x 9, 304 pp, Quality PB, 978-1-58023-113-8 **$19.99**

Tears of Sorrow, Seeds of Hope, 2nd Edition: A Jewish Spiritual Companion for
   Infertility and Pregnancy Loss *By Rabbi Nina Beth Cardin*
   6 x 9, 208 pp, Quality PB, 978-1-58023-233-3 **$18.99**

A Time to Mourn, a Time to Comfort, 2nd Edition: A Guide to Jewish
   Bereavement *By Dr. Ron Wolfson*
   7 x 9, 384 pp, Quality PB, 978-1-58023-253-1 **$19.99**

When a Grandparent Dies: A Kid's Own Remembering Workbook for Dealing
   with Shiva and the Year Beyond *By Nechama Liss-Levinson, PhD*
   8 x 10, 48 pp, 2-color text, HC, 978-1-879045-44-6 **$15.95** *For ages 7–13*

Inspiration

Happiness and the Human Spirit: The Spirituality of Becoming the Best You Can Be *By Abraham J. Twerski, MD*
Shows you that true happiness is attainable once you stop looking outside yourself for the source.
6 x 9, 176 pp, Quality PB, 978-1-58023-404-7 **$16.99**; HC, 978-1-58023-343-9 **$19.99**

The Bridge to Forgiveness: Stories and Prayers for Finding God and Restoring Wholeness *By Rabbi Karyn D. Kedar*
Examines how forgiveness can be the bridge that connects us to wholeness and peace.
6 x 9, 176 pp, HC, 978-1-58023-324-8 **$19.99**

God's To-Do List: 103 Ways to Be an Angel and Do God's Work on Earth
By Dr. Ron Wolfson 6 x 9, 150 pp, Quality PB, 978-1-58023-301-9 **$16.99**

God in All Moments: Mystical & Practical Spiritual Wisdom from Hasidic Masters
Edited and translated by Or N. Rose with Ebn D. Leader
5½ x 8½, 192 pp, Quality PB, 978-1-58023-186-2 **$16.95**

Our Dance with God: Finding Prayer, Perspective and Meaning in the Stories of Our Lives *By Karyn D. Kedar* 6 x 9, 176 pp, Quality PB, 978-1-58023-202-9 **$16.99**

Also Available: **The Dance of the Dolphin** (HC edition of *Our Dance with God*)
6 x 9, 176 pp, HC, 978-1-58023-154-1 **$19.95**

The Empty Chair: Finding Hope and Joy—Timeless Wisdom from a Hasidic Master, Rebbe Nachman of Breslov *Adapted by Moshe Mykoff and the Breslov Research Institute*
4 x 6, 128 pp, 2-color text, Deluxe PB w/flaps, 978-1-879045-67-5 **$9.99**

The Gentle Weapon: Prayers for Everyday and Not-So-Everyday Moments—Timeless Wisdom from the Teachings of the Hasidic Master, Rebbe Nachman of Breslov *Adapted by Moshe Mykoff and S. C. Mizrahi, together with the Breslov Research Institute*
4 x 6, 144 pp, 2-color text, Deluxe PB w/flaps, 978-1-58023-022-3 **$9.99**

God Whispers: Stories of the Soul, Lessons of the Heart *By Karyn D. Kedar*
6 x 9, 176 pp, Quality PB, 978-1-58023-088-9 **$15.95**

Restful Reflections: Nighttime Inspiration to Calm the Soul, Based on Jewish Wisdom
By Rabbi Kerry M. Olitzky & Rabbi Lori Forman 4½ x 6½, 448 pp, Quality PB, 978-1-58023-091-9 **$15.95**

Sacred Intentions: Daily Inspiration to Strengthen the Spirit, Based on Jewish Wisdom
By Rabbi Kerry M. Olitzky and Rabbi Lori Forman 4½ x 6½, 448 pp, Quality PB, 978-1-58023-061-2 **$15.95**

Kabbalah/Mysticism

Awakening to Kabbalah: The Guiding Light of Spiritual Fulfillment
By Rav Michael Laitman, PhD 6 x 9, 192 pp, HC, 978-1-58023-264-7 **$21.99**

Seek My Face: A Jewish Mystical Theology *By Arthur Green*
6 x 9, 304 pp, Quality PB, 978-1-58023-130-5 **$19.95**

Zohar: Annotated & Explained *Translation and annotation by Daniel C. Matt; Foreword by Andrew Harvey* 5½ x 8½, 176 pp, Quality PB, 978-1-893361-51-5 **$15.99**
(A book from SkyLight Paths, Jewish Lights' sister imprint)

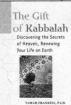

Ehyeh: A Kabbalah for Tomorrow
By Arthur Green 6 x 9, 224 pp, Quality PB, 978-1-58023-213-5 **$16.99**

The Flame of the Heart: Prayers of a Chasidic Mystic *By Reb Noson of Breslov. Translated by David Sears with the Breslov Research Institute* 5 x 7¼, 160 pp, Quality PB, 978-1-58023-246-3 **$15.99**

The Gift of Kabbalah: Discovering the Secrets of Heaven, Renewing Your Life on Earth
By Tamar Frankiel, PhD 6 x 9, 256 pp, Quality PB, 978-1-58023-141-1 **$16.95**
HC, 978-1-58023-108-4 **$21.95**

Kabbalah: A Brief Introduction for Christians
By Tamar Frankiel, PhD 5½ x 8½, 208 pp, Quality PB, 978-1-58023-303-3 **$16.99**

The Lost Princess and Other Kabbalistic Tales of Rebbe Nachman of Breslov
The Seven Beggars and Other Kabbalistic Tales of Rebbe Nachman of Breslov
Translated by Rabbi Aryeh Kaplan; Preface by Rabbi Chaim Kramer
Lost Princess: 6 x 9, 400 pp, Quality PB, 978-1-58023-217-3 **$18.99**
Seven Beggars: 6 x 9, 192 pp, Quality PB, 978-1-58023-250-0 **$16.99**

See also *The Way Into Jewish Mystical Tradition* in Spirituality / The Way Into... Series

Meditation

The Handbook of Jewish Meditation Practices
A Guide for Enriching the Sabbath and Other Days of Your Life
By Rabbi David A. Cooper Easy-to-learn meditation techniques.
6 x 9, 208 pp, Quality PB, 978-1-58023-102-2 **$16.95**

Discovering Jewish Meditation: Instruction & Guidance for Learning an Ancient
Spiritual Practice By Nan Fink Gefen 6 x 9, 208 pp, Quality PB, 978-1-58023-067-4 **$16.95**

A Heart of Stillness: A Complete Guide to Learning the Art of Meditation
By David A. Cooper 5½ x 8½, 272 pp, Quality PB, 978-1-893361-03-4 **$16.95**
(A book from SkyLight Paths, Jewish Lights' sister imprint)

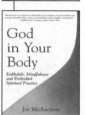

Meditation from the Heart of Judaism: Today's Teachers Share Their Practices,
Techniques, and Faith Edited by Avram Davis
6 x 9, 256 pp, Quality PB, 978-1-58023-049-0 **$16.95**

Silence, Simplicity & Solitude: A Complete Guide to Spiritual Retreat at Home
By David A. Cooper 5½ x 8½, 336 pp, Quality PB, 978-1-893361-04-1 **$16.95**
(A book from SkyLight Paths, Jewish Lights' sister imprint)

Ritual/Sacred Practice

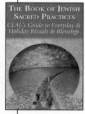

The Jewish Dream Book: The Key to Opening the Inner Meaning of
Your Dreams By Vanessa L. Ochs with Elizabeth Ochs; Full-color illus. by Kristina Swarner
Instructions for how modern people can perform ancient Jewish dream practices
and dream interpretations drawn from the Jewish wisdom tradition.
8 x 8, 128 pp, Full-color illus., Deluxe PB w/flaps, 978-1-58023-132-9 **$16.95**

God in Your Body: Kabbalah, Mindfulness and Embodied Spiritual Practice
By Jay Michaelson
The first comprehensive treatment of the body in Jewish spiritual practice and an
essential guide to the sacred.
6 x 9, 288 pp, Quality PB, 978-1-58023-304-0 **$18.99**

The Book of Jewish Sacred Practices: CLAL's Guide to Everyday & Holiday
Rituals & Blessings Edited by Rabbi Irwin Kula and Vanessa L. Ochs, PhD
6 x 9, 368 pp, Quality PB, 978-1-58023-152-7 **$18.95**

Jewish Ritual: A Brief Introduction for Christians
By Rabbi Kerry M. Olitzky and Rabbi Daniel Judson
5½ x 8½, 144 pp, Quality PB, 978-1-58023-210-4 **$14.99**

The Rituals & Practices of a Jewish Life: A Handbook for Personal Spiritual
Renewal Edited by Rabbi Kerry M. Olitzky and Rabbi Daniel Judson
6 x 9, 272 pp, illus., Quality PB, 978-1-58023-169-5 **$18.95**

The Sacred Art of Lovingkindness: Preparing to Practice
By Rabbi Rami Shapiro 5½ x 8½, 176 pp, Quality PB, 978-1-59473-151-8 **$16.99**
(A book from SkyLight Paths, Jewish Lights' sister imprint)

Science Fiction/Mystery & Detective Fiction

Mystery Midrash: An Anthology of Jewish Mystery & Detective Fiction
Edited by Lawrence W. Raphael; Preface by Joel Siegel
6 x 9, 304 pp, Quality PB, 978-1-58023-055-1 **$16.95**

Criminal Kabbalah: An Intriguing Anthology of Jewish Mystery & Detective Fiction
Edited by Lawrence W. Raphael; Foreword by Laurie R. King
6 x 9, 256 pp, Quality PB, 978-1-58023-109-1 **$16.95**

Wandering Stars: An Anthology of Jewish Fantasy & Science Fiction
Edited by Jack Dann; Introduction by Isaac Asimov
6 x 9, 272 pp, Quality PB, 978-1-58023-005-6 **$18.99**

More Wandering Stars: An Anthology of Outstanding Stories of Jewish Fantasy and
Science Fiction Edited by Jack Dann; Introduction by Isaac Asimov
6 x 9, 192 pp, Quality PB, 978-1-58023-063-6 **$16.95**

Spirituality

Journeys to a Jewish Life: Inspiring Stories from the Spiritual Journeys of American Jews *By Paula Amann*
Examines the soul treks of Jews lost and found. 6 x 9, 208 pp, HC, 978-1-58023-317-0 **$19.99**

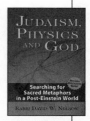

The Adventures of Rabbi Harvey: A Graphic Novel of Jewish Wisdom and Wit in the Wild West *By Steve Sheinkin*
Jewish and American folktales combine in this witty and original graphic novel collection. Creatively retold and set on the western frontier of the 1870s.
6 x 9, 144 pp, Full-color illus., Quality PB, 978-1-58023-310-1 **$16.99**

Rabbi Harvey Rides Again
A Graphic Novel of Jewish Folktales Let Loose in the Wild West *By Steve Sheinkin*
6 x 9, 144 pp, Quality PB Original, Full-color illus., 978-1-58023-347-7 **$16.99**

Ethics of the Sages: *Pirke Avot—Annotated & Explained*
Translation and Annotation by Rabbi Rami Shapiro 5½ x 8½, 192 pp, Quality PB, 978-1-59473-207-2
$16.99 *(A book from SkyLight Paths, Jewish Lights' sister imprint)*

A Book of Life: Embracing Judaism as a Spiritual Practice
By Michael Strassfeld 6 x 9, 528 pp, Quality PB, 978-1-58023-247-0 **$19.99**

Meaning and Mitzvah: Daily Practices for Reclaiming Judaism through Prayer, God, Torah, Hebrew, Mitzvot and Peoplehood *By Rabbi Goldie Milgram*
7 x 9, 336 pp, Quality PB, 978-1-58023-256-2 **$19.99**

The Soul of the Story: Meetings with Remarkable People
By Rabbi David Zeller 6 x 9, 288 pp, HC, 978-1-58023-272-2 **$21.99**

Aleph-Bet Yoga: Embodying the Hebrew Letters for Physical and Spiritual Well-Being
By Steven A. Rapp. Foreword by Tamar Frankiel, PhD and Judy Greenfeld. Preface by Hart Lazer.
7 x 10, 128 pp, b/w photos, Quality PB, Layflat binding, 978-1-58023-162-6 **$16.95**

Does the Soul Survive? A Jewish Journey to Belief in Afterlife, Past Lives & Living with Purpose *By Rabbi Elie Kaplan Spitz; Foreword by Brian L. Weiss, MD*
6 x 9, 288 pp, Quality PB, 978-1-58023-165-7 **$16.99**

First Steps to a New Jewish Spirit: Reb Zalman's Guide to Recapturing the Intimacy & Ecstasy in Your Relationship with God *By Rabbi Zalman M. Schachter-Shalomi with Donald Gropman* 6 x 9, 144 pp, Quality PB, 978-1-58023-182-4 **$16.95**

God in Our Relationships: Spirituality between People from the Teachings of Martin Buber *By Rabbi Dennis S. Ross* 5½ x 8½, 160 pp, Quality PB, 978-1-58023-147-3 **$16.95**

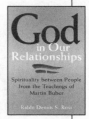

Judaism, Physics and God: Searching for Sacred Metaphors in a Post-Einstein World
By Rabbi David W. Nelson 6 x 9, 368 pp, Quality PB, inc. reader's discussion guide, 978-1-58023-306-4 **$18.99**;
HC, 352 pp, 978-1-58023-252-4 **$24.99**

The Jewish Lights Spirituality Handbook: A Guide to Understanding, Exploring & Living a Spiritual Life *Edited by Stuart M. Matlins*
What exactly is "Jewish" about spirituality? How do I make it a part of my life? Fifty of today's foremost spiritual leaders share their ideas and experience with us.
6 x 9, 456 pp, Quality PB, 978-1-58023-093-3 **$19.99**

Bringing the Psalms to Life: How to Understand and Use the Book of Psalms
By Daniel F. Polish 6 x 9, 208 pp, Quality PB, 978-1-58023-157-2 **$16.95**;
HC, 978-1-58023-077-3 **$21.95**

God & the Big Bang: Discovering Harmony between Science & Spirituality
By Daniel C. Matt 6 x 9, 216 pp, Quality PB, 978-1-879045-89-7 **$16.99**

Minding the Temple of the Soul: Balancing Body, Mind, and Spirit through Traditional Jewish Prayer, Movement, and Meditation *By Tamar Frankiel, PhD, and Judy Greenfeld*
7 x 10, 184 pp, illus., Quality PB, 978-1-879045-64-4 **$16.95**

One God Clapping: The Spiritual Path of a Zen Rabbi *By Alan Lew with Sherril Jaffe*
5½ x 8½, 336 pp, Quality PB, 978-1-58023-115-2 **$16.95**

There Is No Messiah ... and You're It: The Stunning Transformation of Judaism's Most Provocative Idea *By Rabbi Robert N. Levine, DD*
6 x 9, 192 pp, Quality PB, 978-1-58023-255-5 **$16.99**

These Are the Words: A Vocabulary of Jewish Spiritual Life
By Arthur Green 6 x 9, 304 pp, Quality PB, 978-1-58023-107-7 **$18.95**

Spirituality/Lawrence Kushner

Filling Words with Light: Hasidic and Mystical Reflections on Jewish Prayer
By Lawrence Kushner and Nehemia Polen
5½ x 8½, 176 pp, Quality PB, 978-1-58023-238-8 **$16.99**; HC, 978-1-58023-216-6 **$21.99**

The Book of Letters: A Mystical Hebrew Alphabet
Popular HC Edition, 6 x 9, 80 pp, 2-color text, 978-1-879045-00-2 **$24.95**
Collector's Limited Edition, 9 x 12, 80 pp, gold foil embossed pages, w/limited edition silkscreened
print, 978-1-879045-04-0 **$349.00**

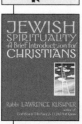

The Book of Miracles: A Young Person's Guide to Jewish Spiritual Awareness
6 x 9, 96 pp, 2-color illus., HC, 978-1-879045-78-1 **$16.95** *For ages 9 and up*

The Book of Words: Talking Spiritual Life, Living Spiritual Talk
6 x 9, 160 pp, Quality PB, 978-1-58023-020-9 **$16.95**

Eyes Remade for Wonder: A Lawrence Kushner Reader *Introduction by Thomas Moore*
6 x 9, 240 pp, Quality PB, 978-1-58023-042-1 **$18.95**

God Was in This Place & I, i Did Not Know: Finding Self, Spirituality and
Ultimate Meaning 6 x 9, 192 pp, Quality PB, 978-1-879045-33-0 **$16.95**

Honey from the Rock: An Introduction to Jewish Mysticism
6 x 9, 176 pp, Quality PB, 978-1-58023-073-5 **$16.95**

Invisible Lines of Connection: Sacred Stories of the Ordinary
5½ x 8½, 160 pp, Quality PB, 978-1-879045-98-9 **$15.95**

Jewish Spirituality—A Brief Introduction for Christians
5½ x 8½, 112 pp, Quality PB, 978-1-58023-150-3 **$12.95**

The River of Light: Jewish Mystical Awareness
6 x 9, 192 pp, Quality PB, 978-1-58023-096-4 **$16.95**

The Way Into Jewish Mystical Tradition
6 x 9, 224 pp, Quality PB, 978-1-58023-200-5 **$18.99**; HC, 978-1-58023-029-2 **$21.95**

Spirituality/Prayer

My People's Passover Haggadah: Traditional Texts, Modern Commentaries
Edited by Rabbi Lawrence A. Hoffman, PhD, and David Arnow, PhD Diverse commentaries
on the traditional Passover Haggadah—in two volumes! Vol. 1: 7 x 10, 304 pp, HC
978-1-58023-354-5 **$24.99** Vol. 2: 7 x 10, 320 pp, HC, 978-1-58023-346-0 **$24.99**

Witnesses to the One: The Spiritual History of the *Sh'ma* *By Rabbi Joseph B.*
Meszler; Foreword by Rabbi Elyse Goldstein 6 x 9, 176 pp, HC, 978-1-58023-309-5 **$19.99**

My People's Prayer Book Series
Traditional Prayers, Modern Commentaries *Edited by Rabbi Lawrence A. Hoffman*
Provides diverse and exciting commentary to the traditional liturgy, helping modern
men and women find new wisdom in Jewish prayer, and bring liturgy into their lives.
Each book includes Hebrew text, modern translation, and commentaries from all
perspectives of the Jewish world.

Vol. 1—The *Sh'ma* and Its Blessings
7 x 10, 168 pp, HC, 978-1-879045-79-8 **$24.99**
Vol. 2—The *Amidah*
7 x 10, 240 pp, HC, 978-1-879045-80-4 **$24.95**
Vol. 3—*P'sukei D'zimrah* (Morning Psalms)
7 x 10, 240 pp, HC, 978-1-879045-81-1 **$24.95**
Vol. 4—*Seder K'riat Hatorah* (The Torah Service)
7 x 10, 264 pp, HC, 978-1-879045-82-8 **$23.95**
Vol. 5—*Birkhot Hashachar* (Morning Blessings)
7 x 10, 240 pp, HC, 978-1-879045-83-5 **$24.95**
Vol. 6—*Tachanun* and Concluding Prayers
7 x 10, 240 pp, HC, 978-1-879045-84-2 **$24.95**
Vol. 7—Shabbat at Home
7 x 10, 240 pp, HC, 978-1-879045-85-9 **$24.95**
Vol. 8—*Kabbalat Shabbat* (Welcoming Shabbat in the Synagogue)
7 x 10, 240 pp, HC, 978-1-58023-121-3 **$24.99**
Vol. 9—Welcoming the Night: *Minchah* and *Ma'ariv* (Afternoon and
Evening Prayer) 7 x 10, 272 pp, HC, 978-1-58023-262-3 **$24.99**
Vol. 10—Shabbat Morning: *Shacharit* and *Musaf* (Morning and
Additional Services) 7 x 10, 240 pp, HC, 978-1-58023-240-1 **$24.99**

Spirituality/Women's Interest

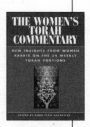

The Quotable Jewish Woman: Wisdom, Inspiration & Humor from the Mind & Heart
Edited and compiled by Elaine Bernstein Partnow
6 x 9, 496 pp, Quality PB, 978-1-58023-236-4 **$19.99**; HC, 978-1-58023-193-0 **$29.99**

The Divine Feminine in Biblical Wisdom Literature: Selections Annotated &
Explained *Translated and Annotated by Rabbi Rami Shapiro* 5½ x 8½, 240 pp, Quality PB,
978-1-59473-109-9 **$16.99** *(A book from SkyLight Paths, Jewish Lights' sister imprint)*

The Women's Haftarah Commentary: New Insights from Women Rabbis on the
54 Weekly Haftarah Portions, the 5 Megillot & Special Shabbatot
Edited by Rabbi Elyse Goldstein
6 x 9, 560 pp, Quality PB, 978-1-58023-371-2 **$19.99**; HC, 978-1-58023-133-6 **$39.99**

The Women's Torah Commentary: New Insights from Women Rabbis on the
54 Weekly Torah Portions *Edited by Rabbi Elyse Goldstein*
6 x 9, 496 pp, Quality PB, 978-1-58023-370-5 **$19.99**; HC, 978-1-58023-076-6 **$34.95**

The Year Mom Got Religion: One Woman's Midlife Journey into Judaism
By Lee Meyerhoff Hendler 6 x 9, 208 pp, Quality PB, 978-1-58023-070-4 **$15.95**

See Holidays for *The Women's Passover Companion: Women's Reflections on
the Festival of Freedom* and *The Women's Seder Sourcebook: Rituals &
Readings for Use at the Passover Seder.*

Spirituality / Crafts

(from SkyLight Paths, Jewish Lights sister imprint)

The Knitting Way: A Guide to Spiritual Self-Discovery
By Linda Skolnick and Janice MacDaniels
Shows how to use the practice of knitting to strengthen our spiritual selves.
7 x 9, 240 pp, Quality PB, 978-1-59473-079-5 **$16.99**

The Quilting Path: A Guide to Spiritual Self-Discovery through Fabric,
Thread and Kabbalah *By Louise Silk*
Explores how to cultivate personal growth through quilt making.
7 x 9, 192 pp, Quality PB, 978-1-59473-206-5 **$16.99**

The Painting Path: Embodying Spiritual Discovery through Yoga, Brush
and Color *By Linda Novick; Foreword by Richard Segalman*
Explores the divine connection you can experience through art.
7 x 9, 208 pp, 8-page full-color insert, Quality PB, 978-1-59473-226-3 **$18.99**

The Scrapbooking Journey: A Hands-On Guide to Spiritual Discovery
By Cory Richardson-Lauve; Foreword by Stacy Julian
Reveals how this craft can become a practice used to deepen and shape your life.
7 x 9, 176 pp, 8-page full-color insert, b/w photos, Quality PB, 978-1-59473-216-4 **$18.99**

Travel

Israel—A Spiritual Travel Guide, 2nd Edition
A Companion for the Modern Jewish Pilgrim
By Rabbi Lawrence A. Hoffman 4¾ x 10, 256 pp, Quality PB, illus., 978-1-58023-261-6 **$18.99**
Also Available: **The Israel Mission Leader's Guide** 978-1-58023-085-8 **$4.95**

12-Step

100 Blessings Every Day: Daily Twelve Step Recovery Affirmations, Exercises for
Personal Growth & Renewal Reflecting Seasons of the Jewish Year
By Rabbi Kerry M. Olitzky; Foreword by Rabbi Neil Gillman
4½ x 6½, 432 pp, Quality PB, 978-1-879045-30-9 **$16.99**

Recovery from Codependence: A Jewish Twelve Steps Guide to Healing Your Soul
By Rabbi Kerry M. Olitzky 6 x 9, 160 pp, Quality PB, 978-1-879045-32-3 **$13.95**

Twelve Jewish Steps to Recovery: A Personal Guide to Turning from Alcoholism &
Other Addictions—Drugs, Food, Gambling, Sex ...
By Rabbi Kerry M. Olitzky and Stuart A. Copans, MD; Preface by Abraham J. Twerski, MD
6 x 9, 144 pp, Quality PB, 978-1-879045-09-5 **$15.99**

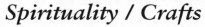

Theology/Philosophy/The Way Into... Series

The Way Into... series offers an accessible and highly usable "guided tour" of the Jewish faith, people, history and beliefs—in total, an introduction to Judaism that will enable you to understand and interact with the sacred texts of the Jewish tradition. Each volume is written by a leading contemporary scholar and teacher, and explores one key aspect of Judaism. *The Way Into...* series enables all readers to achieve a real sense of Jewish cultural literacy through guided study.

The Way Into Encountering God in Judaism
By Rabbi Neil Gillman, PhD

For everyone who wants to understand how Jews have encountered God throughout history and today.
6 x 9, 240 pp, Quality PB, 978-1-58023-199-2 **$18.99**; HC, 978-1-58023-025-4 **$21.95**
Also Available: **The Jewish Approach to God:** A Brief Introduction for Christians
By Rabbi Neil Gillman, PhD
5½ x 8½, 192 pp, Quality PB, 978-1-58023-190-9 **$16.95**

The Way Into Jewish Mystical Tradition
By Rabbi Lawrence Kushner

Allows readers to interact directly with the sacred mystical text of the Jewish tradition. An accessible introduction to the concepts of Jewish mysticism, their religious and spiritual significance and how they relate to life today.
6 x 9, 224 pp, Quality PB, 978-1-58023-200-5 **$18.99**; HC, 978-1-58023-029-2 **$21.95**

The Way Into Jewish Prayer
By Rabbi Lawrence A. Hoffman, PhD

Opens the door to 3,000 years of Jewish prayer, making available all anyone needs to feel at home in the Jewish way of communicating with God.
6 x 9, 208 pp, Quality PB, 978-1-58023-201-2 **$18.99**

Also Available: **The Way Into Jewish Prayer Teacher's Guide**
By Rabbi Jennifer Ossakow Goldsmith
8½ x 11, 42 pp, Quality PB, 978-1-58023-345-3 **$8.99**
Visit our website to download a free copy.

The Way Into Judaism and the Environment
By Jeremy Benstein, PhD

Explores the ways in which Judaism contributes to contemporary social-environmental issues, the extent to which Judaism is part of the problem and how it can be part of the solution.
6 x 9, 288 pp, Quality PB, 978-1-58023-368-2 **$18.99**; HC, 978-1-58023-268-5 **$24.99**

The Way Into *Tikkun Olam* (Repairing the World)
By Rabbi Elliot N. Dorff, PhD

An accessible introduction to the Jewish concept of the individual's responsibility to care for others and repair the world.
6 x 9, 304 pp, Quality PB, 978-1-58023-328-6 **$18.99**; 320 pp, HC, 978-1-58023-269-2 **$24.99**

The Way Into Torah
By Rabbi Norman J. Cohen, PhD

Helps guide in the exploration of the origins and development of Torah, explains why it should be studied and how to do it.
6 x 9, 176 pp, Quality PB, 978-1-58023-198-5 **$16.99**

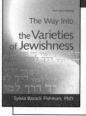

The Way Into the Varieties of Jewishness
By Sylvia Barack Fishman, PhD

Explores the religious and historical understanding of what it has meant to be Jewish from ancient times to the present controversy over "Who is a Jew?"
6 x 9, 288 pp, Quality PB, 978-1-58023-367-5 **$18.99**; HC, 978-1-58023-030-8 **$24.99**

Theology/Philosophy

A Touch of the Sacred: A Theologian's Informal Guide to Jewish Belief
By Dr. Eugene B. Borowitz and Frances W. Schwartz Explores the musings from the
leading theologian of liberal Judaism. 6 x 9, 256 pp, HC, 978-1-58023-337-8 **$21.99**

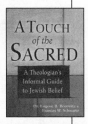

Talking about God: Exploring the Meaning of Religious Life with
Kierkegaard, Buber, Tillich and Heschel *By Daniel F. Polish, PhD*
Examines the meaning of the human religious experience with the greatest theologians of modern times. 6 x 9, 160 pp, HC, 978-1-59473-230-0 **$21.99**
(A book from SkyLight Paths, Jewish Lights' sister imprint)

Jews & Judaism in the 21st Century: Human Responsibility, the
Presence of God, and the Future of the Covenant *Edited by Rabbi Edward Feinstein;
Foreword by Paula E. Hyman* Five celebrated leaders in Judaism examine contemporary
Jewish life. 6 x 9, 192 pp, Quality PB, 978-1-58023-374-3 **$19.99**; HC, 978-1-58023-315-6 **$24.99**

Christians and Jews in Dialogue: Learning in the Presence of the Other
By Mary C. Boys and Sara S. Lee; Foreword by Dr. Dorothy Bass
6 x 9, 240 pp, Quality PB, 978-1-59473-254-6 **$18.99**; HC, 978-1-59473-144-0 **$21.99**
(A book from SkyLight Paths, Jewish Lights' sister imprint)

The Death of Death: Resurrection and Immortality in Jewish Thought
By Neil Gillman 6 x 9, 336 pp, Quality PB, 978-1-58023-081-0 **$18.95**

Ethics of the Sages: *Pirke Avot*—Annotated & Explained
Translation & Annotation by Rabbi Rami Shapiro
5½ x 8½, 208 pp, Quality PB, 978-1-59473-207-2 **$16.99** *(A book from SkyLight Paths, Jewish Lights' sister imprint)*

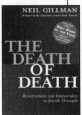

Hasidic Tales: Annotated & Explained *By Rabbi Rami Shapiro; Foreword by Andrew Harvey*
5½ x 8½, 240 pp, Quality PB, 978-1-893361-86-7 **$16.95**
(A book from SkyLight Paths, Jewish Lights' sister imprint)

A Heart of Many Rooms: Celebrating the Many Voices within Judaism
By David Hartman 6 x 9, 352 pp, Quality PB, 978-1-58023-156-5 **$19.95**

The Hebrew Prophets: Selections Annotated & Explained
Translation & Annotation by Rabbi Rami Shapiro; Foreword by Zalman M. Schachter-Shalomi
5½ x 8½, 224 pp, Quality PB, 978-1-59473-037-5 **$16.99** *(A book from SkyLight Paths, Jewish Lights' sister imprint)*

A Jewish Understanding of the New Testament
By Rabbi Samuel Sandmel; Preface by Rabbi David Sandmel
5½ x 8½, 368 pp, Quality PB, 978-1-59473-048-1 **$19.99** *(A book from SkyLight Paths, Jewish Lights' sister imprint)*

Keeping Faith with the Psalms: Deepen Your Relationship with God Using the Book
of Psalms *By Daniel F. Polish* 6 x 9, 320 pp, Quality PB, 978-1-58023-300-2 **$18.99**

A Living Covenant: The Innovative Spirit in Traditional Judaism
By David Hartman 6 x 9, 368 pp, Quality PB, 978-1-58023-011-7 **$20.00**

Love and Terror in the God Encounter: The Theological Legacy of Rabbi Joseph
B. Soloveitchik *By David Hartman* 6 x 9, 240 pp, Quality PB, 978-1-58023-176-3 **$19.95**

The Personhood of God: Biblical Theology, Human Faith and the Divine Image
By Dr. Yochanan Muffs; Foreword by Dr. David Hartman
6 x 9, 240 pp, Quality PB, 978-1-58023-338-5 **$18.99**; HC, 978-1-58023-265-4 **$24.99**

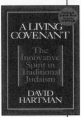

Traces of God: Seeing God in Torah, History and Everyday Life *By Neil Gillman*
6 x 9, 240 pp, Quality PB, 978-1-58023-369-9 **$16.99**; HC, 978-1-58023-249-4 **$21.99**

We Jews and Jesus: Exploring Theological Differences for Mutual Understanding
By Rabbi Samuel Sandmel; Preface by Rabbi David Sandmel
6 x 9, 176 pp, Quality PB, 978-1-59473-208-9 **$16.99** *(A book from SkyLight Paths, Jewish Lights' sister imprint)*

Your Word Is Fire: The Hasidic Masters on Contemplative Prayer
Edited and translated by Arthur Green and Barry W. Holtz
6 x 9, 160 pp, Quality PB, 978-1-879045-25-5 **$15.95**

I Am Jewish
Personal Reflections Inspired by the Last Words of Daniel Pearl
Almost 150 Jews—both famous and not—from all walks of life, from all around
the world, write about many aspects of their Judaism.
Edited by Judea and Ruth Pearl 6 x 9, 304 pp, Deluxe PB w/flaps, 978-1-58023-259-3 **$18.99**
Download a free copy of the *I Am Jewish Teacher's Guide* at our website:
www.jewishlights.com

About Jewish Lights

People of all faiths and backgrounds yearn for books that attract, engage, educate, and spiritually inspire.

Our principal goal is to stimulate thought and help all people learn about who the Jewish People are, where they come from, and what the future can be made to hold. While people of our diverse Jewish heritage are the primary audience, our books speak to people in the Christian world as well and will broaden their understanding of Judaism and the roots of their own faith.

We bring to you authors who are at the forefront of spiritual thought and experience. While each has something different to say, they all say it in a voice that you can hear.

Our books are designed to welcome you and then to engage, stimulate, and inspire. We judge our success not only by whether or not our books are beautiful and commercially successful, but by whether or not they make a difference in your life.

For your information and convenience, at the back of this book we have provided a list of other Jewish Lights books you might find interesting and useful. They cover all the categories of your life:

Bar/Bat Mitzvah	Life Cycle
Bible Study / Midrash	Meditation
Children's Books	Parenting
Congregation Resources	Prayer
Current Events / History	Ritual / Sacred Practice
Ecology / Environment	Spirituality
Fiction: Mystery, Science Fiction	Theology / Philosophy
Grief / Healing	Travel
Holidays / Holy Days	12-Step
Inspiration	Women's Interest
Kabbalah / Mysticism / Enneagram	

Stuart M. Matlins, Publisher

Or phone, fax, mail or e-mail to: **JEWISH LIGHTS Publishing**
Sunset Farm Offices, Route 4 • P.O. Box 237 • Woodstock, Vermont 05091
Tel: (802) 457-4000 • Fax: (802) 457-4004 • www.jewishlights.com
Credit card orders: **(800) 962-4544** (8:30AM–5:30PM ET Monday–Friday)
Generous discounts on quantity orders. SATISFACTION GUARANTEED. Prices subject to change.

For more information about each book, visit our website at www.jewishlights.com